PRACTISING CRITICAL REFLECTION TO DEVELOP EMANCIPATORY CHANGE

This book is dedicated to victims/survivors of sexual assault, particularly those inspirational women who have had the courage to report their experience to the legal system.

This book is also dedicated to those audacious, activist women who work towards the elimination of sexual violence in all its forms and support victims/survivors, particularly those who participated in this research.

Practising Critical Reflection to Develop Emancipatory Change

Challenging the Legal Response to Sexual Assault

CHRISTINE MORLEY
University of the Sunshine Coast, Australia

Routledge
Taylor & Francis Group
LONDON AND NEW YORK

First published 2014 by Ashgate Publishing

Published 2016 by Routledge
2 Park Square, Milton Park, Abingdon, Oxfordshire OX14 4RN
711 Third Avenue, New York, NY 10017, USA

First issued in paperback 2016

Routledge is an imprint of the Taylor & Francis Group, an informa business

British Library Cataloguing in Publication Data
A catalogue record for this book is available from the British Library

The Library of Congress has cataloged the printed edition as follows:
Morley, Christine.
Practicing critical reflection to develop emancipatory change : challenging the legal response to sexual assault / By Christine Morley.
p. cm.
Includes bibliographical references and index.
ISBN 978-1-4094-6258-3 (hardback)
1. Rape--Australia. 2. Rape victims--Legal status, laws, etc.--Australia. 3. Law reform--Australia. I. Title.
KU4202.M67 2014
345.94'05046--dc23

2013039237

ISBN 13: 978-1-138-24842-7 (pbk)
ISBN 13: 978-1-4094-6258-3 (hbk)

Contents

Foreword

Critical reflection is a mindset and a skill that is seen as increasingly necessary in the current economic climate. It involves an ability to uncover the fundamental assumptions on which actions are based, and to examine and change these to improve practice if necessary. In the current climate, professionals are challenged to work more effectively and efficiently with reduced resources, and also to be more accountable for their decisions and actions. This is especially difficult given the restrictions on discretion which many professionals experience in the workplace. There is therefore a high degree of interest, from nearly all professions, in how critical reflection can support and empower practitioners to improve their practice. This is particularly needed when the situations and problems with which professionals deal seem increasingly complex and in fact are less able to be controlled or the outcomes of actions predicted. What happens to the practitioner's sense of integrity and of agency, when confronted with what seems to be an increasingly disempowering work environment? Critical reflection is sometimes believed to be a way of helping professionals not only to learn directly from their own practice, but it can also be a way of helping them engage better with the specific challenges of their own work (Pockett and Giles 2008).

Unfortunately it is difficult to pin down exactly what people mean when they speak about critical reflection, and it is even more difficult to pin down what they actually do. There are many different perspectives on critical reflection, and indeed many different ways of practising it. Whilst having numerous perspectives is healthy, this also means that practitioners can be confused about what critical reflection actually is, and how they can incorporate it meaningfully into their specific jobs and workplaces. This book is an exceptionally welcome contribution to both the theory and practice of critical reflection. It should go a long way towards clarifying in depth how critical reflection can be understood and practised. Not only does Christine Morley develop a clear and strong theoretical base for critical reflection (postmodern feminism). She also describes, and researches, in detail, how it can be used to change practitioners' thinking and practices in work with the legal system.

Working in the sexual assault field and trying to ensure that the legal system responds effectively and sensitively to victim experiences can be especially challenging to workers. Many professionals, in particular female social workers, may feel that the legal system is relatively intractable, and may feel largely disempowered in such a male-dominated field. As Christine ably points out, the attitudes toward sexual assault by many judges, present a huge social barrier towards understanding of female victims' experiences and female workers' perspectives.

This choice of field is therefore an excellent one to illustrate the possibilities for emancipatory change. I was struck and heartened by the deep changes in thinking experienced by the participants, most precisely because it was related to work in the legal system. From this point of view as well, this book provides valuable data on the possible benefits of critical reflection. Again, although much literature attests to perceived benefits, there have been very few studies which provide more concrete evidence of how it can be used by practitioners and indeed what changes come about (Fook and Gardner 2007).

I worked closely with Christine on the initial design of the study, which began some years ago now. At this time there was very little work done on the use of critical reflection as a research methodology itself. Some literature spoke about incorporating a critical reflection stage into action research design (Reason and Bradbury 2001) but this was not the same as using a critical reflection process itself for gathering data. This book therefore is also innovative in its development and use of a critical reflection process as a research method that at the same time brings about emancipatory change for the participants involved in the study.

I therefore heartily commend this book to all of you: practitioners who wish to become more critically reflective and improve their practice; educators of professionals who wish to teach concrete ways of being reflective; and researchers who are interested in ways of researching which incorporate the experience of the practitioner and can bring about transformative change.

Jan Fook
June 2013

Preface and Acknowledgements

All told, this book has probably been close to two decades in the making; not that I knew that when I was undertaking my undergraduate education as a social worker that this book would be the product of the journey I was about to embark on. I was first taught feminism by an inspiring activist called Lee FitzRoy. In many classroom discussions, Lee shared her practice experiences of working with victims/survivors of sexual assault, and it sparked a strong commitment in me to work within and make a contribution to this field.

I was fortunate to complete my final social work field education placement at the Ballarat Centre Against Sexual Assault. I was particularly privileged in this time to be mentored by Shireen Gunn, a remarkable woman who continues to fight for victims/survivors and the centrality of feminism within Centres Against Sexual Assault.

It was during this period that I also became heavily influenced by the work of Professor Jan Fook. Again, I was incredibly privileged to have the opportunity to work closely with Jan at a time when she was developing her ideas about critical reflection and its transformative possibilities. Jan was the principal supervisor of both my Honours and PhD research, and I am particularly grateful to her for encouraging me to undertake this research and supporting me to write this book.

I am also indebted to Fiona Gardner, who similarly contributed greatly to the supervision of the PhD research that substantially informs this book.[1] Fiona was a wonderful supervisor who was able to ground me and motivate me, provide me with continual reassurance, encouragement and support and for really solid, practical advice on how to proceed. The contributions that Jan and Fiona have made to my thinking are evident throughout this book, and I continue to be in awe of their work and their wisdom.

My experiences of working within Centres of Sexual Assault, which I talk more about later in the book, were mixed. The work was dynamic, interesting and challenging. I had a strong sense that I was part of an emancipatory project that was incredibly important and worthwhile, and I met some amazing people: politicised women who were passionate about victims/survivors' rights, and courageous women who had often survived horrendous violence.

I personally struggled with bearing witness to the injustices that these women suffered. The interactions with the legal system were ironically where some of

---

1 Morley, C. 'Sexual Assault and the Legal System: How Does Critical Reflection on Practice Develop Possibilities for Change?' Submitted in the fulfilment of the requirements of the Doctor of Philosophy, La Trobe University, 2010.

those injustices felt most profound. As a practitioner, I often felt powerless and overwhelmed by the level of structural disadvantage that the women faced in trying to seek justice from the judicial system. Although it felt necessary (and therapeutic at times) to descend into the depths of a disparaging and hostile critique of the legal system and its personnel, ultimately this reinforced a fatalistic sense of hopelessness.

And that is the point of this book. We have comprehensive critiques available to us about the plethora of problems with the legal response to sexual assault, but what are we to do about it? The research process, for me, has been an expedition to explore and move beyond my level of 'stuckness' – a state of hopelessness and despair at time that I know was shared by many of my colleagues. There are numerous books dedicated to detailing the problems with the legal system for women who have experienced violence. This book expands on this work by making a contribution to the practical theorising of critical reflection. It demonstrates how critical reflection can be used to reshape ideas that have previously been considered as predominantly theoretical and abstract, to make them accessible for practitioners in ways that can inform new thinking and practice responses to the inadequacies of the system.

The research draws on critical postmodern analysis to develop new ways of thinking about change and new ways to enhance change practices both within and without the legal system. It has been a heartening and re-energizing process for me to engage in because it demonstrates that even in the most restrictive and disempowering contexts it is possible for practitioners to create their own sense of agency and power to bring about change and positive outcomes for the people they work with. I have therefore been left with a much-needed sense of optimism and renewed hope about the possibilities practitioners may create for enacting change. This has been particularly important for me to be able to continue my work as a critical social worker and social work educator, at a time when many critical thinkers are not positive or enthusiastic about the future. I talk daily with students and colleagues about the transformative possibilities of critical reflection, and it has been reassuring to see that it has been able to live up to its promise in this research.

My hope is that the book will be a useful resource for practitioners and researchers who work in the field of sexual assault, and more broadly for practitioners who struggle to work towards emancipatory outcomes in their practice in a variety of contexts. Given that the book sets out to detail practical strategies regarding how to negotiate complex structural problems (using the legal response to sexual assault as an example), it holds relevance for both undergraduate and postgraduate students in social work and related disciplines, though to practitioners, supervisors, managers and academics. I hope that readers will find the lessons that come from the analysis of practitioners' accounts as constructive, useful and inspiring as I have.

The other key use of the book will be for researchers who are interested in understanding and replicating research methodologies that are informed by critical reflection, as a means for developing social research that contributes to social change. This contributes to both the development of social science research methodology, and also practical applications of critical reflection for those wishing to engage in practice-related research.

I especially wish to thank my research participants, who took time from their busy working lives to share their accounts of their practice with great personal and professional generosity. This research would not have been possible without them, and I was continually humbled and inspired by their contributions to the research and their willingness to engage in the critical reflection process, which was often extremely challenging.

I would like to thank the many students, friends and colleagues who have both challenged and affirmed me and contributed to the ideas that are presented here, particularly those who have read drafts and given feedback including Jess Boccia, Karen Marshall, David O'Connor, Jayne Clarke and Kirsty Roberts. Kirsty deserves a special mention in her tireless efforts in assisting me to gain the appropriate permissions from publishers. I would also like to acknowledge Michael Buky who did a wonderful job of editing the research. And finally, I want to thank to my wonderful colleague and companion, Dr Phillip Ablett of the University of the Sunshine Coast, for his continual support and encouragement. Phillip is the person who hears and discusses all the ideas and drafts in their infancy, not just the polished version, which thanks to his wise critical engagement, is a much better product.

Christine Morley
July 2013

List of Abbreviations

ALRC	Australian Law Reform Commission
CASA	Centre Against Sexual Assault
CIU	Criminal Investigation Unit
DHS	Department of Human Services
FMO	Forensic Medical Officer
OPP	Office of Public Prosecutions
NWSLRC	New South Wales Law Reform Commission
PoVSDC	Parliament of Victoria Social Development Committee
RRLC	Real Rape Law Commission
SECASA	South East Centre Against Sexual Assault
SOCAU	Sexual Offences and Child Abuse Unit
VLRC	Victorian Law Reform Commission

Chapter 1
Introduction

This book provides an innovative framework that enables social work and human services practitioners to find hope, agency and practical strategies to work towards change. Many social workers, particularly those who are committed to critical and emancipatory goals, report feeling exhausted, powerless, alienated from the means of change, and hopeless about their capacities to make a difference in the lives of the individuals, groups or communities with whom they work. This is testament to the complex, challenging nature of the work they undertake, the demanding roles they fulfil, and the rapidly changing, uncertain and often, restrictive contexts in which they practice.

However, by demonstrating how critical reflection as an educational tool enables practitioners to envision possibilities for change, the research presented in this book supports and resources practitioners who are interested in continuing the struggle for a more socially just, democratic and equitable world, despite having to work in contexts that appear immutably oppressive. The legal system, particularly in its response to sexual assault, provides a consummate example of this type of context. Hence the research presented in this book explores the work of sexual assault practitioners that are engaged in supporting victims/survivors of sexual assault through the legal process.

It is therefore a book about resistance – not only to the problems embedded in the legal response to sexual assault, but to the full array of dominant discourses (such as neo-liberalism, professionalism, medicalisation, colonisation) that impact the contexts in which social workers operate, and often limit our perceptions of our capacities to resist. The research explores the type of theorising and political engagement that is not limited to dismantling formal structures, but harnesses the potential of critical postmodernism and critical reflection as emancipatory tools that can assist practitioners to critique received wisdom and agitate for change in multiple ways. Specifically, this book presents the findings of original research to demonstrate how a particular model of critical reflection, first developed by Fook (2002) and later refined by Fook and Gardner (2007) and Fook (2012), was used to enable sexual assault practitioners to develop a clear capacity to think about their personal agency to work towards change.

This book makes a solid contribution to the practical theorising of critical reflection, by reshaping ideas that have previously been considered as predominantly theoretical and abstract, to make them accessible for practitioners to inform their thinking and action in meaningful ways. The book demonstrates the contribution that critical reflection makes to professional practice, not only for the field of sexual assault, but also for a range of fields of practice where social workers feel overwhelmed and disempowered by seemingly insurmountable structural barriers to change.

Locating Myself in the Research

The research presented in this book explores counsellors/advocates'[1] perceptions of their capacities to bring about change in the legal response to victims/survivors of sexual assault. Whilst counsellors/advocates are the 'frontline people' to assist victims/survivors, they are typically neglected in the literature (Maier 2008: 786). The research was conducted in the context of the Australian legal system that is widely lamented amongst practitioners who work in the field of sexual assault as unresponsive and hostile to victims/survivors and impervious to change.

The focus of this research emerged from my experiences of working as a counsellor/advocate at a number of Centres Against Sexual Assault (CASA) across regional Victoria. My work predominantly involved short- to longer-term counselling with adult women who had either experienced recent rape or been subjected to sexual assault in childhood.[2] I also worked as an after-hours counsellor/advocate, providing a crisis intervention response for victims/survivors of recent rape, while coordinating police and forensic medical involvement.

My practice in this role spanned just over seven years during which time I supported numerous women through the legal process. Sometimes, in my after-hours capacity, this process included advocating with police and forensic medical professionals for the victim/survivor immediately after an assault. This generally involved supporting the victim/survivor during the forensic examination and the making of an initial report to police.

More comprehensively, the business hours counsellor/advocate response would often follow the legal process in its entirety. The legal aspect of this role included supporting the victim/survivor to make a formal statement to police, ensuring that the victim/survivor was kept informed of the progress of an investigation, being notified if and when a perpetrator was charged and preparing the victim/survivor for the court process. Finally, in those rare cases in which the Office of Public Prosecutions (OPP) decided there was enough evidence to proceed, my role involved preparing the victim/

---

1 This term is used to refer to the practitioners who work in Centres Against Sexual Assault. These practitioners are usually social workers, psychologists or qualified professionals in related disciplines.

2 In particularly acknowledging the experiences of women, I do not wish to deny that men also experience sexual violence (Carpenter 2006, Doherty and Anderson 2004, Graham 2006, Oosterhoff et al. 2004, Rumney and Morgan-Taylor 2004, Stermac et al. 2004, Washington 1999). The use of gendered language in this book, however, is quite deliberate in reflecting the gendered nature of sexual assault in that statistics consistently demonstrate that the overwhelming majority of victims/survivors are women and children (Dekeseredy and Joseph 2006, Gilmore 1995).

survivor for the committal hearing and trial process, including cross-examination, and supporting her through this (see for example Campbell 2006, Yancey Martin 2005). As other practitioners acknowledge:

> The fact that sexual assault is a crime means that as sexual assault counsellors we are working in the context of the criminal justice system. The criminal justice system may exist on the fringes of counselling for victims of sexual assault but it is a constant presence, always there in the background influencing our practice. The consequence being, that we are constantly making decisions in the context of not only competing professional and ethical codes, but also complex legal codes. (Gardiner and Roberson 1995: 229)

Although engagement with the legal system was not the most significant part of my role, it was the aspect that often caused the most frustration and disillusionment. The inappropriateness and failure of the legal system to deliver just outcomes can be devastating, particularly for those who have had the courage to pursue legal justice for the crimes committed against them, but also for the practitioners who are charged with the responsibility of supporting them. These practitioners repeatedly witness the acquittal of perpetrators, and the demeaning legal processes to which victims/survivors are subjected, with a sense of powerlessness.

Despite the countless police statements I have witnessed being taken and the numerous committal hearings and trials I have attended, I never once worked with a complainant of sexual assault whose engagement with the legal system resulted in the conviction of the perpetrator. Of those cases that proceeded to trial, all of the perpetrators were acquitted usually on the basis of lack of sufficient evidence to convict.

I have been present in the court room while defence lawyers have asked the victim/survivor a seemingly endless number of irrelevant and ridiculous questions, demanding that she give precise details, specific dates and times; sometimes when the abuse had occurred more than 10 to 20 years ago, and sometimes when, at the time of the abuse, she may only have been five or six years old. Courts have seemed disinterested in the fact that the energies of that child were understandably dedicated to surviving the abuse at the time, rather than memorising specific details so that they could be recalled exactly in court decades later.

When following the legal process, my work with these women would typically involve responding to the consequences of their experience with the legal system: police who had not believed victims/survivors, trivialised their experiences, or had generally been disrespectful; detectives who did not prioritise their case, and who did not tell them when developments had occurred; long delays; several adjournments; defence lawyers who had intimidated victims/survivors, accused them of fabricating their experience of sexual assault, blatantly used myths about sexual assault to blame victims/survivors and discredit their version of events whilst exonerating the accused; perpetrators who had sneered and disturbingly stared at victims/survivors during the hearing to make them feel intimidated and uncomfortable; magistrates who had blamed victims/survivors and dismissed important evidence; and juries who had not believed victims/survivors and ultimately acquitted the perpetrator. The devastation of this often humiliating and distressing legal process, combined with a legal outcome that denied victims/survivors' experiences, was often interpreted as a secondary assault by the system which caused a level of trauma that rivalled the initial sexual violence.

I always felt apologetic at this point; apologetic that each woman had endured one of the most abhorrent experiences possible and that the legal remedies available to her would almost certainly compound and exacerbate the original injustice. Perhaps more pertinently, I felt apologetic about the fact that my role was to support her but that I was powerless to change her disempowering experience. I despised the fact that my role as counsellor/advocate seemed to position me in the placation of the victims of an unjust system, rather than meaningfully organising for resistance and change. I knew that these women deserved more from me than an acknowledgement that they had been wronged.

I am not alone in these observations. Other practitioners have similarly observed:

> In our counselling and court support with clients over many years, we have witnessed the struggle of many children and adults enduring the legal process. We have also often worked with clients for months after their court appearances in counselling as they address the traumatising effects of their participation in court. (Mitchell et al. 1995: 123)

However, despite the extensive acknowledgement of the inadequacies of the legal response to sexual assault (documented in chapters 2 and 3) victims/survivors have a right to expect that they will not be subjected to processes of secondary victimisation by the criminal justice system. They have a right to be heard, to be treated with respect and integrity, to feel safe during the legal process and a right to a fair trial.

Some practitioners refer to the disparity between victims/survivors' basic rights and their actual experiences in the legal system as a 'crisis of witnessing' (Jarvis and McIlwaine 1997: 3). For some researchers, such experiences have contributed to initiatives to study victims/survivors' experiences in a more systematic way (see for example Carmody and Carrington 2000, D'Arcy 1995, Heath 2007, Mitchell et al. 1995). However, as Carmody (2003: 199) asks, 'How is it that we now know so much about the extent and manifestations of gendered violence, yet remain unable to find ways to stop it happening or at least to reduce its occurrence?'

For myself as a practitioner/researcher, the impact of the experiences that I have witnessed as part of my work heightened my awareness of the need to explore possibilities to create change. My observations fuelled my motivation to research alternative ways to think about the kinds of practices that might assist practitioners to envision their exercise of agency and power, to develop different ways to engage with the judicial system and to create new opportunities to influence legal processes and outcomes for victims/survivors.

The aim of this research, therefore, was to explore how counsellors/advocates conceptualised change within the legal system with a view to formulating strategies that transcended their initial constructions of the problems. The research uses critical reflection to examine the possibilities for those who support victims/survivors of sexual assault to deconstruct and reconstruct their own practices in ways that will enable them to envision possibilities for change. The research question explored in this study was: How does critical reflection on practice develop possibilities for change? Significantly, the findings of the research suggest that even in the most restrictive and disempowering contexts, it is possible for practitioners to create their own sense of agency and power to bring about change and positive outcomes for the people with whom they work.

How Will This Book Be Organised?

Following on from this introduction, Chapter 2 explores some of the most highly criticised aspects of the legal process. The primary concerns with the legal system, its personnel and processes for victims/survivors of sexual assault are examined in detail, highlighting the ways in which the legal system functions to privilege and protect the accused.

This leads to a discussion in Chapter 3 of the impact of inadequacies of the legal response to sexual assault on victims/survivors and, in particular, an exploration of their experiences of secondary victimisation by the legal system. This is followed by a discussion about the important contribution that feminist perspectives make to our theorising of these issues and to our thinking about change. The complexities surrounding the decision to report the crime of sexual assault to legal authorities are also explored.

Given the nature of the problems with the legal system that are addressed in these two chapters, an overwhelming contention to emerge from a review of existing research is that the legal system needs to change in order to be more responsive to the victims/survivors who report crimes of sexual assault. Feminist perspectives point to several sites for change including the broader social and patriarchal context in which the law operates, and the nature and operations of the legal system itself.

This notion of change is thoroughly explored in Chapter 4. The chapter focuses specifically on law reform, presenting the most significant examples of remedial legislative change over the past two decades. Unfortunately, the evaluative research in this area seems to point to the limitations of law reform to achieve the kinds of changes that practitioners and victims/survivors would like to see. This invites us to rethink how we conceptualise change strategies in the field of sexual assault and leads us to consider the exploration of theoretical alternatives. Chapter 4 concludes with a discussion of the ways in which counsellors/advocates think about changing the legal system, and what they perceive as the barriers to bringing about change. This exploration suggests that some aspects of feminist thinking concerning the struggles with the legal system may inadvertently contribute to a lack of a sense of agency in practitioners to challenge its oppressive processes and practices.

Chapter 5 explores the contributions that postmodernism and critical postmodernism make to expanding feminist thinking about change. Critical postmodernism is drawn upon because it holds the promise of overcoming the 'tragic failures' (Davies and Leonard 2004: iv) of modernist traditions by reconstructing possibilities of challenging and changing structurally produced power relations at an interpersonal level (Fook 2012). It is suggested that critical postmodern thinking may contribute to alternative conceptualisations of the problem by transcending some of the unintended consequences of feminist solutions that are grounded in modernist assumptions. I use a postmodernist appropriation of critical theory, critical postmodernism (see for example Allan et al. 2009; Fook 2012), to explore the influences these theoretical ideas might make to understanding practitioners' sense of powerlessness to bring about change in the legal system and to formulate different conceptualisations of change.

The initial focus of the research was therefore broadened from concentrating exclusively on the structural problems and unresponsiveness of the legal system to include an understanding of the ways in which practitioners construct, and are constructed by, their roles in the context of their work with the legal system, and to uncover discourses about their internal sense of agency (Ellermann 1998, Fook and Morley 2005). In approaching the research from a critical postmodern perspective, it was my contention that changing the ways we construct the problem, and our options in relation to it, may free practitioners to work in ways that have not previously been considered. Thus the book elucidates the ways in which critical postmodern perspectives, and the practices these theories imply, enable practitioners to envision possibilities for addressing the structural problems of the legal system at a micro level and therefore connect them with a more localised means of social change. It achieves this by drawing on critical reflection to generate new ways of thinking about the problems. Accordingly, this chapter also introduces the critical reflection model that was used as a method of inquiry in this research. The design of the study will be briefly explained, emphasising the central processes of deconstruction and reconstruction, as integral to the critical reflection method.

Chapter 6 establishes the foundation for the remainder of the book by presenting the stories of the six counsellors/advocates who participated in this research. The overview of these narratives demonstrates the transformative learning processes that each participant engaged in as part of the critical reflection research process. This includes a brief description of their practice example, a summarised deconstruction of their accounts, with particular reference to their implicit assumptions and the consequences of these for their practice, and a reconstructed account of their thinking and practice. This summary highlights each participant's individual journey in formulating new ways to challenge and change inequitable and unjust power relations and structures, and resisting participation in the discourses that sanction the legal system's unjust responses to victims/

survivors of sexual assault. Each practitioner's narrative is presented separately in order to provide a context to understand chapters 7 and 8.

These chapters both present the findings of the research and discuss the ways in which critical reflection on practice developed possibilities for change. Participants' narratives are presented thematically to capture the common, key issues in the collective deconstruction and reconstruction of their accounts. Discussion of these macro themes convincingly demonstrates the possibilities for change that the participants generated from critically reflecting on their practice.

Chapter 9 concentrates on the two most significant themes to emerge from the research findings. These are: 1) that even in the most disempowering contexts, it is possible for practitioners to envisage their own power to bring about change; and 2) that critical reflection is a powerful tool to assist practitioners to connect with this sense of agency. The broader implications of these themes are discussed in connection with relevant literature that assists to contextualise these key findings.

Ultimately, the final chapter begins by explicating how critical postmodern theory was integral to enabling the practitioners to reconstruct their practice. Critical postmodern thinking assisted participants to enhance feminist practice and improve prospects for emancipatory change. This observation may be particularly useful for practitioners who want to incorporate feminist ideals into their work, despite operating in contemporary contexts that may be hostile to goals and values of feminism.

The second part of this chapter discusses some of the contextual considerations when thinking through the implications of this research. It also refers to some potential limitations of the study and makes recommendations for further research. The concluding comments discuss the significance of the research in terms of the contributions it makes to feminist practice, critical postmodern practice and critical reflection in social work and related fields.

Chapter 2
The Legal Response to Sexual Assault

Introduction

This chapter explores victim/survivor's experiences of the Australian legal system's response to sexual assault. It provides a detailed overview of the most challenging aspects of the legal personnel and processes that constitute the judicial system as identified by victims/survivors, researchers and practitioners. Regarding legal personnel, some of the issues explored include the poor response to victims/survivors from police, which implicates them in low levels of reporting and conviction. It also examines the questionable conduct of defence lawyers and magistrates in the context of sexual assault hearings. In terms of legal processes, I will explore the central issues of consent, the victim/survivor's credibility, corroboration requirements, plea bargaining, the forensic examination, adjournments and cross-examination to outline the gravity of the problems embedded in the legal system that create major difficulties for victims/survivors and their supporters. A critique of the ways in which the legal system privileges and protects the accused will also be presented.

I include material as far back as the 1990s here because that was a time when feminist researchers and activists were particularly vocal about the injustices perpetrated against victims/survivors by the legal system (Laing 2008, Mustaine and Tewksbury 2002). Since that time, however, research that explicitly criticises the legal responses to sexual assault has significantly declined. The rise of neo-liberalism, managerial practices, and medicalisation have combined to individualise social issues and shift research agendas towards the treatment, assessment and management of victims/survivors (see for example Morley and Macfarlane, 2008) rather than to analyse their rights and experiences in the legal system.

Although many law reforms have been implemented over the last three decades, laws vary from state to state in Australia and are continually changing. For example, there are currently no universally agreed definitions about the behaviours that constitute sexual assault despite some common elements across jurisdictions (Fileborn 2011). To some extent, this is inconsequential in understanding the current state of the legal system because, as is discussed in Chapter 4, changes to the laws have not resulted in significantly different experiences of the legal process for victims/survivors. Therefore, many of the concerns that were documented earlier still hold currency today. As Heath (2007: 191) laments:

> [i]t is heartbreaking to report that statements about rape made decades ago continue to ring true … even with an impressive record of achieving *legislative* change, the broader goals of feminist rape law reform have not been attained.

Ultimately, she confirms the view that 'institutional responses to sexual assault remain manifestly inadequate' (Heath 2007: 176). This is reinforced by Fileborn (2011), who has undertaken research on behalf of The Australian Institute of Family Studies. She contends that despite significant changes to the law's processing of sexual assault offences in all Australian states and territories, 'victim[s]/survivors navigating the legal system still encounter significant difficulties and barriers throughout the court process, often as a direct result of the way in which criminal offences are structured' (Fileborn 2011: 6–7).

Problems with the Legal Responses to Sexual Assault

The Police Response

Police are the victims/survivors' gateway to the criminal justice system (Page 2004). Given that they are generally the first point of contact with the criminal justice system for the victim/survivor, the initial police response has a significant impact on the victim/survivor's experience of the legal process and on whether the offence is ultimately reported and investigated (Heath 2007). Unfortunately, victims/survivors' main concerns with their initial contact with the legal system include: police disbelief or denial of victims/survivors' experiences; the victim-blaming attitudes exhibited by the police; the impact of these attitudes on the capacity of particular police members to do their jobs appropriately in terms of taking statements, investigating crimes and making recommendations for prosecution; and the concern that sexual assault consequently remains largely under-reported and unprosecuted. Disturbingly, '[v]ictims of sexual assault commonly report that they are treated with disbelief, a lack of understanding, hostility and blame: in fact, a denial of their experience of violent crime' (Jarvis and McIlwaine 1997: 6; see also Heath 2007, Konradi 2001, Maier 2008).

These responses reflect the problematic value and belief systems that inform police attitudes to sexual assault (see for example Jordan 2004, Maier 2008, Page 2004). 'It seems that the police themselves are still highly influenced by the myths surrounding sexual assault and are still uneducated about the true nature of this crime' (Wightman 1995: 257).

Much research indicates that victims/survivors feel judged, blamed, ridiculed and disbelieved by police when they report an experience of sexual assault (see for example Campbell et al. 2001, Filipas and Ullman 2001, Maier 2008, Temkin 2005). Other work emphasises how the blaming and disbelieving attitudes of police result in 'irrelevant and inappropriate questions' being asked of victims/survivors during police inquiries (see for example Page 2004). One victim/survivor described her experience of the police interview process as 'like living a terrible nightmare' (Cripps 1995: 49).

Another victim/survivor described the police as 'aggressive and intimidating'. She reported feeling 'silenced' by the police officer's 'manner' and disappointed that he repeatedly told her that her case was not a priority (Kate 1998: 25). Her concerns with the police included their negligent 'investigation' and threatening behaviour, which resulted in her making a complaint about 'collusion in crimes of sexual violence within families' (Kate 1998: 26). Other allegations range from 'police refusing to even take a statement, to the disappearance or non-presentation of crucial evidence at trial, as well as intimidatory and dismissive treatment of alleged victims' (Kate 1998: 26). All of this may understandably discourage women from reporting, or even cultivate the withdrawal of their statements (Heath 2007: 177, Lievore 2005). It seems that the '... cultural context of their [the police] beliefs is exacerbated by a particularly male and misogynist sub-culture of policing' (Easteal 1996b: n.p.).

While anecdotal accounts provide rich insight into victims/survivors' experiences with the police, other empirical research indicates that 50 per cent of victims/survivors report experiences of feeling intimidated, 'so much so that they were unable to provide accurate statements' (Mitchell et al. 1995: 128). Making a statement should provide victims/survivors with an opportunity to have their version of events documented (Jarvis and McIlwaine 1997). However, in practice it seems that police often reinterpret and translate victims/survivors' stories into 'legal relevancies' (Smart 1989: 11 cited in Grix 1999: 93). Other difficulties with making statements include 'lengthy delays' in the process (Mitchell et al. 1995: 128). For example, one victim/survivor who reported her experience of sexual assault to the police was told to 'go home and to act normal until the police could get to the case!' (Mitchell et al. 1995: 128). Other practical difficulties with making statements concern a lack of both confidentiality and an appropriate private space for victims/survivors to tell their story (Mitchell et al. 1995).

In addition to concerns about how police treat victims/survivors, the police role also appears to have a negative impact on how (or whether) an investigation proceeds. Police are implicated in both low levels of reporting and charges not being laid (Jordan 2008, 2012, VLRC 2008, Maier 2008). Furthermore, there is a strong tendency for rape charges to be withdrawn (Heath 2007, Jarvis and McIlwaine 1997), with research indicating 'that 60 per cent of reports made to the police d[o] not result in any further action, and in 74 per cent of cases it was the police who made the decision not to proceed' (Stuart 1993: 99). Consequently, the overwhelming majority of sexual assaults reported to police do not result in criminal charges (See for example Heath 2007: 175, Jordan 2008).

Regrettably, it seems, '[p]olice make decisions on whether to proceed with a case based on their assessment of the evidence and of the victim's capacity as a witness' (Allen 1996 n.p.). In addition, 'Women often feel that lawyers and the police make decisions about what is and what isn't good for them without actually consulting; and that they are given information that is deemed "suitable" rather than all of the information about the process and their situations' (Martin and Angel 1995: 99).

Moreover, policing is informed by dominant social myths about sexual assault. (These myths are explored in Chapter 3). The factors that increase the likelihood of police pursuing an investigation include: a witness who can verify the victim/survivor's story; when the offence is considered severe, for example, if a weapon was used; when the perpetrator was not previously known to the victim/survivor (See for example Maier 2008: 788); if the victim/survivor incurred physical injuries during the assault (Du Mont et al. 2003); and whether she physically resisted her assailant (Du Mont and Myhr 2000). Essentially, the research indicates that police adhere to stereotypical notions about how 'genuine' the victim/survivor appears to be in order to judge the merits of the case (see for example Jordan 2008, Maier 2008). As one victim/survivor states: '*Why is a victim of sexual assault not believed ... I know why, because the police need ... evidence: they want bruises, cuts, evidence that physical violence occurred, broken bones even better, and lastly they want witnesses*' (cited in D'Arcy 1995: 138, italics in original).

A further complaint is that the needs of the victim/survivor after an assault 'often take second place to the investigative and administrative priorities' (McKelvie and Heenan 1993: 7; see also Bargen and Fishwick 1995: 46, Maier 2008). The result is that police may 'fail to enquire after a victim's welfare and make her feel like "just another piece of evidence"' (McCulloch 1998: 17). In addition, 'benign actions' by the police 'often leave the victim feeling absolutely devoid of any personal control' (Nelson 1995: 293, Maier 2008), or worse: 'Some police actively discourage women from proceeding' (McCulloch 1998: 17; see also Heath 2007).

Low Levels of Reporting and Conviction

Given victims/survivors' experiences with the police, it is not surprising that between at least 75 per cent (Heath 2007: 175) and 85 per cent (Fileborn 2011) of women who are raped choose not to report their experience of a serious indictable crime to police. Sexual assault is therefore a 'massively underreported' offence (Townsend 1996: 7; see also Fileborn 2011, Heath 2007, VLRC 2008).

The most frequently cited reason for victims/survivors' decision to avoid reporting an assault is 'a lack of confidence in the legal system' (Jarvis and McIlwaine, 1997: 6). Related reasons include victims/survivors' fears of being identified and blamed, not being believed, being made to feel that they contributed to the assault in some way (see for example Brown 2007, Jordan 2008, 2012), traumatising interactions with the police, fear of loss of privacy, poor conviction rates, and a lack of appropriate training on the part of legal personnel involved in the process (Bargen and Fishwick 1995: 26, Brown 2007). In summation, the choice by most victims/survivors not to engage in the legal system can be attributed to 'a quite accurate perception that the legal system may not support them' (Martin and Angel 1995: 97; see also Jordan 2008, 2012).

In addition to low reporting rates, the rate of convictions for sexual assault is continuing to decline in Australia (Carmody 2003: 200, Cook 2002–3, Philadelphoff-Puren 2005, VLRC 2008), which hardly serves as an incentive to report. In the 1990s, '... the reality [was] that only one in three sexual assaults at best [were] likely to be reported to the police ... [and] a mere 6 per cent of all assaults committed end in conviction in our courts' (Corbett and Larcombe 1994: 140). More recent research suggests that levels of reporting and conviction are still 'unacceptably low' (Heath 2007: 101; see also Fileborn 2011) and constitute an even bigger problem now, with, for example, less than one in seven reports of penetrative child sexual abuse resulting in prosecution (VLRC 2008: 3), less than two per cent of reported incidents (of rape in South Australia, for example) resulting in a conviction (Heath 2007: 175), and 85 per cent of sexual assault offences remaining unreported (Fileborn 2011). Australia is not alone in these unacceptable statistics: similarly low levels of reporting and conviction have been documented in the United States (Anderson 2001, Monroe et al. 2005). Heath (2007: 185–6) suggests that low rates of reporting are tied to low rates of conviction because detectives often make decisions to proceed with investigating a complaint based on 'a reasonable prospect of gaining conviction'. She highlights how the 'underenforcement of the law of rape ... is justified with reference to the low rate of conviction' (Kelly 2001: 185 cited in Heath 2007: 186), which becomes a 'self-perpetuating cycle' (Heath 2007: 185–6). Commenting on the South Australian experience, Heath states that the lack of law enforcement promotes the perception that sexual assault is acceptable. She ultimately contends, 'there is little evidence that it [rape] is actually illegal' (Heath 2007: 176).

The Responses of Other Legal Personnel

In addition to poor police conduct, and low levels of reporting and conviction, inappropriate and problematic responses from other legal personnel seem to occur at all levels of the legal system. Research indicates, for example, that prosecutorial decision-making is based on similar factors to police decision-making, which is highly reflective of certain social myths (Beichner and Spohn 2005, Frazier and Haney 1996, Page 2004). This is particularly concerning as '... the attitudes and ideology of legal system personnel are ... crucial to the way ... sexual abuse cases are dealt with ...' (Scutt 1991: 128). If, for example, a victim/survivor is represented by legal counsel who does not believe her or does not think her assault was serious, it is likely that her allegations will not even be raised (Scutt 1991). More recent research indicates that prosecutorial decision-making is also highly influenced by the prosecutor's perception of the victim/survivor's credibility (Beichner and Spohn 2005), which has major implications as to whether a case will proceed to trial.

Magistrates at committal hearings have been similarly accused of acting as 'gatekeepers' because of their capacity to filter cases from the legal system (Martin and Angel 1995: 95). Often, victims/survivors' experiences are 'reinterpreted by the male dominated judiciary in this country to fit with their picture of the world' (Aldunate, 1995: 177). The literature highlights the 'attitudinal problems and the ignorance so often exhibited by the legal system' (Hunter 1995: 249). For example, many complainants report feeling 'blamed by the judge's summation to the jury' (Mitchell et al. 1995: 130) and distressed by 'unfair comments' offered by judges to the jury throughout the trial process (Mitchell et al. 1995: 131). One study reports that victims/survivors 'viewed the language and the comments made in the summation as prejudicial and, at times, reflecting societal myths about what constitutes "real" rape' (Mitchell et al. 1995: 130; see also Erlich, 2001). These 'findings replicate the notorious examples of judges' comments that have been given prominence in the media' over the last two decades (Mitchell et al. 1995: 130). More recent commentary indicates these concerns are still just as valid (Beazer 2008).

Perhaps some of the most abhorrent responses that have attracted media attention have come from trial judges whose comments reflect misogynist social myths about sexual assault. One magistrate stated that, 'the crime [of rape] when committed against prostitutes ... is not as heinous as when committed, say, on a happily married woman living in a flat in the absence of her husband when the miscreant breaks in and commits rape on her' (*R v. Hakopian 1991*, County Court, Melbourne cited in Scutt 1996: n.p.). Justice Bollen's assertion that it is acceptable for husbands to use 'rougher than usual handling' of their wives who do not consent to fulfil his supposed conjugal rights is equally disturbing (Aldunate 1995: 179, Gilmore 1995). Similarly, a forensic expert rendered rape an 'oxymoron' in stating, '[i]t is to be recollected that many women will not consent without some force' (Clark 1987: 71 cited in Gilmore 1995: 51). In highlighting the legal system's complicity with violence against women at an international level, Madame Justice Wilson, a Canadian Supreme Court Judge stated:

> ... it was not so long ago that the law not only failed to protect women from battering, but positively sanctioned this form of injury to women through the device of the "rule of thumb" under which it was permissible for a man to beat his wife so long as he did so with a stick no longer than his thumb. Apparently Welsh law had an even more precise standard: the rod had to be no longer than a man's forearm. (cited in Gilmore 1995: 51)

While many of these examples attracted media attention in the 1990s, more recently, the Victorian director of public prosecutions publicly reprimanded Michael Kelly, a Victorian county court judge for his insensitivity in dismissing a complainant's victim impact statement as a 'waste of time' (Beazer 2008: 8). Such an example indicates that concerns about the conduct and perceptions of judges in sexual assault cases continue to be valid. It appears that police, magistrates and legal personnel frequently operate upon 'gendered (mis)assumptions [which] have plagued the law governing violence against women to the detriment of the victim'

(Gilmore 1995: 51). I now continue to explore this theme of legal injustice with specific reference to legal processes that are identified as particularly problematic.

Consent

Consent is often the most central issue in rape trials (see for example Grey 2007: 128, Fileborn 2011). Section 37 of the Victorian Crimes (Rape) Act 1991 states that for consent to be given the person must communicate 'free agreement' to the particular act. The recently amended Crimes Amendment (Consent – Sexual Assault Offences) Act 2007, enacted in 2008 also created a statutory definition of '"consent" as being a free and voluntary agreement to sexual intercourse' (Wells 2008: 1). As McKelvie and Heenan (1993: 10) state, the Victorian legislation indicates that judges should warn jurors:

> not to assume that a complainant freely agreed just because: there is no evidence of physical resistance; she did not protest; she did not sustain any injury; or she had freely agreed to sex with the accused or another person on another occasion. (McKelvie and Heenan 1993: 10)

Despite this, the issue of consent continues to be invoked as the most commonly used defence in rape cases (see for example, Grey 2007: 178, Philadelphoff-Puren 2005). This 'means that the victim's character is put on trial in ways that are unparalleled in other areas of the law' (NSW 1992 Sexual Assault Phone-In Report, quoted in Mitchell et al. 1995: 132; see also ALRC 2010, Malloch 2004). Several authors argue that the issue of consent is largely underpinned by prevalent social myths that falsely stereotype male and female sexuality, including the implicit assumption that women are always consenting (see for example Brown 2007, Garcia and McManimon 2011). This has been linked with discourses that conflate rape with romance, and seduction with aggression (Philadelphoff-Puren 2005).

The matter of consent therefore obstructs victims/survivors' access to a fair trial (Easteal 1996b). It is based on the continuation of key concepts that are constructed within a masculine, non-victim reality (Malloch 2004). For example, in law, a victim/survivor is required to make the refusal of consent explicitly known (O'byrne et al. 2006). In most circumstances, however, this requirement is not realistic due to the impact of gendered power imbalances between the victim/survivor and the offender (Malloch 2004). Furthermore, the inclusion of *mens rea* means that in order for a conviction to occur, the prosecution must prove beyond reasonable doubt that the defendant knew that the victim/survivor was not consenting (Fileborn 2011). The implications of this are twofold: 1) it is not the victim/survivor's experience that defines whether the sexual assault has occurred, but the 'defendant's mental state and knowledge' (Fileborn 2011: 7) and 2) 'the issue of consent shifts a jury's attention from the actions of the accused, ensuring that the victim/survivor's conduct 'remain[s] the point of focus in the criminal trial' (Fileborn 2011: 7; see also ALRC 2010). However, research indicates that men have a refined ability to understand very subtle, non-verbal sexual refusals (Philadelphoff-Puren 2004). Therefore, it should not be necessary for a woman explicitly to say 'no' to indicate that she is not consenting (O'byrne et al. 2006, Philadelphoff-Puren 2004).

Despite this, for women who have been sexually assaulted, the issue of consent often causes hostile, unjust and humiliating treatment by the police and courts (see for example Malloch 2004). Juries assess whether a complainant has consented based on their own 'common sense' understandings that are largely informed by the dominant patriarchal ideologies responsible for creating and maintaining myths about sexual assault in the first place (Corbett and Larcombe 1994, Taylor 2004). For example, one legal case study described how the issue of consent was responsible for the acquittal of a stranger who broke into a woman's flat and raped her in the middle of the night: 'Questions focused on her credibility as a witness in relation to her assertion that she had not consented. In order to "assess" this credibility the inquiries focused on her lifestyle, past experience and behaviour before and after the assault' (Allen 1996: n.p.). Clearly, these are all circumstances that hold no relevance either to the perpetrator's actions or to the assault, yet they act to make the victim/survivor culpable for the assault.

In addition, the issue of consent may be particularly complicated for victims/survivors who are disadvantaged in other ways such as having a disability (Phillips 1996, VLRC 2008). For a victim/survivor with a hearing impairment, for example, there may be significant gaps in appropriate and adequate information about the law and the victim/survivor's rights (Phillips 1996). Furthermore, if a person is hearing impaired, they 'miss out on a lot of information and therefore, view the world in a slightly different way to hearing people. Each extra disability compounds the situation, and further changes your view and understanding of how the world works' (Phillips 1996: 186). Therefore, for people with disabilities, due to early and consistent experiences of directional learning, '… a direction or order given by a hearing or non-disabled person is usually met with compliance' (Phillips 1996: 186). In a court of law, compliance is interpreted as consent. It is therefore probable that police would not proceed with charging an offender who had ordered a victim/survivor to commit sexual acts with which she felt compelled to comply (Phillips 1996).

Closely connected to the issue of consent, the victim/survivor's credibility is often attacked due to 'common law's archetype of the "reasonable" rape victim' (Grey 2007: 173). Referring to a case study to demonstrate how credibility is linked to consent, one researcher states: 'That the woman lived alone, had had previous boyfriends, was not a virgin, was unmarried and did not immediately report [the attack] would not have assisted in the assessment' (Allen 1996: n.p.). Frequently informed by dominant gender role stereotypes of women that influence the 'jury's subjective criteria', credibility is often judged by 'the extent to which she behaved according to how they believed a "proper" woman should' (Allen 1996: n.p.; see also Jordan 2008). For adult complainants of sexual assault, the issue of credibility is often decided on the basis of whether the sexual intercourse was consensual.

For children, credibility is judged on whether their evidence can be believed (ALRC 2010).

These constructions of credibility influence not only juries but also the prosecutors and police (ALRC 2010, Beichner and Spohn 2005, Jordan 2008). Feminist sociologist Smith (1990: 14–18) parallels this analysis in medicine, education and mental health where she demonstrates how the 'relations of ruling' in historically male-dominated, administrative domains, systematically define universal standards according to patriarchal norms, excluding or distorting the concrete and particular lived-experiences of women.

In the same way, common sense notions of the credible witness ensure that:

> the woman's voice is unheard and *her* meaning of the experience is denied. Instead, it is mediated, reinterpreted and redefined by the dominant discourses of the law. The questions which are asked, how a woman's versions of events is listened to and understood, are undoubtedly constrained by conceptions of blame and responsibility … The consequence for women whose lived experiences do not match that "truth", is that they are neither heard nor understood; their reality is not witnessed. (Jarvis and McIlwaine 1997: 8, italics in original)

Clearly women are subjected to archaic expectations to be morally virtuous and sexually conservative, or face being discredited as victims/survivors of sexual assault in court (see for example Larcombe 2002). For example:

> A woman who reports her assault and has her case taken to court is most often violently assaulted by a man known to her socially, and she has evidence of injury to substantiate her claim of resistance. If her behaviour in any way violated "good girl" social norms she can expect a supreme court trial in front of a jury where [the] conviction rate is low. These cases receive extensive publicity and support the public image of loose women and/or exceptional men (i.e., unemployed, drunk, young jerk). (Yurchesyn et al. 1992: 77)

Female complainants of sexual assault are therefore not treated as 'normal, functional and truthful human being[s]' (Martin and Angel 1995: 100; see also Grey 2007, Stevenson 2000). The concept of 'Incredible Woman Syndrome' has been used to understand how 'the legal system has generally been sceptical of women's ability to tell the truth' (Scutt cited in Martin and Angel 1995: 100; see also ALRC 2010). Whilst some commentators argue that such scrutiny of the victim/survivor is necessary to ensure fairness to the accused (Grey 2007, Orth and Maercker 2004), others contend that these '[j]udicial attitudes reflect and reinforce the lessened credibility for women' (Mack 1998: 145). For example, one researcher suggests that 'it is intrinsically easier for society and the legal system to disbelieve or refuse to listen to survivors than to confront the fact that sexual assault is very prevalent in our society … female victims/survivors are treated as "invalid and unreliable witnesses"' (Mack 1998: 148) and as 'less credible, even when accurate and honest' (Mack 1998: 146). Another woman, reflecting on her own experience of being rendered 'incredible' during cross-examination contends that the defence lawyer's 'aim right from the start was to intimidate me and make me look like a liar' (Cripps 1995: 52).

In short, '[w]omen have been met with disbelief by the legal system and severely marginalised by the law's claim that credibility equals male. In matters of sexual assault specifically, women are viewed as less than competent in relaying their stories' (Martin and Angel 1995: 100). Similarly, in relation to child sexual assault cases '... the survivor's credibility will be on trial, rather than the perpetrator's crimes'. Judges also use the increased public awareness of child sexual assault to 'cast doubt' on victims/survivors' testimonies' (Martin and Angel 1996: 100; see also ALRC 2010).

Corroboration

Inextricably linked to the issue of credibility is the requirement for corroboration, which also significantly impacts legal proceedings in sexual assault cases. Corroboration is defined as 'evidence which tends to confirm the evidence of a complainant or other witness on the matter or issue' (Naylor 1985: 4). Historically, corroboration requirements have directed judges to warn jurors of the dangers of convicting the perpetrator on uncorroborated evidence. Such warnings are also used to caution juries about the impact upon the accused of a delay between the assault and the trial process (Grey 2007: 172).

Perhaps the most contentious issue about corroboration requirements are that they appear to have a significant impact on if and how a trial proceeds. Unless the victim/survivor can give a perfect account, the *Longman* direction is given to juries.[1] This direction states that it is unsafe or dangerous to find the accused guilty based on uncorroborated evidence (Grey 2007, Young 1995). Corroboration requirements therefore 'fortify police "scepticism" and reinforce the view that evidence of complainants in sexual assault cases is potentially so unreliable that it must be independently confirmed' (Naylor 1985: 14; see also Grey 2007).

As with most legislation pertaining to cases of sexual assault, the rules about Longman warnings differ from state to state. In Western Australia, for example, prior to 1988 and the introduction of the Evidence Act, there was a rule that judges must warn juries in rape cases that, while they may act upon the word of a female complainant alone, considerable caution should be exercised because of the 'ease' with which such a charge is made and the difficulty that attends its rebuttal (Tannin 1996). Historical support for this view dates back to 1736 (Tannin 1996). Steeped in social mythology:

---

1 *Longman v The Queen* (1989): in this decision, an appeal relating to the conviction of the accused (Longman, who was convicted more than 20 years after the offence), was upheld on the basis that the trial judge should have warned the jury that the long delay meant the evidence could not be adequately tested (Tannin, 1996).

> [t]he traditional reason for warning the jury about the evidence of a complainant of sexual assault is, first, that she (or he) may deliberately lie … give false evidence out of jealousy, spite or shame for a sexual act done with consent [or that] women may be deluded, neurotic, hysterical and believe in the reality of their rape fantasies. (Naylor 1985: 14)

Unfortunately, this view seems to have retained its currency. In recent years, the federal and Victorian law reform commissions have collaborated in a more uniform approach to limiting judicial discretion over corroboration requirements. However, the New South Wales Law Reform Commission has defended 'unfettered' judicial discretion in order to protect the accused person's right to a fair trial (Grey 2007: 172). 'The maxim that rape allegations are "very easy to fabricate, but extremely difficult to refute" … and other gendered assumptions' continue to justify the 'requirement that judges warn the jury about convicting on the basis of a woman's uncorroborated evidence' (Grey 2007: 173).

Even when there is independent corroboration of the victim/survivor's testimony, 'the law's ideology of truth' may still regard these facts as inadmissible (Taylor 1996: n.p.). This provides the accused a strong advantage in that medical files, for example, may be ruled inadmissible when they are perceived as 'deny[ing] fairness to the accused' (Taylor 1996). In addition, what is considered relevant as evidence for the prosecution is 'vastly different to that which is regarded as relevant to the defence' (Taylor 1996).

Current corroboration requirements make the prosecution of child sexual assault significantly more difficult because evidence given by children is usually required to be independently corroborated, thus resulting in the preclusion of children's testimonies and other relevant evidence (see for example VLRC 2008). This contributes to the trauma suffered by children if the matter does reach court (Grey 2007, Naylor 1985). Corroboration rules mean that a young child who is sexually assaulted in the absence of witnesses, and whose attacker makes no admissions, will rarely receive the protection of the criminal law. In fact, it is likely that a prejudgment will be made about whether the required corroborative evidence exists and that no prosecution will be launched (Naylor 1985: 15; see also Grey 2007: 178, Heath 2007). The myths about women and children being 'incredible' witnesses have therefore elevated corroboration warnings to the status of a legal ruling (Taylor 1996).

Ultimately, there is no basis on which to believe that complainants of sexual assault are unreliable and juries should be able to consider the evidence in the same manner as in other types of cases. Sexual assault should continue to be dealt with by the courts but the faults of the legal system, including an over-reliance on corroboration requirements, should not be 'an excuse for "decriminalising" … sexual assault' (Naylor 1985: 12).

Plea Bargaining

Another legal practice that highlights the difficulties for victims/survivors of sexual assault in attaining a successful prosecution of the perpetrator is plea bargaining (see for example Mack 1998). The preference for guilty pleas and the associated plea bargaining is problematic because it often results in accepting arguments propagated by the defence that the victim/survivor has some responsibility for the crime (for example, the perception that she was a willing participant or provoked the perpetrator). Some suggest that the practice of plea bargaining constitutes an attempt to reduce the 'public exposure' and 'stigma' of sexual assault. However, if plea bargaining takes place, 'the outcome is most likely a conditional discharge or light sentence' (Yurchesyn et al. 1992: 80). Where there is little evidence available and the accused denies the charge or the victim/survivor is labelled as 'seductive … there is a high probability that the accused will be acquitted' (Yurchesyn et al. 1992: 80).

Consequently, from the victim/survivor's perspective, numerous problems are associated with the strong judicial preference to settle out of court (Mack 1998). A major concern is that the Office of Public Prosecutions (OPP) enters into plea bargaining and often accepts pleas of lesser charges without consulting the victim/survivor, adding to her trauma during the legal process. As one woman who was on the receiving end of this practice commented: 'plea bargaining is a compromise – where's the sense of justice?' (Mitchell et al. 1995: 129).

The Forensic Examination

The forensic examination provides another example of a problematic aspect of the legal process for many victims/survivors. The difficulties include being subjected to an 'invasive' gynaecological examination for the purpose of collecting potential forensic evidence, which can serve to remind the victim/survivor of the assault (Maier 2008: 790; see also Jordan 2008). The forensic examination process has been described as reducing victims/survivors' bodies to being the '"site" of the crime' (Jarvis and McIlwaine 1997: 7). As one victim/survivor commented, '[t]he medical examination itself was very frightening. It was like reliving the assault all over again' (Cripps 1995: 49).

Moreover, there is considerable pressure to have the examination done immediately, delaying the victim/survivor's departure from the crisis care unit[2] after an assault (Jordan 2008, Maier 2008). The difficulties are captured by this victim/survivor's statement: '*So even if you do get to hospital remember*

2 Crisis care unit is the terminology used by counsellors/advocates to describe the after-hours crisis response to victims/survivors of sexual assault. This typically involves meeting with the victim/survivor and the police at a neutral location, such as a hospital, to support the victim/survivor during the initial crisis and provide her with information regarding medical and legal options.

not to drink, urinate, wash or move, until at least 3 hours has passed and the forensic [doctor] has arrived to examine you. Anyone who can hold their bladder that long under stress is a remarkable person ...' (victim/survivor quoted in D'Arcy 1995: 138, italics in original).

Another problem with forensic examinations is that, despite the additional trauma they cause, they usually fail to produce any conclusive evidence. If specimens such as traces of semen are found (and they are often not), it may only testify that intercourse has occurred, but not rape. The issue of consent may therefore undermine forensic evidence. This means that the trauma associated with the intrusive examination may well be worthless for legal proceedings and ultimately very disappointing (McCarthy 1995).

Adjournments and Delays

Delays in the legal process such as adjournments are another factor contributing to victims/survivors' sense of powerlessness and sense of dissatisfaction with the legal system. 'Protracted delays' are common (Townsend 1996: n.p.), with committal hearings also identified as elongating the process (VLRC 2008). Research indicates that 60 per cent of cases that go to trial take more than 12 months to be heard and nearly one-third of cases take more than two years to conclude. 'For many women, the recovery process is difficult, if not impossible, especially while the pressures of a trial [are] hanging over their head' (Townsend 1996: n.p.).

Similarly, many women identify 'the lengthy time delay between the assault and the trial as the worst aspect of going to court' (Mitchell et al. 1995: 133). As one report comments, '[d]elays are too lengthy for victims who need to start rebuilding their lives following the assault' (Mitchell et al. 1995: 133). Another victim/survivor recounts the devastation of preparing for the court case only to have it adjourned, confirming the sense of powerlessness that characterises victims/survivors' experiences of the legal process (Cripps 1995).

Cross-Examination

A further difficulty for victims/survivors is cross-examination, which is regarded as one of the most challenging aspects of the legal process for complainants of sexual assault. 'Cross-examination is the most distressing part of court proceedings for victims ... [as] questions are designed to cast doubt on her version of events' (McCulloch 1998: 18). During cross-examination '... the law, formally and informally, denigrates women and devalues their testimony when they speak of being sexually assaulted' (Mack 1998: 147). Research participants have reported that defence lawyers often interact with complainants in ways that are 'rude, sarcastic and threatening' (Mitchell et al. 1995: 129). The Australian Law Reform Commission has acknowledged that 'cross-examination may take on particularly personal dimensions that may not be seen in other criminal proceedings' (ALRC 2010: 5).

For these reasons the impact of cross-examination has been identified as causing a secondary victimisation for complainants of sexual assault (see for example Campbell 2006, VLRC 2008). These victims/survivors state the court process: 'made me feel raped all over again' (Corbett and Larcombe 1994: 132); 'was more painful than the rape itself' (Mitchell et al. 1995: 131), and 'took me longer to get over … than the actual rape. I was treated as the criminal' (Stuart, 1993: 100). Others explain: '[e]ven though I was the victim, everything in that court procedure worked to place me on trial' (Stuart 1993: 102); '[t]here is no difference between being raped and giving evidence as a key witness at the trial of your alleged rapist, except that this time it happens in front of a crowd' (cited in Stuart 1993: 101). Furthermore, '[c]ross-examination may last for several hours or even days' (McCulloch 1998: 18). Research suggests that cross examination is longer in duration in sexual assault trials than trials concerning other offences (ALRC 2010).

Victims/survivors of sexual assault are particularly vulnerable during cross-examination:

> One of the main differences between survivors of sexual offences and other criminal offences is the intensely personal and violating nature of the crime. This means that to access the criminal justice system, victims/survivors must be prepared to reveal highly intimate and personal details, and often have to listen to defence arguments that denigrate them. (D'Arcy 1995: 142)

Consequently, victims/survivors' overall experience of cross-examination is one of 'retraumatisation' (Mitchell et al. 1995: 129). Common experiences include:

> the frustration of having everything taken out of context; the fact that the defence will use anything possible to discredit you … the implication … that you are not convincing enough as a witness or you are too convincing as a witness; that you're going ahead with it because you hate the perpetrator. The defence will also drag up all of your personal history … or alternatively they will imply that you are doing too well in your life now for your story to hold. (Mitchell et al. 1995: 110)

In order to discredit the victim/survivor the defence will use items such as birthday cards from the perpetrator, for example, to imply the existence of a loving relationship (Martin and Angel 1995). 'Basically, there is nothing they will not use' (Mitchell et al. 1995: 110). While victims/survivors have spoken about 'their distress at having past life experiences and sexual histories being used in court as evidence of their character' (Mitchell et al. 1995: 129), defence lawyers have also been accused of portraying the victim/survivor as 'a person of low intelligence or of low moral fibre whose story should not be believed' (Stuart 1993: 102).

Disturbingly, in some cases perpetrators have represented themselves in the court process, thereby being personally allowed to cross-examine witnesses

(VLRC 2008: 8–9, Brown 2007, D'Arcy 1995). Whilst this has recently been removed in some jurisdictions, such as New South Wales (NSWLRC 2009), such practices have allowed the court to 'license abuse' of victims/survivors by allowing lengthy attacks on their character including questions relating to their personal hygiene, and types of nightwear or underwear worn (Taylor 1996: n.p.). As one woman comments, 'I was a little girl both blamed and left unprotected ... such a situation leaves me with a permanent sense of disbelief and horror' (Kate 1998: 24).

In Favour of the Accused

As has been demonstrated any discussion about the problems with the legal response to sexual assault nearly always highlights how the legal process favours the accused whilst actively disadvantaging the victim/survivor. The historical context for this emerged in the twentieth century, in which Freud and other theorists reconceptualised sexual behaviour and sexual deviation to propose that 'rape was a perversion and rapists were mentally ill' (Donat and D'Emilio 1998: 37), thus reducing the perpetrator's responsibilities for his actions. 'In other words, rape was reconceptualised from the perpetrator's point of view. Their focus was on understanding the plight of the man, not the woman; her victimisation was simply a by-product of his pathology' (Donat and D'Emilio 1998: 37–8).

Within this dichotomous understanding, power and privilege lie with the accused in the context of the law. For example, a prominent researcher in this field argues that the 'scales of justice' are weighted more heavily on the side of the defendant in cases of sexual assault (Easteal 1996b, n.p.). Gender-biased understandings of sexual violence are also referred to as 'tip[ping] the scales of justice' (Allen 1996: n.p.). While the explicit goal of the legal system is to protect the rights of the complainant and the accused to a fair trial (see for example VLRC 2008: 3), it is argued that the principle of a fair trial is 'synonymous with fairness to the accused' (Grey 2007: 176). As Stuart (1993: 101) explains: '[T]he rape trial amounts to a gruelling test of the victim/survivor's credibility, where the honesty and integrity of the parties are pitted in a legal struggle weighted overwhelmingly in favour of the accused.' Other research highlights '[t]he multiplicity of ways in which the "woman" who has been sexually assaulted is processed by the criminal justice system and "the law" – and *not* the way the offender is' (Grix 1999: 93, italics in original). Often, victims/survivors do not understand 'why their own character could be questioned, but not the character of the offender – especially when the offender had prior convictions and the charges were against him' (Mitchell et al. 1995: 129). Confirming this, repeated legal processes and outcomes 'display the eagerness of male judges to blame the victim and put the rights of rapists above the rights of their victims' (Wightman 1995: 252). A prominent Australian feminist lawyer, Jocelyn Scutt (1995: 322) states that:

> It is the absence of the voice of the survivor, or the ignorance of that voice, which has allowed the voice of the rapist to dominate in courts where, when

> violence against women is an issue, not only is justice not being seen and heard to be done, it is not being done.

Concluding comments from one research project affirm her observations: 'Victims are not positive about the legal system in general. They perceive that defendant's rights are given precedence over their own, that the system is unfair, and that they are not given enough information' (Frazier and Haney 1996: 625).

Another disadvantage for victims/survivors of sexual assault is their lack of legal advocacy in the courtroom: 'unlike the accused, she has no legal team working on her behalf' (Easteal 1996b: n.p.). This is because it is not her case. She is positioned as a meagre witness for the prosecution. The effects of this are clear in the following personal account from victim/survivor:

> His barrister swung questions at me. I was only supposed to give a yes or no answer. If I paused even in the slightest the barrister would answer the questions for me … he kept insisting it was one of those boy meets girl affairs when it wasn't like that at all … I became increasingly confused. It was just as if he was able to tear me apart and lie and get away with it and no-one stopped him. I looked to the prosecutor. She didn't say anything, she just kept her head down taking notes … With all this happening I went even further into a state of shock … In the end I just agreed with everything that his barrister said. (RRLC cited in Stuart 1993: 100)

Further evidencing the privileging of the accused are the specific legal rules that grant more protection to men accused of sexual offences than any other crime (Heath 2007: 187). For example, the burden of proof lies with the prosecution, who must be able to prove the charge, which can usually not be corroborated by independent witnesses, beyond reasonable doubt. At the same time, women who withdraw statements of sexual assault, may be convicted of perjury, whereas this is far more unlikely for other offences (Brown 2007: 13). Citing some specific examples of this, Scutt (1991: 136–7) writes:

> Despite most sentences for perjury being non-custodial, the Supreme Court imposed sentences of eighteen months with a minimum of six months … The view that women and children are not to be believed where sexual offences are in question is firmly entrenched in the British system of justice, and that entrenchment has transported itself into the Australian system … Innocent men (and women) can be wrongly accused of all manner of crimes, but it is only where the crime is a sexual offence, the victim a women or child, that special rules have been instituted granting men more "protection" than exist in any other area of the criminal law.

The issues of consent, the victim/survivor's credibility and corroboration requirements are also implicated in protecting perpetrators. Analysis of judges' decisions reveal a continuing regard for the position of the man against whom allegations of sexual abuse have been made, and an assumption that such allegations are easily made (Grey 2007: 178). Evidentiary requirements of corroboration, arguably developed to support the right of an accused person to a fair trial, have been defended because changing them would be assumed to deny the fundamental right of the accused to defend himself against malicious allegations (ALRC 2010, Grey 2007).

The concern to protect a defendant from false allegations is placed above a woman's right to justice after being violated (Scutt 1991). The tension between these two competing positions 'is hardly a delicate one when for most victims, justice is just about as remote as the moon' (Corbett and Larcombe 1994: 139), and the principle of a fair trial privileges fairness for the accused (Grey 2007: 176). This focus on the rights of the perpetrator has attracted criticism from feminist commentators who believe that corroboration warnings are 'gender specific discrimination' (Taylor 1996: n.p.). Given that most victims/survivors are female, the judiciary assume a need for independent corroboration of a woman's story. Moreover, highlighting the disadvantages for women accessing the legal system, some researchers argue that '[l]aws requiring physical evidence of penetration, the need for corroboration, and allowing testimony about the victim's sexual history in court trials ha[ve] the effect of placing the victim on trial' (Donat and D'Emilio 1998: 39–40).

Another example of legal rules that favour and protect perpetrators of sexual violence is the situation in which a perpetrator found guilty and convicted of sexual assault can appeal to a higher court against sentencing. This can lead to the whole trial process having to be repeated. The prosecution, however, are unable to appeal an acquittal (Brown 2007: 113). A successful appeal against a conviction can result in the charges being dismissed (Brown 2007) while the prosecution can only appeal against sentences they consider too lenient (McCulloch 1998).

Subpoenaing Case File Notes

Another legal practice that advantages the accused at the expense of the victim/survivor is the subpoenaing of case file notes. In some jurisdictions, case file notes and all other confidential documentation relevant to victims/survivors of sexual assault that access support services are allowed to be subpoenaed for use by the defence at the trial judge's discretion and used as admissible evidence in court (VLRC 2008). For example, Queensland currently has no legislation to protect or restrict access to confidential records that have been documented as part of the victims/survivors' private counselling processes, while communications made prior to charges of sexual assault are not covered by protection legislation in Tasmania or South Australia (Fileborn 2011). In addition, medical records are excluded from protective legislation in most states and territories in Australia (Fileborn 2011). This practice parallels the increasing use of disclosure rules in

Canada and England that enable the defence to gain access to medical records and case file notes (Murphy and Whitty 2000).

Since counsellors/advocates have a counselling, support and advocacy role, and not an investigatory one, counselling notes are largely irrelevant to legal proceedings. However, because the judicial process expects the presentation of evidence, particularly if there is a misguided perception that the evidence might indicate that a complainant consented, counselling records are often subpoenaed. The admission of these notes indicates a failure by the legal system to acknowledge that counsellors are not investigators, but are more concerned with the victim/survivor's recovery process (Townsend 1996: n.p.).

Whilst counselling notes only ever contain the counsellor's impressions and interpretations of the victim/survivor's experience (Gardiner and Roberson 1995), they do articulate information about the victim/survivor's feelings, which can easily be manipulated or misrepresented by the defence. For example, in internalising the dominant mythology about sexual assault, victims/survivors frequently express self-blame. 'An insensitive reading of these statements could inappropriately construe them as evidence of consent' (Townsend 1996: n.p.). As these researchers explain:

> [T]aken out of context, it can end with a devastating result … such action could lead to the victim being discredited and the case against a perpetrator of sexual assault lost … When the defence subpoenas our case files in an attempt to discredit our client, the perpetrator not only has access to the confidential information, he also has the ability to use it against the victim. The very fact that the perpetrator can get his hands on the client's confidential case sets up a vulnerability for violation through a symbolic form of re-perpetration. (Gardiner and Roberson 1995: 230)

It is therefore not surprising that the practice of subpoenaing case file notes has been condemned as tantamount to 'perpetrat[ing] patriarchy as if wielding a weapon and to take our client's private information and use it against them' (Gardiner and Roberson 1995: 238). File notes are inappropriately used to discredit the victim/survivor in the search for admissions of self-blame, guilt, feelings of shared responsibility for the abuse, and discrepancies between records of times and dates. For example, one researcher poses the question: 'To what extent is the goal of a "fair trial" facilitated by the launching of a "fishing expedition?"' (Allen 1996: n.p.). Others ask equally pertinent questions: [W]hy are client files increasingly subpoenaed and used in ways that not only damage the prosecution's case and benefit the defence, but also have the potential to cause harm to the victim of crime?' (Gardiner and Roberson 1995: 236–7).

For Queensland, the public interest should be central to the decision to introduce protection legislation, and public interest immunity should be considered. This means that a court will not order a document to be produced, even if it is relevant, if it could be injurious to the public to disclose it (Tannin 1996). Certainly, counselling notes remaining unprotected from subpoena could be argued as contrary to the public interest given that victims/survivors may avoid counselling or refrain from accessing the legal system out of fear that knowledge of their very personal experiences may end up being given to the perpetrator and exposed in court. It is of fundamental importance in establishing a relationship of trust between counsellor and victim/survivor that the details of counselling sessions remain confidential. Understandably, victims/survivors must feel confident that any information they disclose in the context of counselling will not be used against them (Gardiner and Roberson 1995: 234).

While the victim/survivor's right to privacy is constantly weighed against the defendant's right to a fair trial, Townsend (1996: n.p., italics in original) states that law reformers need to understand:

> that the principle of a fair trial should not be equated with advantage to the accused. A fair trial should hinge upon the consideration of all *relevant* evidence, not simply every document relating to the complainant that the defence can possibly subpoena.

Additional Disadvantage

In addition to the specific problems with the legal system, gendered, structural inequalities are further exacerbated when the victim/survivor belongs to a socially marginalised group.

Adolescents, for example, as a marginalised group in comparison to adults, suffer further structural disadvantage in the legal system (Wightman 1995, Young, 1995). Children too, face additional barriers when attempting to exercise their rights in the justice system (VLRC 2008). In particular, sexual assaults on children are more likely to be uncorroborated (Young 1995).

People with physical disabilities and intellectual disabilities are also disadvantaged in the legal system (Phillips 1996, Haag 2000). Research indicates that people with intellectual or psychiatric disabilities have 'even less recourse than most to the criminal justice system' (D'Arcy 1995: 141; see also Keilty and Connelly 2001). Additional barriers to accessing the criminal justice system also exist for Indigenous women and women from culturally and linguistically diverse backgrounds (see for example Douglas 2005, VLRC 2008,). For these victims/survivors, gender is secondary to racism in compounding levels of systemic discrimination perpetrated by the legal system. For women

> who don't speak the lingo and look the part … the experience of bias is amplified through cultural stereotyping, language barriers, a lack of understanding of cultural factors, and racist attitudes. (Aldunate 1995: 178).

In short the legal system fails women from all backgrounds, but women facing structural disadvantages in addition to gender, such as: women in prison

(Trounstine 2001), women from low socio-economic backgrounds (Haag 2000), those who are unemployed, older, or suburban (Avakame 1999) and women who live in rural areas (Logan et al. 2005) are likely to be disadvantaged to an ever greater degree when attempting to access justice from the legal system.

Conclusion

This chapter has provided an overview of the main problems concerning responses of the legal system – its personnel and processes – to victims/survivors of sexual assault. Overwhelmingly, the legal response to sexual assault appears to privilege and protect the accused at the expense of a fair trial to the victims/survivors. Since one of the aims of this book is to explore how counsellors/advocates working in the field of sexual assault think about the possibilities for changing legal practices, it has been necessary to explore the factors that are most in need of change. There are a myriad of factors including: concerns about police responses to sexual assault; the impact of this on low levels of reporting and ultimately on conviction rates; reservations about other legal personnel, especially magistrates who preside over sexual assault cases; the issue of consent; the emphasis on the credibility of the victim/survivor; the issue of corroboration; the practice of plea bargaining; the intrusive nature of the forensic examination; adjournments and other delays in the legal process; and the imposition of cross-examination for victims/survivors. In addition, systemic problems within society appear to exacerbate victims/survivors' negative experiences with the legal system, especially if she a child or young person, has a disability, is from a minority cultural or linguistic background, or impacted by other structural disadvantages.

Cumulatively, such experiences represent secondary victimisation (see for example Heath 2007: 117). The following chapter explores the impact of this secondary assault that is perpetrated by the legal system and begins to theorise these issues using a feminist analysis.

Chapter 3
Theorising the Impact and Thinking about Change

Victims/Survivors' Experiences of the Legal System

> Unlike the victim, everyone, including the accused, is entitled to remain present throughout the hearing …
> … unlike the victim, the accused along with the rest of the crowd is entitled to hear the forensic medical evidence, the description of genitalia, the markings on nipples, the colour and size of bruises on buttocks, the presence or absence of semen on legs or in the mouth, the finding of the internal gynaecological examination …
> … unlike the victim, they can hear about the presence or the absence of loosened pubic hair, or flakes of skin under fingernails, or sexually transmitted diseases …
> … unlike the victim, they are entitled to hear the doctor's impression of the victim's state of mind …
> … unlike the victim, the accused hears the doctor's findings …
> … unlike the accused, the victim is never told. (Gilmore, public meeting Real Rape Law Coalition (RRLC) quoted in Stuart 1993: 95)

In the previous chapter, the problems with the legal response to sexual assault were examined in detail. In this chapter, these problematic legal processes and outcomes will be further explicated by delineating their impact on victims/survivors. A particular emphasis will be placed on how the legal process frequently results in experiences of secondary victimisation for victims/survivors. This type of secondary trauma that is perpetrated by the legal system, permeates every stage of victims/survivors' contact with the judicial process (see for example Campbell 2006, Maier 2880, VLRC 2008).

'Despite formal legal recognition of her need for protection, a woman who is raped, assaulted or battered by a man may find herself victimised again by police, state and medical agencies … This refusal to recognise a woman's experience can appear to many as secondary assault' (Radford 1987: 135 cited in Stuart 1993: 99). The following discussion will theorise the impact that these injustices create from a feminist perspective and consider the particular contribution that feminist perspectives make to our thinking about change.

Secondary Victimisation

Many victims/survivors find it horrendous to try and cope not only with the ramifications of the sexual assault itself, but also with the difficulties presented by engaging with the legal process (Jordan 2008, VLRC 2008). '[W]omen who have already been victimised by an assault are victimised again by the systemic responses to that crime (Jarvis and McIlwaine 1997: 3).

The experiences of victims/survivors who access the legal system are tantamount to a 'war against women' (Stuart 1993: 96). Adjectives such as 'intrusive', 'judgmental', 'damaging', 'disempowering' (Stuart 1993: 99) 'distressing' (McCulloch 1998) and 'aggressive' (Maier 2008: 789) are consistently used to convey the sense of 'loss of control' that victims/survivors of sexual assault experience during the legal process (Maier 2008 : 797, Stuart 1993: 99). It is well known that victims/survivors feel 'confused, fearful and powerless' during interactions with the legal system (Mitchell et al. 1995: 129). Some of the factors attributed to causing these feelings include:

> sitting opposite the offender, the language used in the court (legal terminology and/or sexually explicit language), being unable to have nominated support people in the court room, offenders laughing, smiling during the giving of evidence, and a lack of understanding as to why some parts of their statement were inadmissible or why they were being asked to leave the court during legal argument. (Mitchell et al. 1995: 129)

Other reasons given by victims/survivors for their dissatisfaction with the legal system include an 'inappropriate legal outcome for the offender', 'a fear of the offender' and of his 'power and proximity' in the courtroom (D'Arcy 1995: 139, see also Fileborn 2011, Heath 2005), as well as an unfamiliarity with, or confusion about, court proceedings. 'Women's experiences testify that the courtroom environment and the mystique of the legal system generally, are threatening to women due to the inaccessibility of the language and procedures and its male dominated milieu' (Grix 1999: 87).

The adversarial nature of the court process is particularly difficult (see for example Cripps 1995). Other problems include the victim/survivor being offered only brief contact with the prosecutor before the trial (Townsend 1996). Victims/survivors who do not have the opportunity to meet the crown prosecution until the day of the trial experience a 'heightened … level of confusion and … sense of powerlessness' (Mitchell et al. 1995: 128). In addition, they do not have adequate opportunities for debriefing after the trial (Townsend 1996).

Further contributing to feelings of powerlessness and a sense of being devalued, is the sense that victims/survivors are relegated to a very marginal or peripheral role within the legal process:

> Most women feel completely alienated from the management of their own case … survivors of sexual assault often feel as if they are completely incidental to the justice system. Their very personal and traumatic experience is manipulated, by both the prosecution and the defence, in the playing out of a complex courtroom drama from which they are effectively excluded. (Townsend 1996: n.p.)

Historically, for many victims/survivors, the legal system has 'operated to censor, ignore, humiliate women who seek justice following an experience of sexual violence' (Jarvis and McIlwaine 1997: 7). During the legal process the victim/survivor becomes merely a 'witness' for the prosecution (see for example Cook 2002–3), or is reduced to being just another 'piece of evidence' (Heenan 1995: 284). Victims/survivors are repeatedly referred to as 'lost' (Lifchitz 1995: 240) in the process and rendered 'invisible' (Townsend 1996). As these researchers explain, '[o]ne of the things that becomes apparent after you make a complaint is that it is not your case – you are just the witness' (Martin and Angel 1995: 94, see also Jordan 2008). Contrary to their needs after a sexual assault, victims/survivors are pushed 'back into that position of being powerless and having someone else in control' (Martin and Angel 1995: 94); 'all too often the needs of the victim/survivor get lost in the process' (D'Arcy 1995: 138). In summary: '… the very nature of the criminal trial process … operates to effectively exclude sexual assault survivors from any active role in the justice system' (Townsend 1996: n.p.). Complainants of sexual assault become 'invisible survivors' in the legal process. As this victim/survivor explains:

> You become missing from the process, your world, your context becomes interpreted to the extent that you are lost from it. It is a strange experience to sit in a court room and hear judges and lawyers arguing about your motives while there is no forum for you to talk except through examination and cross examination. (Martin and Angel 1995: 94)

Even the capacity to have input into the trial during cross-examination is flawed: 'The trial presents an opportunity for her to stand in court, but not necessarily to be heard' (Jarvis and McIlwaine 1997: 7). In highlighting the impact of this on victims/survivors another researcher states, 'The trial is truly Kafkaesque for the woman who has experienced terror and/or humiliation but who is treated like a bystander to the events which she apparently willed upon herself and for which she is seen as seeking an unjustified and malevolent revenge' (Grix 1999: 83).

In addition to feeling excluded, feelings of powerlessness and a loss of control also result from the sense that:

> the victim/survivor has very few rights in the criminal trial … She has *no* choice but to testify and submit to cross-examination. She *cannot* instruct legal counsel, and will have had little, if any, preparation for giving evidence. She will have no knowledge of the defence claims or even of other prosecution evidence. She will

> have waited, perhaps for several days, until the court attendant finally comes to usher her into the courtroom, past the expectant audience. She will see the accused again, and will have to speak with him watching her. She will probably have been told to leave the court as soon as she has given her testimony. She will go home and continue waiting. (Stuart 1993: 101, italics in original)

Ultimately, many feminist researchers concur that the secondary assault perpetrated by the legal system: 'judicial rape', as it has come to be known, 'can be more damaging than an actual rape, "masquerading" as it does "under the name of justice"' (Erlich 2001: 1 citing Lees 1996: 36).

A Feminist Analysis of Sexual Assault

So, how do we make sense of these issues? The research that I have drawn upon thus far to critique the legal responses to victims/survivors of sexual assault, and present the perspectives of the latter and of practitioners, is largely drawn from feminist work. This is not surprising given that there has been a strong history of feminist research and activism that has heightened awareness of the injustices perpetrated against victims/survivors by the legal system over the past 30 years (Jordan 2012, Laing 2008, Larcombe 2005).

There are a multiplicity of feminisms, but the goals of acknowledging women's rights as human rights; freedom from gender-based violence and oppression; rejecting the uncritical acceptance of stereotypical gender roles; exposing and critiquing ostensibly natural social arrangements created by patriarchy; and challenging dominant structures and power relations with the aim of producing greater gender equity, unite many feminists (Bell and Klein 1996, Dominellii 2002, Fook 1993, Laing 2008, Marchant and Wearing 1986, Martin et al. 2006). In brief, feminism places women's experiences and gendered power relations at the forefront of analysis (Dominelli 2002, Weeks 2003). Feminists have extensively highlighted the gendered inequalities entrenched in social institutions and policy, raised awareness of the organisation of society along gender-specific lines and elucidated the inequalities that result from the relegation of women to the private sphere (Bryson 2002, Dominelli 2002, Morley and Macfarlane 2008).

From a feminist perspective, sexual violence against women is a structural problem and the institutions of the state are implicated in supporting the social arrangements that sanction such violence (Allen 1996, Larcombe 2005). Gendered discrimination, exploitation and abuse are enshrined in legislation and underwritten by social policy (see for example Morley and Macfarlane 2008, Phillips 2006). Consequently, the factors responsible for creating the conditions for sexual assault are deeply embedded in our society and challenging these conditions requires changing dominant power structures, institutions and relations in society.

Feminist analyses highlight the links between the gendered nature of sexual assault and the patriarchal institutions and relations that characterise dominant social arrangements in Western society by examining the structural power disparities between men and women (see for example Malloch 2004). Making explicit the links between the broader socio-political context and women's personal experiences of violence, research indicates that 'the extent to which a society is male dominated is positively correlated with the incidence of sexual abuse' (Easteal 1996a: 6). Sexual assault is thus understood as a gendered crime (see for example CASA House 2007, Campbell and Wasco 2005, Dekeseredy and Joseph 2006).

While feminist perspectives highlight disparities of power between perpetrators and victims, they draw our attention to a broader context: 'violence against women is not just about the oppression of individual women but also forms part of a broader picture of power and oppression, and human rights violations' (Aldunate 1995: 76, see also Laing 2008). This is the case in both the Australian and international contexts (Bell and Klein 1996, Dominelli 2002, Weeks 2003). Although the oppression experienced by the majority of Western women is arguably not as extreme as that experienced by women in developing countries (Hastings 2002, Menon 2003), the acts of violence committed against Western women are on the 'same continuum which sees women ... facing discriminatory treatment in the legal system [and] domestic violence [going] unchallenged, rapists ... given lenient sentences [and] the perpetrators of incest [going] free because of some legal technicality' (Aldunate 1995: 175–6). For feminists, this continuum is evident in all aspects of women's lives (Dominelli 2002, Morley and Macfarlane 2008).

Most feminist commentary therefore identifies patriarchal structures, power relations and social arrangements as the cause of sexual assault against women and children (see for example Bell and Klein 1996, Brownmiller 1975). This perspective directly links patriarchal relations to the incidence and prevalence of sexual assault. Furthermore, since rape is seen as an act of violence intended to institute power and control over women, feminist commentators highlight the social control functions that sexual assault serves (Donat and D'Emilio 1998, Parliament of Victoria Social Development Committee (PoVSDC) 1998: 344).

Feminists articulate the ways in which a culture of male violence has developed that legitimises a gender-based organisation of power, in which men are dominant and women are subordinate (Gil and Anderson 1999, Malloch 2004). This culture is embedded in everyday social attitudes and structures that 'allow a rape culture to flourish' (Brisbane Rape Crisis Centre cited in Stuart 1993: 97). This culture is frequently developed and perpetuated through the media (see for example Modisett and Dreyer 2005) and other cultural phenomena such as traditional gender role stereotypes and competitive male sports (Adams-Curtis and Forbes 2004, Safai 2002). Social myths that have been internalised by individuals, families, communities and other social institutions, including the legal system, are also central to the maintenance of this culture (Page 2004). Whilst in broad societal terms social myths function to deny the incidence and prevalence of sexual assault, blame the victim and exonerate the perpetrator (Garcia and McManimon 2011, Geiger et al. 2004), manifestations of these myths also clearly influence the legal system, its processes and personnel (Aldunate 1995, Allen 1996, Easteal 1996a, Gilmore 1995, Graycar 1994). As one researcher comments: 'women lack power and are disadvantaged in the world at large and in the legal system' (Mack 1998: 150).

Social Myths

Feminist scholars argue that social myths effectively determine how victims/survivors are constructed and treated by the legal system. These myths also appear to have a direct effect on legislation, legal proceedings, and, ultimately, on the experiences of those who report sexual assault. Numerous feminist scholars assert that social myths are powerful determinants in maintaining the current inadequacies and injustices of the legal system, in that the patterns of thought that they produce in the community at large effectively block change from occurring (see for example Beech et al. 2005, Bohner et al. 2009, Douglas 2005, Garcia and McManimon 2011). To take one example: while we know that perpetrators of sexual violence are much more likely to be family members or people in positions of trust rather than strangers, critics of the law suggest that legal processes and personnel appear to perpetuate the myth that most victims/survivors are attacked by a stranger in a violent assault (see for example ALRC 2010, Corrigan 2006). A consequence of the 'stranger myth' is that few women seek assistance to report a sexual assault committed by someone who is known to them, because this experience does not match the dominant construction of a 'legitimate' rape (see for example Brown 2007). Moreover, because this myth obscures the fact that most sexual violence occurs in the private realm of the family, it conceals the historical, social, and cultural contexts in which men have exercised ownership rights over women and children. This myth constructs rape as acceptable when it occurs in a context of male ownership of women and children, where men have certain rights and women have certain duties (Garcia and McManimon 2011, Scutt 1998,).

Historically, sexually assault crimes were treated as property offences. The notion that women were the property of their husbands or fathers 'remained enshrined in law until as late as the 1980s when marital immunity to rape was [finally] abolished in Australia' (SECASA 2009 cited in Fileborn 2011: 7; see also ALRC 2010).

Social myths about male ownership of women and conjugal rights are strongly embedded in wider social expectations, and research conducted in this area seems to indicate fairly widespread community ignorance of the social mythology surrounding sexual assault (ALRC 2010, Bohner et al. 2005, Scutt 1990, 1995). In terms of the expression of these myths in the legal system, one feminist lawyer comments:

> All legal institutions – police, courts, the legal profession – are so strongly imbued with the notion of ownership, combined with "male right", that requiring the legal system to respond to children's and women's needs, rather than to maintain privilege, is no easy task. (Scutt 1991: 118)

Paralleling these myths is the belief that no real harm is done if the victim/survivor does not incur serious physical injury during an assault (Easteal 1996a, Fileborn 2011, Yurchesyn et al. 1992). Although we know that victims/survivors suffer multiple harms during and after such an assault, (see for example Bohner et al. 2009, Corbett and Larcombe 1994, Harvey et al. 2007, Kappler 2012) this myth means that if a woman does not sustain serious physical injuries during a sexual assault, then the law may not recognise the harm of the assault while the offender's culpability is frequently minimised (McKelvie and Heenen 1993: 10). In this case, the notion of physical harm is linked to resistance, leading defence lawyers to frequently make the argument that the victim/survivor must have been consenting (Fileborn 2011).

Another myth that holds women responsible for their own victimisation is the belief that sexual violence is linked to male sexuality. This too, effectively shifts responsibility for the assault from the perpetrator to the victim/survivor by raising questions about the woman's conduct and dress (Cossins 1995, Easteal 1996a, 1996b, Whatley 2005). These myths are used to justify legal processes such as cross-examination in which a woman must stand up to rigorous interrogation in order to prove she was not responsible for, or complicit with, the violence perpetrated against her.

Other myths, such as that women and children lie about sexual assault, are equally damaging (ALRC 2010). Feminists contend that Freudian psychoanalytic theory 'and the public understandings which it has promoted, would have us believe that females cannot be trusted, that they should not be listened to, that they fantasise, fabricate and mislead' (Scott et al. 1991: 202; see also Garcia and McManimon), supporting the mythology that complaints of sexual assault should be met with scepticism and not taken seriously (Grey 2007: 173), or at best, 'considered suspect' (Davies 1999: 99). This myth, combined with the notion that allegations of sexual assault are easily made, tends to invalidate disclosures of sexual assault and justify requirements for independent corroboration of the victim/survivor's testimony (Grey 2007: 273). It also legitimates the 'burden of proof' resting with the prosecution, which must be able to prove beyond reasonable doubt that a sexual assault took place (Brown 2007, McCulloch 1998). (Some of these concerns will be further elaborated later in this chapter with regard to changes proposed to the legal system.)

The myths that women and children lie about sexual assault, and that it is an easy allegation to make, also influence perceptions of credibility (Grey 2007: 178). As Martin and Angel (1995: 100) explain: 'Women have been met with disbelief by the legal system and severely marginalised by the law's claim that credibility equals male. In matters of sexual assault specifically, women are viewed as less than competent in relaying their stories.' Moreover, such myths affect 'the jury's subjective criteria for credibility' (Corbett and Larcombe 1994: 133) insofar as credibility is judged by the degree to which women behave according to certain stereotypes (Allen 1996, Garcia and McManimon 2011, Mack 1998). Juries make subjective judgments based on their own assumptions (Golding et al. 2003) and are left to determine issues of guilt or consent, for example, based on their own 'common sense' understandings, and 'dominant social attitudes, myths and custom, the very social attitudes, myths and customs … that tolerate rape … the sexist attitudes and beliefs that are responsible for rape and sexual assault in the first place' (Corbett and Larcombe 1994: 134). Thus, not only are social myths central influences on the legal process, they also 'have a serious impact' on how people view the victims/survivors of sexual assault and the perpetrator, and on the implementation of law reform (Easteal 1996b: n.p.).

Feminist analyses highlight how some of the more subtle and insidious expressions of power and implicit workings of patriarchy function through social mythology (Lee and Auburn 2001, Page 2004, Wightman 1995). From a feminist perspective, violence against women, and the way that we think about it, is not a private matter but a structural problem and therefore, a community responsibility. As such, it requires both interpersonal and structural responses, major education programs to expose and debunk social myths, and broad macro structural changes (Pearce 2003).

Feminist Analyses of Sexual Assault and the Law

Feminist analyses have much to contribute to our understandings of the legal response to sexual assault, both in terms of the identification of the nature of the problems embedded in the system, and the impediments to change. Gender bias inherent in the composition of the legal system's personnel is but one notable point (see for example Allen 1996). Another issue concerns the false presentation of the law as fair, neutral and objective, when in reality, 'the law operates with a strict division of labour, with men dominating decision-making, interpretation and administration', while masking the implicit patriarchal norms and social myths that the system upholds (Neave 1995: 184).

Several writers suggest that despite the use of objective, gender-neutral language, the law continues to be defined according to normative standards of male experience (Easteal 1996a, Grix 1999, Stephen 1994). Examples include: 'Notions of "force" and "resistance" [which] are … defined according to male standards' (Stuart 1993: 104). Furthermore, what is considered 'reasonable' and 'ordinary' in the context of the legal system continues to deny women's experience (Grey 2007: 173). Numerous examples illustrate the effect of these assumptions on the formulation of legal processes and principles. As one researcher explains:

> Gendered assumptions can be found in the criminal law dealing with sexual offences, in the law's failure to provide adequate remedies to women beaten by their spouses and in the law's refusal to recognise the economic value of domestic labour in dividing property at the end of a marriage or de facto relationship. (Neave 1995: 185)

Another feminist researcher suggests that male norms in the legal system 'mirror the power that males have and use to maintain a stranglehold on the institutions and structures of Australian culture … masculine language in turn affects or even directs how we see the rest of our reality, including sexual assault and the law' (Easteal 1996a: 4). Legal discourse is firmly embedded in and reproduces masculine-centred thinking, in that it is situated in a phallocentric cultural context. Phallocentrism is 'the premising of concepts on the behaviour and characteristics of men which are falsely represented as universal and abstract *norms* for all humanity' (Stephen 1994: 225). The legal processes operate 'as a … "regime of truth" [*sic*] which subjugates women's own interpretations of their experiences of violence' (Jarvis and McIlwaine 1997: 3) Normative male standards reflected in the law result in the exclusion of women's experiences. 'Common law's archetype of the "reasonable" rape victim' (Grey 2007: 173) is but one example.

The immediately preceding arguments have several implications for how we understand the barriers to justice that victims/survivors of sexual assault face when pursuing justice through the legal system and how, or whether, changing them might be possible. One is that the law is heavily implicated in perpetuating a narrow definition of violence against women (Bargen and Fishwick 1995, Corrigan 2006) that may ultimately discourage women from reporting an incident of sexual assault to the police in the first instance (Heath 2007: 177). As Corbett and Larcombe (1994: 136) explain, '[t]he law focuses on types of violence which reflect man's physical superiority over females … and ignores other types of violence which reflect man's economic, organisational and social "superiority"'.

Invoking the centrality of social myths, narrative approaches have been used to deconstruct pre-court and court documentation, highlighting how they are constructed in accordance with dominant mythologies that prevent 'the legal system from adequately addressing women's experiences of sexual violence' (Kaspiew 1995: 350). For example, '[t]he legal system dominates the official process of defining what behaviours constitute sexual assault' (Stuart 1993: 99). Consequently, '[w]omen's experiences of assault … are often not recognised' (Corbett and Larcombe 1994: 136). As a 'self-regulating, "scientifically based" male constructed and male dominated discourse, law retains the power to determine what knowledge and experience is inferior and what knowledge and experience is valid, and to construct the various parties according to this discourse' (Taylor 1996: n.p.; see also Erlich 2001). This brings the legal logic of 'you find the facts, you apply the law to the facts, and then you have a judgment!' (Brown cited in Kumar 1995: 94) into serious question because '[f]acts and evidence do not exist in their own discrete manner but in a context which is value laden and is presented, and therefore processed, in a manner consistent with reinforcing of these values' (Allen 1996: n.p.). While 'fact-finding' is presented as a 'common sense' process (Gans 1995: 221), '[t]his is not the case. The legal system is, and functions as, part of the broader society and the illusion of pure technical rationality is even more dangerous because it obscures that operation of bias from attention' (Allen 1996: n.p.).

Deconstruction of legal narratives identifies how the legal system advantages dominant interests, privileges the stories of the powerful and silences those of the subordinate (Erlich 2001, Kaspiew 1995). Decision makers do not choose certain stories over others according to their validity and objectivity, but because they comply with dominant social myths, ideologies and discourses (Kaspiew 1995). Research demonstrates the ways in which victim/survivor's stories become circumscribed, regulated and shortened, and the process by which 'stock' stories, or rape myths, replace women's own stories in legal discourse. The researcher (Kaspiew 1995: 253) uses material from six Victorian cases to illustrate that though the legal process purports to uncover 'truth', it does not. The 'law as a social-political construct, [is] both determined by, and determining wider social-political discourses' (Kaspiew 1995: 253). This analysis 'eschews traditional forms of legal theorizing in favour of focusing on what is said in legal discourse, how it is said, and who says it', thus dismantling claims of objective 'truth' (Kaspiew 1995: 253).

There must be an exploration of 'the validity of the so called "objective" nature of the [legal] process' because 'the whole system assumes a level playing field, neutral processes, and fair, logical and rational arguments as the key mechanism for decision-making' (Allen 1996: n.p.). Given the inherent biases and limitations within the legal system, '[m]any rape trials inevitably turn almost entirely on the fact-finder's assessment of the complainants' credibility' (Gans 1995: 221).

The feminist literature on sexual assault illustrates the unfairness of the hidden, pre-existing bias towards patriarchal norms and standards. Kaspiew (1995: 374) sums this up:

> The legal system's failure to allow women to tell unedited stories about the experiences of sexual violence creates a vacuum which the legal process fills with other stories that are about women and their relationship with men … [which] have a long history in the legal discourses on rape and reflect masculinist perceptions which discount, denigrate and disqualify women's experiences.

Therefore, what 'masquerades as "point of viewlessness" in the legal rape story reflects the masculine point of view and masculine subjectivity' (Kaspiew 1995: 381; see also Erlich 2001). It is these 'apparently benign' legal processes which 'are complicit in obstructing women's access to the justice system in relation to sexual violence' (Allen 1996: n.p.). In addition, within this patriarchal, legal context, women have been constructed as 'inherently inferior, incorrigible and inept' by positivist, objectifying, 'male-stream theories' which connect the 'biological reproductive capacities and sexuality of women with a positive correlation to physical pathology and madness' (Taylor 1996: n.p.). Phallocentrism is a useful concept to draw upon to deconstruct the 'sexing of women through rape law', and to highlight the heterosexist, essentialist assumptions of phallocentric sexuality, and the way in which 'women are seen as emotional, weak, dependent ... and intimately bound to their reproductive functions ... [that are] meant to complement men's [sexuality] which is powerful, active and dominant' (Stephen 1994: 225). Within phallocentric cultural understandings women are 'sexed', and 'rape' is constructed according to inherent patriarchal interests and social myths (Stephen 1994: 25; see also Bargen and Fishwick 1999, Grix 1999, Taylor 1996). This construction of sexual assault complainants operates in tandem with the social mythology outlined earlier to effectively invalidate women's testimonies (Bargen and Fishwick 1995, Jarvis and McIlwaine 1997, Stephen 1994). The law denigrates complainants of sexual assault and undermines their testimony 'through an ownership of discursive knowledge' that is 'able to silence women's experiences in the very forum where [they] should be spoken' (Taylor 1996: n.p.). This 'refusal to hear women, to take us and what we say seriously, to accord women the same respect and credibility men automatically receive, is one of the major barriers to achieving equality' (Mack 1998: 145).

Feminist Approaches to Change

Given that feminism is a modernist emancipatory project that seeks to end the gendered oppression and exploitation of women, feminist projects seek such change through social and political reform via the development of liberty, democracy, human rights, the eradication of poverty and oppression (Francis 2000: 23). Feminist conceptualisations of change suggest that women need to stand together in solidarity against patriarchal forces that attempt to dominate. Feminist politics demand unity and action on defined women's issues and assume that women are an essential entity with similar interests (Forcey and Nash 1998, Stromquist 2000). Such universalist analyses and collective action are seen as necessary for the transformation of the legal system, and have been successful historically in effecting other positive changes for women, including the areas of childcare, safe abortion and equal pay (MacDonald 1996). Collective action usually implies broad-scale activism and macro-level interventions to change the cultural, social and political patriarchal contexts seen as the main arenas for changing society at large, and therefore, the legal system (Carmody and Carrington 2000, Easteal 1996b). In Australia, feminist campaigners have effectively targeted social policy as a site for potential change (Sawyer 1993, Yeatman, 1990). 'Anti-violence has been a key focus of these political activities and led to an active engagement with the state to try and bring about a reduction in violence against women' (Carmody 2003: 199). Redressing the power disparities between men and women and challenging the broader patriarchal context in which laws are made, interpreted and implemented are seen as crucial to facilitating change. Changes in the context of the legal system that reflect these sorts of commitments are analysed in the following section.

Changes to Remedy the Legal System?

Given the gender bias in the composition of the judiciary and numerous legal processes, the appointment of more women judges has been suggested as one potential solution (Neave 1995). It is thought that redressing this imbalance may contribute to the law being more objective and impartial by helping to eliminate gendered assumptions, and thus altering the content of substantive legal rules or changing, inter alia, dispute resolution procedures (Neave 1995). The Senate Standing Committee on Constitutional and Legal Affairs recommends that entrenched forms of gender bias should be remedied by broadening judicial selection to ensure that judges are appointed from a diverse range of backgrounds, and encouraging them to undertake gender awareness education (Neave 1995: 183).

In theory, introducing a more equitable representation of women in the legal system would mean that women's experiences and perspectives would be included in the adjudication process and gender bias in the law would be reduced, thus improving the quality of justice. Research indicates that men are more likely to accept the social mythology surrounding sexual assault than women (Neave 1995). 'Women judges ... may vote [*sic*] differently in cases involving sex and race discrimination and issues of particular concern to women' (Neave 1995: 191). In addition, altering the composition of the judiciary to ensure that it is more representative of women and minority groups may contribute to a more equitable legal system (Easteal 1996b, Neave 1995).

Gender education for the judiciary, including all police, judges and lawyers is another feminist strategy for change (Easteal 1996b, Taylor 1996, VLRC 2008, Young, 1995). 'Better education on the nature of gender bias and its impact, for judges as well as other members of the legal profession, is an essential step in this change' (Mack 1998: 150). Continuing community education has also been identified as an important contribution to change (see for example Heath 2007). There are also calls to develop a national response to violence against women and a uniform criminal code to be adopted by all Australian jurisdictions (Grey 2007). This would include consultation with gender experts throughout the legal process, and a dedicated unit within the Federal Attorney General's Department to promote strategies to address violence against women (ALRC 2010).

Suggestions concerning the taking of police statements indicate that police should place greater emphasis on privacy and confidentiality; ensure that interpreters, where required, are appropriately qualified; wear plain clothes while taking statements; and keep interruptions and delays to a minimum (Mitchell et al. 1995). Participants in the Mitchell et al. (1995) research also stated that the Office of Public Prosecutions (OPP) should keep victims/survivors informed of developments in their case; give them the opportunity to attend a pre-trial conference with the Crown prosecutor as well as ensure continuity of representation by this prosecutor; be better informed about the impact of sexual assault on victims/survivors; and be more aware of the emotional impact of the court experience on victims/survivors. They also indicated that police, counsellors and the OPP should familiarise victims/survivors with the courtroom and legal processes prior to the trial (Mitchell et al. 1995: 133). The findings point to the need to limit the amount of time between offences being reported to the police and the completion of a trial, and for victims/survivors to be provided with a free transcript of the court hearing (Mitchell et al. 1995). Other research proposes that victims/survivors be treated fairly, be provided with a safe environment during the legal process, be supported by a counsellor/advocate (D'Arcy 1995); and be kept informed about the progress of an investigation (VLRC 2008).

Additional resources would help to improve the legal system's response to victims/survivors of sexual assault, including increasing funds to the Office of the Public Advocate to train Independent Third Persons and ensure that their role is professionalised (Phillips 1996). Increasing resources for the investigation of cases may thus increase the number of reports that result in charges being laid (Frazier and Haney 1996). Increased funding would also enable support services to improve their responses to complainants who are socially marginalised (VLRC 2008).

Finally, a 'Women's Justice Outreach Service' has been proposed to improve the quality of legal service delivery for victims/survivors of sexual assault through 'purposeful collaboration between solicitors and counsellors/advocates' and 'valuing of the quality of the process of legal service delivery, as much as the outcome' (Hunter 1995: 245). Employing a lawyer as an advocacy worker in sexual assault services is another proposed strategy to improve the experience of the legal process for victims/survivors (Lifschitz 1995).

Civil Options as Solutions?

Some of the international literature moves away from discussing change in the criminal court to look instead at options in civil proceedings. The *Violence Against Women Act* that became United States legislation in 1994 'allows survivors of gender based violence to bring a civil suit against their attackers in a State or Federal court and sue them for violation of civil rights' (Townsend 1996: n.p.). If the accused loses the case, he is 'compelled to compensate the survivor for all the harm resulting from his attack, such as lost income from missed days of work, medical expenses and the cost of any counselling. The court may also award punitive damages, impose injunctive relief such as a restraining order' (Townsend 1996).

Although Australia has a compensation system in which victims/survivors can be awarded small payments, changes similar to the US Act could be 'important in the sense that [they would allow] a forum for the legal acknowledgment of the pain and suffering of survivors … which … is often crucial for women who feel as if they have not received justice or recognition through the criminal system' (Townsend 1996).

Proposed Law Reform

Other research has suggested specific legislative changes, including the use of independent observers in court; reassessing rules of evidence in relation to relevance of particular material; allowing representation evidence that would permit victims/survivors to discuss the history and context of the abuse; the removal of corroboration warnings in legislation and in practice; and protection of victims/survivors from verbal character assaults in court (Taylor 1996). Essentially, these are calls for greater emphasis to be placed on the behaviour of the rapist, rather than the actions of the victim (Corbett and Larcombe 1994, Taylor 1996).

Additional proposed remedial changes include: assuring the confidentiality of client notes and counsellor records (VLRC 2008: 12); the provision of advocates for people from culturally and linguistically diverse backgrounds (Aldunate 1995); changes to the rules of evidence in order to prevent the discrediting of complainants, and the tightening of legislation to shield women in respect to past sexual history (Mitchell et al. 1995, VLRC 2008); allowing victims/survivors to testify *in camera*; the introduction of a positive standard of consent where the notion of free agreement replaces consent (Wells 2008); the reduction of police, jury and judicial discretion (Corbett and Larcombe 1994, Grey 2007); and the introduction of mandatory directions such as the Longman warning (as discussed in Chapter 2) (Easteal 1996b, Corbett and Larcombe 1994, Grey 2007). Legislation aimed at allowing expert evidence to assist understanding of the experiences of trauma and its effect on memory would also improve the capacity of the legal system to offer justice (Jenkins 1996, Phillips 1996), as would enabling vulnerable witnesses such as children or complainants with cognitive impairments to give evidence and be cross-examined via closed circuit television (VLRC 2008: 8).

With phallocentric beliefs and patriarchal social myths covertly informing the ostensibly objective legal processes, scrutinising more closely the legal processes that are generally invisible to analysis has also been suggested as a strategy to reform the criminal justice system's handling of facts in rape trials. This includes asking both the prosecution and defence to articulate 'the precise relevance of any piece of evidence in a way consistent with other arguments put forward by that side' (Gans 1995: 26–7). One approach to this would be to develop a pre-trial hearing where both parties would be required to 'justify the relevance of proposed evidence and cross-examination' (Gans 1995: 26–7). This would potentially challenge the 'common sense' elements of the law which contribute to unarticulated gender biased assumptions and the reproduction of rape myths in legal decision making, processes and outcomes (L'Heureux-Dube 2001).

The Decision to Report

Such changes, as a minimum will be necessary if victims/survivors' experiences of the legal process are going to improve. As it stands, the legal system has been described as 'unworkable for women and children' (Heath and Naffine 1994: 48 cited in Jarvis and McIlwaine 1997: 6). Research indicates that one third of victims/survivors who chose to participate in the legal process would not, in hindsight, repeat their decision to report the assault (Heath 2007, Lievore 2005). Other research indicates that overall, 81 per cent of victims/survivors are dissatisfied with their court experience (D'Arcy 1995). Of the 32 sexual offences that had been tried and represented in this research, only one victim/survivor indicated that she was satisfied with her court experience. Her reason for this was '*I didn't have to go to court as he pleaded guilty*' (quoted in D'Arcy 1995: 139, italics in original).

However, despite the inadequacies of the legal system, it represents the 'only formal channel of redress for the victim/survivor and provides the most legitimate and resounding means of validating the woman's experience' (Stuart 1993: 99). Importantly, it provides the potential for victims/survivors to have the opportunity to place blame for an assault with the offender (Brown 2007). As one victim/survivor states when recounting her own experience of the legal system after being sexually assaulted: 'I so desperately wanted recognition from the courts that my efforts hadn't been for nothing, and for them to recognise that I had been sexually assaulted' (Cripps 1995: 52). This is why finding strategies to change victims/survivors' experiences of the legal process is so important.

Women report their experiences of child sexual assault to legal authorities for a variety of valid reasons. These include: concern that the perpetrator has access to other children and may also perpetrate abuse against them; and, the fact that these women are now adults and it has therefore become safer to report because they can no longer be violated as children. In addition, the legal system offers the opportunity to place blame for the abuse with the perpetrator and hold him accountable for his actions, and to 'break … the silence' (Martin and Angel 1995: 98) by challenging the secrecy that was imposed on them by the perpetrator. The legal system also potentially offers a sense of justice, which contributes to restoring some faith in the world (Martin and Angel 1995: 98). Despite the problems, women who report their experiences of sexual assault to legal authorities do so 'out of a sense of the present legal system being the only legitimate, legal way of attempting to seek justice' (Mitchell et al. 1995: 131).

Given this, the legal process represents a powerful system 'which can play a fundamental role in offering meaningful remedies to victims of sexual assault' (Jarvis and McIlwaine 1997: 3) through formally acknowledging women's experiences and providing an avenue for seeking justice. Therefore, '[i]t is crucial to the recovery of the victim that post-assault interventions do not contribute to the client's existing feelings of violation, helplessness and powerlessness' (Gardiner and Roberson 1995: 234). Yet the legal system often does not deliver the validation and justice that victims/survivors seek. Instead, the majority of victims/survivors find the legal process and response highly unsatisfactory, and experience it as re-inscribing the original assault (see for example Campbell 2006, Cook 2002–3, Heath 2007, Maier 2005).

This observation parallels the perspectives of magistrates, barristers and solicitors, who concur that the legal system is unsatisfactory for complainants of sexual assault (Jarvis and McIlwaine 1997, Mills 1996). Research indicates that 'five out of thirteen magistrates said they would advise a friend who was a victim of date rape or rape by a *de facto* not to report the rape; five out of eight solicitors and 40 per cent of barristers agreed with those magistrates' (Heenan and McKelvie 1997 cited in Jarvis and McIlwaine 1997: 7). This represents 'a crisis of faith' in the legal system's response to victims/survivors of sexual assault (Jarvis and McIlwaine 1997: 7). 'Sadly, much of the relevant research on sexual assault, and anecdotal evidence from counsellors and lawyers involved in sexual assault cases, demonstrate … often the best option for women who have been raped/sexually assaulted is not to report to the police' (Bargen and Fishwick 1995: 27). On the whole, '[w]omen appear to be very reluctant to advise other women who have been raped/sexually assaulted to proceed with a court case' (Bargen and Fishwick 1995: 108; see also Heath 2007: 177, Lievore 2005). This understanding resonates with my experience of working in the field and became the impetus for this research.

Conclusion

In summary, theorising the inadequacies of the legal system from a feminist perspective uncovers the complexity of endemic structural, institutional, communal and interpersonal problems that contribute to victims/survivors' experiences of oppression in the legal system. Chapter 2 highlighted the multitude of ways in which the legal response is manifestly inadequate for victims/survivors, and the feminist analysis presented in this chapter elucidates a host of additional ideological problems that constitute significant barriers to changing the legal responses to sexual assault. Feminist analyses are useful in assisting us to understand the impact of patriarchal ideology on workings of the legal system, and how this is borne out in specific legal processes and problems. Given the extent of the problems identified, most research points to the need for the legal system to be changed in order to be more responsive to the women who report sexual assault.

The difficulties for practitioners engaged in supporting victims/survivors who access the legal system have been described as 'a crisis of witnessing' (Jarvis and McIlwaine 1997: 3). The significant problems in the legal system are not discrete, but intersect to compound disadvantage for victims/survivors in multiple and complex ways. For example, cross-examination might not be so problematic if consent were not so central to sexual assault trials. Similarly, plea bargaining and settling out of court might not be as common if the victim/survivor's credibility was not so undermined and corroboration was not a legal requirement. Perhaps none of the legal processes or rules would be as consequential and harmful as they are if the judicial personnel interpreting and implementing them were not influenced by the dominant social mythology surrounding sexual assault. In short, the structural problems with the legal response to sexual assault are not only embedded in the legal system, but throughout every level of society, and the impact of this for victims/survivors is an experience of sexual violence followed by secondary victimisation perpetrated by the system.

Despite the problems with the legal response, reporting sexual assault to the legal system represents the only formal channel of redress for victims/survivors to pursue justice for the crimes committed against them. Whilst feminist perspectives point to a number of proposed changes that range from greater gender equity in the composition of legal system, to greater participation of women in society more broadly, it is necessary to understand the implications of remedial legislation that has been introduced over the last couple of decades. This will be discussed in the following chapter, along with the obstacles that counsellors/advocates believe are preventing changes in the legal system.

Chapter 4
The Need for Law Reform

Introduction

The previous chapters have highlighted the problems with the legal response to sexual assault and identified the impact of these problems on victims/survivors. Feminist theories point to multiple sites for change: the broader social (patriarchal) context in which the law operates; the patriarchal nature and operations of the legal system itself; and specific legislative change. This chapter will begin by focusing on the latter in exploring how legislative reforms have been expressed through changes and improvements to the law and its processing of sexual assault. Given the limitations of law reform, I will briefly return to reconsider the broader social context as a significant determinant for change. However, this circular process clearly has limitations for advancing effective change strategies. This chapter concludes by pointing to the need to develop alternative ways to think about and respond to the problems regarding the legal response to sexual assault.

Law Reform

This section outlines some of the most notable examples of remedial legislative changes that have been achieved in the past two decades. Some authors write enthusiastically about these law reforms. Mack (1998: 147), for example, states:

> Many of the formal barriers in law, the special rules diminishing women's credibility when testifying about rape, such as the expectation of recent complaint, the use of sexual history, or requirements of warning of a need for corroboration, have been re-examined and changed by the statute.

Reforms concerning: the victims/survivors' sexual history; recent complaint evidence; the issue of consent; adjournments; closed courts; hand-up briefs; and the introduction of police code of practice, are among those discussed.

Sexual History and Delayed Reports

The prevention of information relating to the victim/survivor's sexual history being accessible to the defendant's counsel and hence being revealed to the jury is seen as a major step in law reform. For example, rape shield laws have been introduced in some Australian jurisdictions to prohibit courtroom questioning of the victim/survivor's sexual history (Brown 2007: 117, Gans 1995, McCulloch 1998, Townsend 1996). Other research indicates that the reporting of rapes committed in Australia has slightly increased since 1990, suggesting some enhanced accessibility of the legal system for victims/survivors (Clay-Warner and Burt 2005).

Similarly, improvements have been cited with regard to delayed reports. In relation to how delays in complaints of sexual assault have been regarded by the judiciary, specific reference is made in the NSW Crimes Act 1995 s 405 B(2) which states that when there is a 'delay in complaint the judge must inform the jury that there may be good reasons why a victim of sexual assault may hesitate in complaining about it' (cited in Martin and Angel 1995: 95). Section 61(b) of the Act specifically states that the trial judge is mandated to 'inform the jury that delay in complaining does not necessarily indicate that the allegation is false'.

Recent Complaint Evidence

Also regarded as an indication of improvement in terms of weighting the evidential balance more fairly towards the victim/survivor is the establishment of 'recent complaint' evidence. This means that 'evidence of a complaint of sexual assault having been made as soon as possible after the incident, is admissible – not as evidence that the assault in fact occurred, but as to the consistency of the complainant's account of the incident' (McKelvie and Heenan 1993: 10). Researchers in this area assert that these developments in law reform make 'it more difficult for the defence to successfully argue that a delay in complaining is evidence of the falsity of the complainant's allegation of sexual assault' (McKelvie and Heenan 1993: 10).

Clarification of Consent

Victorian government law reforms introduced in the early 1990s are cited for clarifying the concept of consent, reaffirming 'the fundamental right of a person not to engage in sexual activity, and to provide victims/survivors "greater protection" in judicial proceedings' (McCulloch 1998: 16). Such reforms have the potential to re-educate the community by exposing some of the myths that contribute to prevalent understandings of sexual assault and force jurors to challenge preconceptions they may have regarding the reporting of complaints of sexual assault and how and when they are made (McKelvie and Heenan 1993, Wells 2008,).

Reduction of Trial Delays and Adjournments, Closed Courts and Hand-Up Briefs

Changes that minimise delays and adjournments in the legal process are also designed to improve the experience of victims/survivors. For example, '[i]n some jurisdictions, such as Victoria, there are legislative time limits upon serious sexual assault trials. In other jurisdictions, procedural measures have been implemented to minimise delays with the aim of ensuring sexual assault trials take place within 12 months of charges being laid' (Townsend 1996: n.p.).

In addition, as part of the attempt to overcome the difficulties that young witnesses have demonstrated, the practice of 'hand-up briefs' has been introduced. Hand-up briefs assist the prosecution to prepare written statements to be presented to the court during committal hearings without cross-examination. This practice enables the child witness to avoid giving evidence until the matter proceeds to trial (Scutt 1991: 130).

Closed courts are also seen as a way to potentially make the legal process more equitable (Scutt 1991). While court hearings are usually open to the public, closing the court theoretically means that victims/survivors do not have to disclose information that is 'distressing or embarrassing' in front of members of the general public (Scutt 1991: 131).

The Police Code of Practice

Changes to the policing of sexual assault have also been welcomed as addressing some of the problems with the legal response to sexual assault (Heenan 1995, McKelvie and Heenan 1993, Townsend 1996). Reforms introduced include the appointment of police officers who specialise in sexual offences and who have completed gender awareness training (Maier 2008, McKelvie and Heenan 1993, Townsend 1996, VLRC 2008). Significantly, the reforms also include the introduction of a Police Code of Practice in relation to sexual assault in Victoria in March 1992. This is recognised as an effort to rectify some of the problems of the police response to victims/survivors of sexual assault. This Code emerged from the VLRC's review of sexual assault laws that highlighted the need to develop a 'co-ordinated service response' for victims/survivors of sexual assault. The Police Code of Practice is a 'document that explicitly recognise[s] the importance of involving "outside" agencies to ensure that victims' emotional and medical needs [a]re being met' (Heenan 1995: 284). It provides guidelines for police who receive an initial report of sexual assault in terms of how to take the statement and conduct the investigation. 'A major emphasis of the Code is for police members to respond sensitively and to provide support to victims, but more importantly to leave as much control over the reporting process as possible with the victim/survivor herself' (Heenan 1995: 184). It also imposes a two-hour time limit from when a report is received to when victims/survivors are taken to a crisis care unit.

Arguably, the Code assists in clarifying the role of counsellors/advocates and prioritising the emotional and medical needs of the victim/survivor. Also significant is the 'spirit' of the Code 'which clearly attempts to challenge the traditional assumptions which have long since governed community attitudes towards rape victims/survivors, rapists and the offence itself' (McKelvie and Heenan 1993: 8). As the researcher who conducted a review of the Police Code states, 'of considerable importance [is the fact that] police are told not to presume that an allegation of rape is false … the guidelines are endeavouring to specifically break down some of the longstanding stereotypes regarding sexual assault' (Heenan 1995: 285). The Code has an educative function for police in explicitly making reference to information that they will need if their responses are to be remotely sensitive or adequate. It states, for example, 'Remember that people react differently to traumatic events. A victim may appear very composed and be able to calmly discuss the incident' (Police Code of Practice for Sexual Assault Cases cited in Heenan 1995: 285). Such statements educate police to understand that victims/survivors may legitimately respond in a variety of different ways to the trauma of sexual assault and that they should not infer that the victim/survivor must be falsifying a story if she does not react in a way consistent with their expectations (Heenan 1995). The Code states that, 'every police member involved in the investigation must be sympathetic and supportive, and that victims/survivors should be allowed as much control over the situation as possible' (McCulloch 1998: 17). It also emphasises the need for victims/survivors to be kept informed of developments in the investigation. Importantly, the Code also has a feedback mechanism that ensures any breaches can be formally reported to senior police for accountability (Heenan 1995). In general, the Police Code of Practice is seen as an important and effective document in ensuring improved service responses for victims/survivors of sexual assault.

Civil Options

Finally, civil options have also been referred to as an improvement in the legal response to sexual assault. Significantly, the possibilities for victims/survivors to avail themselves of options outside the criminal justice system, including the possibility for victims/survivors to sue the perpetrator for damages in civil action proceedings, is seen as a positive step towards legal justice for victims/survivors (McCulloch 1998).

The Limitations of Law Reform

So far this chapter has outlined some of the legislative changes that have been implemented in the Australian legal system since the 1990s. A number of significant changes have been made to the law with the aim of improving the experience of engaging with the legal system for victims/survivors. However, despite these legislative changes, responses from the legal system to victims/survivors remain incredibly poor and inadequate (see for example Heath 2007, Grey 2007). This indicates that legislative reform may not be the most effective strategy for change. In fact, most of the research seems to indicate that the impact of legislative changes on victims/survivors' experiences of the legal process is negligible, owing to the powerful influence of the dominant social mythology surrounding sexual assault. As one research report states: 'The recommendations for improvements to the legal system that were reported in this research are in many instances, already a matter of existing policy. However, in gathering this material, it is clear that policy is not always being put into practice' (Mitchell et al. 1995: 134). The gap between criminal law and practice have been referred to as the 'implementation gap' (ALRC 2010: 1); examples of which are identified in jurisdictions around the world (Beichner and Spohn 2005, Mertus 2004, Munaaaba 2004, Yancey Martin 2005). It is contended that the 'implementation gap' between the law and its practice, which is consistently demonstrated by research, 'highlights the resistance to change evident in the legal system through its legal players who may still hold views about sexual assault characterised by myths and misconceptions' (ALRC 2010: 1). As Larcombe (2005: 136) explains:

> No longer the paternalistic protector of the fairer sex … the criminal justice system now stands accused of, at best, failing to live up to its promises, at worst, being an active perpetrator of sexual violence. Law's contribution to the "licensing" of rape through the perpetration of myths about female sexuality and the silencing or muting of women's complaints of sexual violence is now persuasively documented.

This has systemic implications regarding the conservative and unsatisfactory nature of the investigatory/legal processes and outcomes for victims/survivors.

The Police Code

Numerous authors have noted the limitations of the Victoria Police Code of Practice. Firstly, it is the only one of its kind that is operating in Australia. This means that other states and territories have no equivalent protocol in place. Moreover, it is focused on recent adult survivors and therefore largely neglects past assaults and assaults on children (McKelvie and Heenan 1993). An evaluation of the Code (Heenan and Ross 1995 cited in Heenan 1995) revealed that members of Sexual Offences and Child Abuse Units (SOCAU) were generally familiar with the Code. However, knowledge of it was much less satisfactory among uniformed police and detectives while knowledge of the Code has declined generally among police since its implementation in 1992 (Heenan and Ross 1995 cited in Heenan 1995: 287). The evaluation also revealed evidence of non-compliance with the Code by police such as exceeding the two hour time limit to arrange a crisis care unit for the victim/survivor, as a result of police prioritising administrative and investigative matters over the victims/survivors' welfare. There was also evidence that victims/survivors were made to give detailed statements and assist in identifying a perpetrator or details at the crime scene before receiving medical attention or support and information from a counsellor/advocate. 'There continues to be a perception among some police that adherence to the Code will be to the detriment of the investigation' (Heenan 1995: 289). Heenan (1995: 289) concedes that:

> the success of the Code depends upon police members accepting the principles underlying the guidelines, and their recognizing that the Code is not an attempt to place the victim's medical care and emotional needs in competition with the role of the detective to investigate the crime.

Other research is slightly more critical:

> Unless appropriate implementation of the Code of Practice occurs, through systematic and ongoing training and education for police as well as breaches being related with the abhorrence they deserve, we will see little change in the police response to victims/survivors of sexual assault. (Stuart 1993: 100)

Research has also found that one-third of police did not believe the victim/survivor was telling the truth about their experience of being sexually assaulted. This increased to 44 per cent when detectives from the Criminal Investigation Unit (CIU) were interviewed (Heenan 1995: 282). Confirming this scepticism, Detective Training School Notes are cited in the literature:

> The investigator must first satisfy himself [sic] that a crime has been committed and secondly, that it was apparently committed by the accused. He must remember at all times that complaints in sexual assault cases are easily made. False accusations resulting from sexual neuroses, fantasy, jealousy, spite or simply a girl's refusal to admit that she consented to an act of which she is now ashamed often place the person accused in the position where he has great difficulty establishing any defence. (quoted in Heenan 1996: 282 cited in Jarvis and McIlwaine 1997: 6)

Given that it is the police who are often responsible for implementing law reforms, questions are hereby raised about their effectiveness (Page 2004).

Corroboration Requirements

Changes to mandatory corroboration requirements are also identified as ineffective in transforming the legal process for victims/survivors. While the 'old evidence rules which treated rape complainants in a special manner, such as the compulsory corroboration rules and the recent complaint rule' (Gans 1995: 224) have been abolished, the common practice of trial judges giving corroboration warnings to juries continues despite the changes to legislation which supposedly abolished or eliminated such a practice (Grey 2007). In Western Australia for example, the requirement for corroboration warnings was abrogated by s 50 of the Evidence Act (WA), which prohibited a judge from giving the warning 'unless … satisfied … such a warning is justified' (Tannin 1996: n.p.). It was understood that corroboration warnings would only be given in the most exceptional circumstances. Similarly, corroboration requirements were officially abolished in New South Wales by the introduction of s 164 of the Evidence Act 1995 (NSW) which allows for the trial judge's discretion as to whether corroboration warnings are given to the jury (Martin and Angel 1995: 97). However, unofficially 'unfettered judicial discretion over Longman warnings' continues to cause 'systemic prejudice' against victims/survivors (Grey 2007: 172) and the current position of the New South Wales Law Reform Commission is that judges must retain this discretion in order to protect the defendant's right to a fair trial. This is despite a recommendation by the Victorian and Australian Law Reform Commissions that the practice be abolished (Grey 2007: 175). Numerous cases cited in the literature suggest that if judges do not give the warning, then the case will be overturned on appeal (Aldunate 1995, Gans 1995, Martin and Angel 1995). As Mack (1998: 145) states,

> an examination of Australian appellate cases shows that trial judges have continued to warn juries that it is unsafe to convict without corroboration, after legislation has removed the requirement for such a warning or even forbidden such an instruction. In cases where judges have not warned juries to be careful of women testifying about sexual assault, apparently in accord with the legislative directions, convictions have been overturned on the basis that warnings attacking the women's credibility were needed in the particular circumstances of the case, as a matter of the court's discretion, thereby undoing the impact of the remedial legislation.

Despite the clarity of the Acts that supposedly eliminate judges' provision of corroboration warnings to juries, current court practice is influenced by the High Court decision in Longman v The Queen (1989). The principle espoused in this case holds that a warning is required to be given to juries 'if … the evidence discloses any circumstances which suggest that the evidence of the complainant may be unreliable' (Tannin 1996, n.p.). It appears that:

> according to the law, a woman's word alone is insufficient. Her evidence needs to preferably be supported by medical evidence or the evidence of somebody else. This is an extremely problematic notion considering that … sexual assault often occurs in private, without witnesses, often systematically over a long period of time, and without necessarily leaving physical evidence. (Martin and Angel 1995: 97)

Low rates of conviction can therefore be directly linked to the legal discourses that construct the complainant's testimony as 'uncorroborated evidence' (Gans 1995: 226).

Despite the High Court's critique of the rationale underpinning corroboration warnings – that women are prone to make false complaints of rape – it remains common practice for the defence counsel to request a trial judge in a sexual assault case to give what has come to be known as a 'Longman warning', and failure to do so adequately is a 'fruitful ground for appeal' (Tannin 1996: n.p.). This supports the notion that women and children cannot be believed (Scutt 1995) and practically rules out the conviction of a perpetrator if there is no independent corroboration of the victims/survivors' story (Grey 2007, Taylor 1996). The fact that corroboration can be 'discerned in various common law directions to the jury … despite successive restrictions in legislation around Australia' (ALRC 2010:2) confirms the failure of remedial legislation to produce its intended outcomes.

Hand-Up Briefs, Closed Courts, Sexual History and Civil Options

The introduction of hand-up briefs for young witnesses, in which the victim/survivor's statements are presented to the court, is also quite limited in terms of improving the experience of participating in the legal process for victims/survivors. Invariably, legal practices still require victims/survivors to be witnesses in court despite the introduction of hand-up briefs (Scutt 1991).

In addition, the notion of a closed court is also a fallacy given that, even in a closed court, a minimum of 23 individuals are still present (Scutt 1991). Hence the notion of having a closed court to offer a degree of privacy for the victim/survivor, who may be distressed or embarrassed at discussing intimate details of a sexual assault, is not really achieved by this reform.

In addition, laws that aim to restrict the ability of the defence to construct the victim's/survivor's sexual history and behaviour as evidence of consent (recently introduced in Victorian legislation, for example), do not seem to prevent the sexual history and reputation of the victim/survivor being introduced as part of the trial (Heath 2005, Heenan 2002). Even though various jurisdictions prevent sexual history information to greater or lesser degree, currently 'there is no state of territory legislation that imposes a total ban on the introduction of sexual history as evidence in sexual assault trials' (Fileborn 2011: 9, italics in original).

Paralleling this, civil options, which were also believed to represent an improvement in alternatives available to victims/survivors of sexual assault, have similarly been criticised. Whilst remedies available through civil law potentially increase the flexibility, speed and accessibility of the legal system to victims/survivors, they ultimately fail to hold perpetrators responsible for their criminal behaviour (Laing 2008).

Failure to Change the Social Context

While some researchers argue that many of the most highly criticised elements of sexual assault legislation have now been amended, Townsend (1996: n.p.) contends that, '[w]hat they fail to acknowledge is that mere legislative change is not enough to secure equal treatment before the law'. The apparent increased accessibility of the law, for example, evidenced by a steady increase in the number of sexual assaults in Australia reported since 1990, is challenged by the acknowledgement that these statistics predominantly relate to aggravated rape.

Sexual assault involving aggravated violence is treated differently in the legal system because of social myths that see physical evidence as important, whereas the greater proportion of assaults do not produce this level of tangible proof (Clay-Warner and Burt 2005). Similarly, sexual assaults are less likely to be reported if the perpetrator is from an Anglo-Saxon/Celtic cultural background, suggesting that myths about ethnicity influence and racialise legal processes (Carbone-Lopez 2005, D'Alessio and Stolzenberg 2002, Warner 2004).

Mirroring the Australian experience more broadly, in other Western countries such as Canada, the United Kingdom some states of America, 'there has been clear evidence of the failure of the courts to properly implement laws which attempt to control the use of sexual history of women who accuse men of rape' (Mack 1998: 148). Hence, despite remedial legislative change, the social and political context in which the laws are interpreted and implemented has not significantly changed, resulting in the continuation of many of the problems described with the legal response (Carmody 2003, Heath 2007).

Highlighting the failure of law reform, one researcher argues that laws that do not specifically exclude 'sexist, discriminatory and ill-informed attitudes and beliefs' will continue to 'tacitly condone rape, condemn women to suffer in silence' and perpetuate the harm caused by sexual assault (Stuart 1993: 104–5). Thus, it will remain virtually impossible for victims/survivors to obtain a just response from the legal system unless the system becomes more aware of the impact of gender, power 'and the realities of women's lives, rather than to continue perpetuating a system based on myths/stereotypes, dishonesty and injustice' (Martin and Angel 1995: 101). While some writers credit changes to the law with shifts in social attitudes (see for example Cook 2002–3), within the context of cultural 'masculocentrism', legal reform must be understood as limited (Easteal 1996a: 4; see also Allen 1996, Grey 2007, Hovdestad 2001).

Could Law Reform Be Damaging?

Despite the law reforms that have been made, changes are not being interpreted or implemented correctly; the result is little or no improvement to victims/survivors' experiences of the legal process, and possibly even detrimental effects (see for example Grey 2007). Mack (1998: 147) observes that:

> an examination of the treatment courts have given these legislative changes shows the limited impact of law reform in this area, the tenacity of the legal system's distrust of women and a continuing acceptance of false beliefs about women and rape throughout the judiciary.

There is also concern that:

> a reform strategy implemented on its own may not only be limited, but may even compromise progress if it operates in isolation, and by so doing allows the

> State to absolve itself of the responsibility to address the issue from a broader perspective. If the State is allowed to rationalise inaction in other areas by reference to its activity in the area of law reform, then other strategies will be compromised and the process of the overall challenge to sexual assault/abuse will be obstructed. (Allen 1996: n.p.)

Allen (1996) contends that relying on sexual assault law reform to produce change, without paralleling this with social action aimed at transforming patriarchal power relations and structures, may 'create a smokescreen by reference to which the State can obscure inaction'. Another researcher echoes these concerns arguing that 'law reform by its very nature compels the framing of demands that liberal law reform might not be able to deliver' (Heath 2007: 176). Hence, demands 'are reduced again and again until they are polite and realistically attainable requests: requests that might find their way through the maze of legal impediments' (Heath 2007: 176). Allen (1996) has taken this argument further: 'Confronted with a legal system that refuses to recognise all women as equal to men, a battle has been fought to change laws rather than acknowledge that the problems lie in the very nature of law, the dominant ideology and those who interpret it.' An example lies in the analysis of evidence in fact-finding processes in criminal trials. This is different from other parts of the trial according to Gans (1995: 221) who says it is 'almost entirely ungoverned by detailed rules'.

> Lawyers traditionally divide rape law into three parts: substantive law, evidentiary law and procedural law. Rape law reforms, to date, have operated within each of the three traditional divisions. However the fact-finding process stands largely outside of these categories. As a consequence, modifications to the fact-finding process have been, at best, indirect. (Gans 1995: 221)

This is because uncovering the 'facts' is seen as a 'common sense' process, taken for granted and unchallengeable (Gans 1995: 221). Thus, dominant patriarchal norms and assumptions operate as the hegemonic discourse in which meanings related to sexual assault are socially constructed by dominant ideologies, and are therefore not questioned (Kaspiew 1994).

Concerning the goal of changing the legal system and its current responses to victims/survivors of sexual assault, commentators suggest that 'there is no optimum strategy' (Allen 1996, italics in original). Instead a 'linked strategic diversity' is advised, which includes reforms to address institutionalised inequity, public advocacy and policy development that challenges patriarchal structures: 'a unitary approach to addressing sexual assault and abuse is limited in that it has insufficient breadth to impact significantly unless it is augmented by complementary strategies' (Allen 1996).

The Need for Social Change

Consideration of the role of social change returns us to where we commenced at the beginning of Chapter 3 in exploring the contribution of feminism. Because feminist perspectives link the personal with the political and locate the underlying sources of the problems in the legal system within the broader context of patriarchal society, feminists focus on macro social change strategies' impact on the law. As Mack (1998: 150) suggests, '[t]he full remedy for gender inequality lies in broad social change so that the context in which women speak enables them to be heard'. Others concur that the courts are generally 'lagging behind the community in the recognition of rape as a crime of sexual aggression against women' (Scutt 1995: 319). A strong theme in the literature reflects the belief that structural change regarding gender inequality must occur in society before the legal system becomes more responsive to victims/survivors (Yurchesyn et al. 1992). Indeed, social transformation represents a new target for change, given that there have been very 'few publicly advertised moves to make changes in responding to allegations of rape other than law reform' (Heath 2007: 189, italics in original).

Allen (1996) reinforces this assertion by highlighting the need to challenge social mythology that informs dominant (mis)understandings of sexual assault. 'Ideology and mythology can tilt a level playing field. This same ideology also underpins the processes and procedures by which the system itself operates'. Others similarly assert the need to replace patriarchal ideology with a more socially just and inclusive alternative (Townsend 1996: n.p., Yurchesyn et al. 1992: 84). Easteal (1996b: n.p.) says:

> We must break down such false beliefs so that tomorrow's victims will know that they are not responsible for their victimisation. To do that, the community needs to look at sexual assault with less trivializing, less blaming of the victim or survivor and a less narrow definition of what sexual assault is … we must eradicate gender inequality throughout our society.

When maintaining the focus for change not just on the legal system but also on patriarchal social arrangements, some feminist commentators suggest that addressing gender bias in the legal system, for example, needs to be much broader than the appointment of more female magistrates. Change should also aim to achieve greater representation of women in senior policy positions (Allen 1996, Stephen 1994). Stephen (1994: 225) suggests that 'to address sexism alone is not enough to eliminate gender bias and initiate real change, but that phallocentrism in which the law is deeply embedded must also be addressed to reach the core of the problem'. The appointment of more women to the judiciary and requiring all judges to attend gender awareness classes will simply not suffice to address the problems (Allen 1996, Stephen 1994).

Modernist Notions Of Change

Understanding the legal responses to victims/survivors of sexual assault as deeply and structurally ingrained has significant implications for how we think about the possibilities for transforming the legal system. Although change is certainly needed, the opportunities for effecting that change seem limited and the strategies employed by feminists to date appear to fall short of their intended aims:

> Numerous rounds of legislative reform, increased penalties for sexual offences, revised health, welfare and police procedures and several decades of community education have been achieved. These gains were not easily won but despite their best intentions they have failed to deliver the much hoped for deterrence in crimes being committed or significant changes in the behaviour of those who continue to perpetrate violence against women. (Carmody 2003: 119–20)

While feminist values and commitments remain constant, the context in which counsellors/advocates work is always changing. Consequently, some researchers argue that feminist ideals have lost their contemporary relevance (see for example Featherstone 2005, Phillips 2008). On the basis of the arguments presented in the previous chapters, which were largely informed by feminist analyses, I argue here that despite the emancipatory intentions of feminism, some aspects of feminist analyses of the research problem – which emphasise, for example, the power of the legal system and powerlessness of victims/survivors and practitioners – may unintentionally compound a sense of disempowerment for both victims/survivors and practitioners. I also contend that some of the ideas inherent in feminist conceptualisations of change might unintentionally contribute to a sense of powerlessness in practitioners to change the legal response, and therefore an ironic lack of change.

Very little feminist literature, for example, makes explicit reference to how practitioners who work in the field of sexual assault might work towards facilitating change in a practical sense. Change is largely constructed abstractly, consisting of aspirations to dismantle patriarchy and the related social mythology. Ironically, the emancipatory aims of feminism for change to structural, institutional and historically entrenched belief systems may unwittingly reinforce notions of powerlessness by constructing such change as remote, distant and virtually impossible, thereby distancing both victims/survivors and practitioners from the means of change (Fook and Morley 2005, Healy 2000, Morley 2004). Given that patriarchy is unlikely to be completely eradicated in the near future, feminist thinking about this problem seems to consider positive and meaningful change to the legal system as outside the realms of possibility. Feminist thought appears to be somewhat stuck in terms of providing concrete strategies for change (Carmody 2003).

Some researchers, for example, have noted that violence against women appears to be largely resistant to decades of feminist activism (Larcombe 2005).

As Healy (2000: 37) states, 'despite the relevance of these contemporary theories within the social work literature, their influence on social work, particularly day to day practice … is limited'. This leads us to ask whether theorists and practitioners who critique the legal system using modernist feminist constructs are inadvertently contributing to the problems rather than creating possibilities for changing them. As Fook (2000: 130) cautions, '[a]lthough the stated principles of perspectives that hold to a critical condition are clearly emancipatory, the ways in which they have functioned and are experienced may in fact be disempowering'.

If we continue to demand that change must occur in structural and legal domains, what are the possibilities for practitioners for effecting such changes? Is change an intangible, remote process outside our work as counsellors/advocates that we hope will simply eventuate in time? Are we limited to supporting the processes of change in indirect ways, from a distance? Does conceptualising change to the legal system purely in terms of institutional transformation result in limiting the possibilities for developing other emancipatory responses? While aspiring to dismantle patriarchy and the related gendered inequalities in Western society, what do we do in the meantime as we work with victims/survivors participating in the legal process? Is it possible that as feminist theorists, practitioners and researchers in the field of sexual assault, we have written ourselves out of meaningful participation in change?

Exceptions to the Feminist Narrative about Change

Importantly, there are some voices and acts of resistance that position victims/survivors and counsellors/advocates quite differently from the dominant constructions. Jarvis and McIlwaine (1997: 6), for example, state that:

> women who do choose to participate in the legal process are exercising their agency to bring in to the public domain what is mostly a very private experience … The telling of the sexual assault itself acts to undermine the power that maintains and sanctions it.

Unlike the dominant voices in feminist commentary, they point to 'women's agency and power' in challenging and changing the legal system (Jarvis and McIlwaine 1997: 3).

Similarly, other research indicates that victims/survivors do not 'trust the legal process' but believe they 'should use it so as to bring pressure to bear upon the system and by so doing, eventually change it' (Mitchell et al. 1995: 131). This inspires hope about the possibilities of effecting change within the legal system. Recounting her own experience of cross-examination, one victim/survivor describes how, even under the highly adverse circumstances of having to face the perpetrator in court, she summoned the courage to find a narrative that displayed strength rather than powerlessness: 'I felt that if he got convicted it would serve him right. I was becoming more determined to see that I got justice for what he'd done to me' (Cripps 1996: 52). Despite feeling intimidated by the defence lawyer's cross-examination, this courageous complainant says that she was able to resist being rendered powerless or victimised a second time, by dismissing him as 'an arrogant jerk' (Cripps 1996: 52).

Whilst sexual assault workers are rarely portrayed in the research literature as powerful advocates, there are examples of counsellors/advocates challenging the structural inequities in the legal system (Allen 1996, Jarvis and McIlwanie 1997, Morley 2009). Providing perhaps one of most pertinent demonstrations of this, Allen (1996) documents her protest in court against the subpoenaing of files. Others explain how sexual assault workers have adopted a number of covert strategies in attempts to create files that meet legal requirements but could not be used to compromise the complainant if subpoenaed. Such approaches, which attempt to address 'the dilemma that exists when aiming to provide confidential case notes with the possibility of files being subpoenaed' (Gardiner and Roberson 1995: 232), have taken the form of Post-Traumatic Stress Disorder (PTSD) files: files that contain information related to responses of the sexual assault that are consistent with the Diagnostic Statistical Manual (DSM-IV); the 'dual/shadow' file, which involves keeping one file for court and one as the counsellor's working notes (this is labour-intensive and illegal, but it is one option that is documented in the literature); the 'bland' file, which contains minimal information; the 'cryptic' file, which can only really be understood by the counsellor recording the notes; and, the 'Clayton's'[1] file, which records dates and time of sessions, but no other details (Gardiner and Roberson 1995). While all of these options have limitations, including illegality, they represent acts of covert resistance at the local level.

Furthermore, just because subpoenae of case file notes and warrants to search for confidential information are issued, does not mean that counsellors/advocates are diligently complying with unreasonable requests. As one researcher indicates, '[w]omen's groups and service providers have been very vocal in seeking a clarification of the law in regard to the admissibility of rape counselling notes' (Townsend 1996: n.p.). The following quote illustrates the determination to resist legal dicta:

> Such "fishing expeditions" as they have come to be known, have extended to a search warrant being issued to search the premises of a Sydney metropolitan sexual assault service. We are yet to hear the outcome of this matter as the keys to the file storage area were lost at the time the police turned up with the search warrant. (Gardiner and Roberson 1995: 236)

---

[1] This is an Australian colloquial term that refers to a soft drink that has the appearance of being an alcoholic beverage. It is often used as a term to create an illusion. In this case, a file, that is not really a file.

Conclusion

Analysis of the law reforms presented in this chapter suggests that targeting legislation may not be the most effective strategy for change. Following a feminist logic, the broader social and political (patriarchal) context of our society also needs consideration as an important site for change, given it is this context in which the laws are made and implemented.

However, if we focus specifically on broader social change, what practical opportunities does that afford us for making a contribution to change processes as individual practitioners? Do feminist analyses of the issues potentially exacerbate the problems, and at the same time make practitioners feel more removed from being an active part of the solution? Whilst there are some exceptions to the modernist, feminist narratives about change, such acts of resistance are arguably made more visible through critical postmodern theoretical frameworks.

The following chapter will explore the contribution that critical postmodern theorising might make to feminist understandings of the problems. It will also discuss the ways in which critical reflection was used as the method of inquiry in this research in order to put the emancipatory potential of critical postmodern theorising into practice.

Chapter 5

Alternatives for Thinking about Change: Critical Postmodernism and Critical Reflection

Introduction

This chapter explores the contribution that postmodernism and critical postmodernism make to expanding feminist thinking about change. I use a postmodernist appropriation of critical theory, critical postmodernism (see for example Allan et al. 2009, Fook 2012), to explore the influences these theoretical ideas provide in understanding practitioners' sense of powerlessness to bring about change in the legal system and in formulating different conceptualisations of change.

This chapter also introduces the model of critical reflection that was used as the method of inquiry in this research. I will argue that critical reflection, based on critical postmodern theorising, can assist practitioners to reconceptualise possibilities to work constructively with the legal system towards change. The design of the study will be briefly explained, emphasising the central processes of deconstruction and reconstruction, as integral to the critical reflection method.

Postmodernism

While there is a significant body of literature that argues that the principles of a postmodern analysis are problematic for feminism (see for example Bell and Klein 1996, Fawcett 2008) condemning its: 'potential for epistemological and socio-political nihilism' (Holmes and Warelow 2000: 90); its complicity with capitalism, patriarchy and globalisation; its political neutrality (Kermode and Brown 1996, Stromquist 2000); its fragmentation of universalist feminist arguments (Bulbeck 1994, Hare-Mustin and Maracek 1994, MacDonald 1996, Stephenson 1994) and its potential to undermine the need to mobilise for social transformation (Francis, 2000; Fraser and Briskman, 2005), postmodern thinking provides an alternative to the feminist belief that emancipation can occur only through changing the structures that produce oppression (Fook 2012, Morley and Macfarlane, 2012). This perspective therefore offers other possibilities for conceptualising change.

Postmodernism refers to a broad range of theoretical developments that emerged in the social sciences and humanities in the late twentieth century (Healy 2000, Weedon 1987), particularly the intellectual movement against deterministic structural analyses (poststructuralism) in France in the 1960s. It is a critique of universal ideas, singular truths and logocentrism, that is, unified ways of thinking (Fook 2012). 'Poststructuralists are concerned to move away from notions of "essential" meanings or beliefs in a fixed, singular, logical order' (Featherstone and Fawcett 1994: 27). In broad terms, postmodernism extends modernist ideas by critiquing their exhaustive truth-claims and showing that 'knowledge is always provisional, incomplete and perspectival' (Seidman 2013: 169). While modernist perspectives, such as feminism, are based on 'fixed, universal explanations of reality' (Sands and Nuccio 1992: 492; see also Macey 2000, Parton and O'Byrne 2000), postmodern analysis rejects universal and totalising ways of knowing, and can create different opportunities for thinking about legal practices and how we may create change.

'Postmodernism presents itself as a celebration of the multiplicity of individual [and collective] experiences ... It encourages a multiplicity of views and approaches to understanding. It supports the view that knowledge is contextual and localised and it rejects generalised ways of knowing' (Kermode and Brown 1996: 376). It potentially enables us to transcend the thinking that changing patriarchal structures and eradicating social mythology are the only possibilities for creating change. Postmodern thinking is therefore 'less concerned with the search for universal laws than with building broader understandings' (Weber 2006: 35).

Similarly, postmodernism questions the usefulness of the feminist tendency to universalise women's experiences and position women as a disadvantaged or disempowered social category. As Seidman (2013: 215) explains:

> Postmodern feminists posed a broad challenge to the core premise of the women's movement: the idea that "women" refers to a shared essence or common identity that forms the necessary basis of feminist knowledge and politics. They raise doubts about appealing to "women" as the foundation of the women's movement on the grounds that such a concept is incoherent, excludes certain women and creates norms of the good woman.

From this perspective, some of the grand narratives associated with feminism can be interpreted as unintentionally disempowering due to casting individuals as passive victims at the mercy of abstract structures (Healy 2000, Leonard 1994, 1997). 'Postmodernists such as Foucault and Derrida argue that the self is only a "position in language"' (Rosenau 1992: 43) and not an essentialist identity incapable of conscious change. What this means for thinking about practice in the field of sexual assault is that the ways in which practitioners and victims/survivors are positioned in dominant narratives about the problems with the legal system, are understood to be a mere 'effect of discourse' (Rosenau 1992: 43) and not an inevitable fate. For example, the notion that practitioners are powerless, and the view that victims/survivors are invisible and peripheral to legal proceedings, are understood simply to be constructs of discourse. Given that discourses are not 'real' in an objective sense, but socially constructed, and multiple, it renders these received 'truths' challengeable and amenable to change. This postmodern thinking therefore potentially creates opportunities to rethink our participation in the unintended, unhelpful consequences of feminist thinking.

Postmodern analysis considers reality to be a social construction: *a* truth, rather than *the* truth (Fook 1996, 2012). While feminist theories offer a universal, singular truth about how women experience structural disadvantage in relation to men because of patriarchal social arrangements that contribute to the epidemic of sexual violence against women (see for example Brownmiller 1975, Larcombe 2005), from a postmodern perspective, reality is constructed through discourse (Seidman 2013). Postmodern analysis thus suggests that all situations can be understood by any number of discourses, and that therefore multiple interpretations of reality exist. Postmodernists similarly emphasise our own personal engagement with discourses that construct us in disempowering terms (Parton and O'Byrne 2000) and focus on the nature of language in creating reality. This creates the 'conceptual space' (Rossiter 2005: 1) in which we can develop other ways of thinking about the problems of the legal response to victims/survivors, and invites questions such as what are the discourses that have been unintentionally silenced, marginalised or excluded by feminist thinking about change? What possibilities for change have also been precluded by this thinking? And how might we develop different understandings and opportunities for change by viewing the research problem through different discourses?

Using postmodern thinking to analyse some of the language used in feminist understandings of the problems with the legal responses to sexual assault, highlights a number of important considerations. For example, because feminist narratives, despite their liberatory aims, appear to construct practitioners and victims/survivors as powerless, and the goal of changing the legal system as hopeless, some of the dissenting voices that are more hopeful about the potential for change are subjugated. Using postmodern thought to deconstruct 'reality' through analysis of discourse, we can consider the possibilities for critically reconstructing unhelpful and disenabling discourses that construct women as powerless, passive victims at the mercy of the legal process and its personnel. The idea of 'reconstruction' (further explained later in this chapter) originates in the critical theory of Jürgen Habermas (1979: 95), who defines it as taking a theory or discourse 'apart and putting it back together again in a new form in order to attain more fully' its intent, in this case an emancipatory intent. It is this emancipatory-reconstructive project, in the wake of deconstruction that distinguishes critical postmodernism from other postmodern approaches.

Is it possible, for example, that some victims/survivors have at times felt more supported, empowered, aware of their rights and able to exercise them, than dominant narratives suggest? Indeed, research indicates that victims/survivors who were supported by a counsellor/advocate following a sexual assault were more likely to have police statements taken, receive a more positive response from the police and more care from medical personnel, as well as reporting less distress from interactions with police and medical practitioners (Campbell 2006, Maier 2008, Shaw and Campbell 2011, Wasco et al. 2004).

Agency, in this context, is a person's awareness of their capacity to exercise power or influence over a situation (Fook 2012). If instead, the personal agency of practitioners is emphasised, it is possible to conceive, for example, that practitioners may be able to assist victims/survivors to understand their experiences of sexual violence and the legal responses to them within discourses that they can create and deploy, rather than accepting the 'facts' as dominantly constructed by the social mythology surrounding sexual assault. This is perhaps indicative of some gaps in the dominant narratives that, in the main, fail to document comprehensively the courage and strength of victims/survivors, and the inspirational acts of resistance captured in the change-oriented work practised by many counsellors/advocates.

Part of the role of this book is to extend this marginal commentary on local acts of resistance. This will be done partly by privileging the expressions of counsellor/advocate agency and victim/survivor empowerment, and involves uncovering possibilities for envisaging their personal agency in responding to legal system injustices.

Critical Postmodernism

A critical and postmodern theoretical framework facilitates the extension of this marginalised commentary, as it preserves the social justice value commitments and emancipatory visions of feminist perspectives on the problem, while incorporating selected postmodern ideas to enhance feminist thought on the issues. A number of social theorists have explored the possibilities for a critical approach that brings together the emancipatory possibilities of both feminist and postmodern perspectives (see for example Butler 1989, 1992, Fraser and Briskman 2005, Healy 2000, Leonard 1997, Morley and Macfarlane 2012, Mullaly 2007, Pease and Fook 1999, Yeatman 1994). As Fook (2012:18) explains,

> a postmodern and critical social work practice is primarily concerned with practising in ways which further a society without domination, exploitation or oppression. It will focus both on how structures dominate, but also on how people construct and are constructed by changing social structures and relations, recognising that there may be multiple and diverse constructions of ostensibly similar situations. Such an understanding of social relations and structures can be used to disrupt dominant understandings and structures, and as a basis for changing these so that they are more inclusive of different interest groups.

The combination of critical theories informing this book includes structural and feminist analyses as well as an interpretive framework whereby the links between the individual and the social context are made explicit through an analysis of how language and social practices produce and construct meaning (Ife 1997).

In drawing on critical postmodern thinking to inform this research, I understood that this perspective has the potential to identify and reconstruct the limitations and unintended consequences of modernist conceptions of power, identity, dichotomous categories and universal narratives (Fook 2012) that are inherent in feminist thinking. Critical postmodernism has been shown to transcend some of the limitations of modernist, critical theories by reconstructing the possibilities to challenge and change structurally produced power relations at an interpersonal level. This offers the potential for practitioners working with victims/survivors of sexual assault to examine and reject personally internalised social messages that are contrary to our interests and the interests of the people with whom we work. As Fook (2004: 16) states, critical postmodern thinking

> might potentially unsettle some of our assumed ways of thinking about ourselves in relation to the social structure. It is possible that this unseating of taken-for-granted ways of understanding of ourselves in our social worlds might in fact provide a means and a site for challenging and resisting different forms of domination.

Changing the ways we see the problems with the legal system, and our options in relation to it, may therefore free practitioners to work in ways that have not previously been considered. Consequently, my research explored questions such as: what capacity do we have to envision agency and to change how we construct the problems with the legal response to sexual assault? How might we reconstruct our roles and our practices in more enabling and empowered terms so that we can have a greater capacity to improve legal processes and outcomes for the women who have the courage to access the legal system, albeit within the patriarchal context in which the legal system operates? And what are the possibilities to construct new ways of thinking and related practices that provide new strategies to respond to the difficulties victims/survivors experience with the legal process that enhance our broader commitments to progressive social change? As such. the research investigated the implications of drawing upon critical postmodern thinking for counsellors/advocates who support victims/survivors of sexual assault in the legal system.

The incorporation of critical postmodern perspectives broadened the initial focus of the research from concentrating specifically on the structural problems and (un)responsiveness of the legal system, to include understanding the ways in which practitioners construct and are constructed by their roles in the context of their work with the legal system, and to uncover discourses about their internal sense of agency to enact change (Ellermann 1998, Fook and Morley 2005). Part of this included exploration of whether critical postmodern thinking and practice might enable individual practitioners to envision alternative strategies to address the structural problems in the legal system and therefore connect them with the means of social change. DiAngelo (1997: 7) describes this process succinctly: 'to transform power structures, we must first transform ourselves.' I therefore needed to find a method of inquiry that would enable the emancipatory potential of critical postmodernism to be put into practice. I needed to choose a methodology that could be transformative and that was capable of analysing discourses to produce change. Critical reflection was ultimately chosen as the research methodology, as it has been shown to meet these requirements (See for example, Fook 2004, Fook and Napier 2000, Pockett and Giles 2008).

Critical Reflection

Whilst critical reflection is a contested concept that can be understood in a myriad of different ways, the approach used in this book draws on Fook (2002) (developed later by Fook and Gardner 2007, Fook 2012). This model coalesces a number of different theoretical traditions including: reflection (see for example Boud et al. 1985, Dewey 1933, Kolb 1984); reflective practice (Argyris and Schon 1976; see also Schon, 1983, 1987); reflexivity (Gouldner 1970, Taylor 2006, Taylor and White 2000); critical and experiential approaches to learning (Brookfield 2005, Mezirow and Associates, 1990) and critical postmodern analysis (see for example Fook 2012). More recent iterations of this model of critical reflection may also draw upon spirituality and Eastern religions, cognitive approaches to transformative learning and relational approaches (Fook 2013). This critical reflection model has primarily been identified as an educational tool for learning about professional practice (Fook 2013), but more recently has also been adapted and developed into a research methodology (Allen 2013, Askeland, Fook 2011, Gardner 2013, Morley 2008a, 2013a).

Critical reflection, in this tradition, is a process that enables us to identify the ways in which we might unwittingly affirm discourses that work against us and the people we are working with through examining our implicit assumptions (Fook 2000). It involves self-reflection on how our thoughts and perceptions have been constructed, and can therefore be deconstructed, resisted, changed and reconstructed (Fook 2012). More specifically, '[c]ritical reflection … is about understanding the technologies of power, language and practice that produce and legitimate forms of moral and political regulation' (Fook et al. 2006: 10). As Fook (2002: 98) puts it: 'The prime purpose of critical reflection is to unearth how we ourselves participate in discourses which shape existing power relations.' Through creating 'conceptual space' (Rossiter 2005: n.p.), it may free us from hegemonic, 'fixed and potentially restrictive ways of thinking, and may indicate avenues for change' (Fook 1996: 199).

This '"learning from experience" aspect … is transformative in that it allows a fundamental reworking of experience (in an enabling way), which also functions as to provide new guidelines for action and an improvement of practice' (Fook 2013:7). In addition, it is contended that critical reflection creates a personal sense of power or liberation (Fook and Askeland 2006) and has the potential to provide emotional and social support to practitioners (Ruch 2007). As a method of inquiry, critical reflection therefore offered a number of valuable characteristics for the research participants/practitioners who were feeling overwhelmed and disenfranchised by the legal system, yet wanting to use the research process to explore possibilities for change within their own practice.

Some of the concepts involved in critical reflection therefore involve 'certain uncertainty', 'thoughtfully unthinking' and a 'process of letting go' – a mechanism of unlearning many of our previous assumptions that restrict and limit our potential (Bolton cited in Fook et al. 2006: 16). This involves attempting to step outside familiar theories and practices, to make them appear unfamiliar or 'strange' so that they can be properly interrogated and so that we can 'develop the capacity to resist and transgress' (Fook et al. 2006: 10). These processes were central to this research as some of the modernist assumptions inherent in feminist thinking (as highlighted by critical postmodern analyses) were functioning to compound practitioners' sense of powerlessness and difficulties with the legal system. Critical reflection helps address this issue by activating a process of identifying and analysing how our use of language, participation in discourse and social practice may indicate the influence of dominant discourses (Fook 2012). Considering the aims of this research were to assist practitioners to develop alternative thinking and practices for change, critical reflection was therefore an ideal method of inquiry.

While critical reflection has been criticised as being little more than 'benign introspection' (Woolgar cited in Taylor 2006) that 'does not take the process far enough' (Taylor and White cited in Tseris 2008: 30), Fook and Napier (2000: 224) contend that 'it can have very real externalised outcomes'. Numerous authors attest to the value of critical reflection for developing new insights into professional practice (see for example Baldwin 2004, Fook 2012, Morley 2004, 2011, 2012, 2013b, Taylor 2006). Given that my aim was to explore how practitioners might envisage challenging and changing the legal response to sexual assault, critical reflection became crucial because it 'can provide a means for reconstructing, and thus changing, the ways in which individuals perceive and relate to their social worlds. In this sense, critical reflection holds emancipatory possibilities' (Fook 2004: 16). As Fook and Askeland (2006: 42) explain, '[t]he central idea is that the new insight and knowledge gained through reflection would result in societal changes'.

Rationale

Whilst building theory inductively from critical reflection on practice departs significantly from dominant, objectivist research paradigms (Allen 2013, Morley 2013a), there were sound epistemological reasons for using critical reflection as the method of inquiry in this project. For example the research question: 'How does critical reflection on practice develop possibilities for change?' did not require me to prove anything. Nor did the research aim to simply discover 'the truth' about problems with the legal response to sexual assault. In fact, as outlined in the previous chapters, there is already a wealth of feminist research comprehensively documenting the impact and inadequacies of the legal response to victims/survivors of sexual assault. In order for this research to make an original contribution to the existing knowledge base in this field, it needed to go beyond the well-known critiques of the legal system to formulate alternative thinking and practices about change.

Questioning of the assumed supremacy of objectivist paradigms that continue to dominate approaches to research was one of the first steps in this process. These dominant paradigms separate the researcher from the research and assume that what we know, can be known independently of the knower (Arnd-Caddigon and Pozzuto, 2006). They assume that an objective 'truth' can be discovered with the right (external, distant and unbiased) technical treatment of data (Arnd-Caddigon and Pozzuto, 2006). However, this contention would be severely limiting for research that aims to generate new knowledge that can contribute to emancipatory changes. Indeed accepting the 'truth', as presented by dominant ideologies, would have us believe that reconstructing practitioners' agency to challenge and potentially change the legal system is not a realistic goal (Morley 2011, 2012, 2013b). Dominant research paradigms would therefore simply reinforce the assumed powerlessness and fatalism of the situation for practitioners.

Consequently, the method of inquiry used in this research had to be able to incorporate critical and postmodern/social constructionist principles into the analysis of practitioners' stories. For critical approaches to research, there is a virtual, historical reality that has been shaped by structural factors over time (Denzin and Lincoln 2000: 165). This is necessary to acknowledge the patriarchal, structural context in which the legal system has developed and operates. At the same time, in order to move beyond reproducing the familiar critiques of the system and context, the postmodern/social constructionist approach to research suggest that realities are locally produced and specifically constructed (Denzin and Lincoln 2000: 165). Hence an analysis of practitioners' narratives seeks to uncover alternative understandings of the 'reality' in which the potential for more critical practice and emancipatory outcomes could be highlighted. This privileges an exploration of how individual practitioners construct, interpret, engage with and make sense of the structural context and their agency within it, without capitulating to relativism (Rossiter 2005).

This involved questioning the relationship between being and knowing, and recognising the social, cultural and political relationships implicated in the construction of 'truth' (Arnd-Caddigon and Pozzuto, 2006). Such a recognition can create the possibilities for alternative discourses about problems in the legal system and how we understand the potential for change. From the perspective of a postmodern analysis, facts and knowledge are social constructions that are culturally and historically determined by dominant power structures and relations. One of the issues targeted by the critical reflection methodology was therefore an examination of how the social positioning and biography of the participants influenced their perception of their practice incident, and the world more broadly. The language they used to describe particular social phenomena was similarly scrutinised (Ellermann 1998, White 2001: 102). As Ellermann (1998: 36) explains, 'far from capturing pre-existing meanings, it is language itself that constructs meanings and creates truths'.

Critical and postmodern/social constructivist research paradigms are also designed to produce knowledge that contributes to an agenda of social change. This combination blends critical theory's goal of emancipatory transformation with the postmodern/social constructionist goal of understanding and deconstruction: the fusion of both approaches leading to reconstructed possibilities. United, yet held in tension, these approaches aspire to 'chang[e] the world and not be content with merely describing it' (Acker et al. cited in Wuest 1995: 135).

The research therefore aimed to 'understand social reality in ways that provide insights towards the creation of a more emancipatory society' (Popkewitz 1984: 50 cited in Goodman 1998: 55) and to 'share in the joint process [between the research participants and myself] of knowledge construction as a basis for achieving change' (Powell 2002: 25). Such an approach intends to uncover the operations of the particular discourses, and to additionally critically reflect on this knowledge in ways that actively challenge, disrupt and reconstruct dominant oppressive power relations and structures (Fook 2012).

Reflexivity

Reflexivity acknowledges that as the researcher, I am part of the social world that I am studying, and my own internal assumptions, values and biases will shape the way I approach the research, engage with it and interpret and present the information that emerges from my interactions with the participants (Loftus et al. 2011). Reflexivity is a crucial component in evaluating the worth of research located within these critical and constructivist qualitative paradigms (Fook 1999b). It appears in the research literature as an alternative to positivist notions of reliability and validity (Allen 2013). While reflexivity is defined in different ways, most authors emphasise the impact and influence of the researcher, the importance of self-reflection and critique, (see for example Taylor 2006) and the researcher's positioning in terms of the 'politics of location' (Lipp 2007: n.p.) in producing the research. Reflexivity is the critical gaze focused upon 'researcher's struggle with the epistemological, methodological and political issues that are always inherent in critical research … and the … impact of the researcher on the intention, processes and outcomes of the research' as well as the 'intersections between the researcher's values and the research processes' (Smyth and Shacklock 1998: 1). Many writers concur that because the researcher is part of the text, it is unavoidable that the self is incorporated into the inquiry (Allen 2013, Loftus et al. 2011, Morley 2013). Consistent with this principle, in this research I took a reflexive stance in using critical reflection as a methodology to conduct semi-structured interviews with research participants.

I also chose to critically reflect one of my own practice experiences as part of the research in order to engage in a parallel process of critical reflection alongside the other participants. This decision mirrors auto-ethnographic approaches to research (Allen 2013, Ellis and Bochner 2000), yet the critically reflective focus is slightly different given the emphasis on exploring participants' capacities to envisage challenging dominant power relations. While I critically reflected on my own account, because critical reflection is a practice that you perform on yourself (Fook 2012), I also facilitated a critical reflection process for the other five participants involved in the study to assist them to unsettle and examine their own hidden assumptions and rework ideas about professional practices. In this way, the research participants became the researchers of their own practice experiences.

Design of the Study

In practical terms the research involved analysing six case studies of counsellors/advocates' practice in the context of the legal system when supporting victims/survivors of sexual assault. The case studies were narratives about practice that were provided by practitioners in interviews, including my own narrative about a critical incident. As Frost (2006: 113) explains:

> Narratives are personal constructions that enable us to explore how … relationships work in ways that help to understand how we, as professionals, understand and explain what we do. This approach sees the role of the practitioner merging in dialogue with (in relation to) "others".

The narratives concern 'critical incidents'. Analysis of critical incidents has been widely used in education as a tool for transformative learning (Benner 1984, Flanagan 1954, Fook et al. 2000). Critical incidents are 'idiographic in that they are brief and concrete, contextually specific descriptions on incidents that are significant' (Brookfield 1990: 180). Given the focus of this research, participants were asked to select a case or critical incident that typically illustrated the problems that they experience with the legal system. I asked the participants to think about a particular case or incident that had been critical for them in some way: that they may have felt troubled by, experienced as challenging and difficult, or one in which they had ethical conflicts (Fook 2012). I met with practitioners individually, on two separate occasions, to talk with them about their chosen critical incident or case. Each interview took between 60 and 90 minutes to complete. Like Taylor (2006: 80), I was 'concerned with what the writer produced as a version of themselves as a practitioner, and possibly a person, as well as a version of the service user'.

The participants were counsellors/advocates who had worked in the field of sexual assault for a minimum of two years, and had been engaged in supporting victims/survivors of sexual assault through the legal process in the context of their role at a Centre Against Sexual Assault (CASA). The emergence of CASAs in Australia in the 1970s and 1980s paralleled the Second Wave of Feminism in the United Kingdom (Jones and Cook 2008) and the anti-rape movement in the

United States (Shaw and Campbell 2011). These first centres emerged from the grass roots organising of volunteers with the intention of supporting victims/survivors of sexual assault and working towards social change (Maier 2005, Shaw and Campbell 2011).

Purposive sampling was used to recruit the participants (Denzin and Lincoln, 2000). Since I have worked as a counsellor/advocate at two CASAs in Victoria, some of the potential participants were known to me personally through professional networks. I approached them and invited them to participate as individual professional practitioners rather than as agency representatives. Two interviews were carried out with all participants with the exception of one (Andrea), who, due to chronic illness, participated in the first interview only.

I asked each participant to make some brief notes about their chosen critical incident and bring them to our first meeting. Both written notes and verbal text were deconstructed and reconstructed in line with Fook's (2002) model of critical reflection (updated in 2012). As Brookfield (1990: 180) states, the benefit of analysing critical incidents is that 'specific responses to critical incidents often have the generic embedded within'. As he explains, 'the critical incident technique is rooted in the phenomenological research tradition and presumes that learners' general assumptions are embedded in, and can be inferred from, their specific descriptions of particular events' (Brookfield 1990: 180). In addition, researching practitioner's narratives about a case or incident that is critical to them provides 'incontrovertible sources of data giving insights into learners' assumptive worlds in expressions that are indisputably the learners' own' (Brookfield 1990: 180). When using critical incidents and cases as a part of a critically reflective process, 'the incident [or case] and its "telling" become the "story" of the person which is deconstructed or reflected on' and later reconstructed (Fook 2002: 99). In this process, '[p]ractice is conceptualised as research, and the moments of "not knowing" are prized for what they can generate' (Napier and Fook 2000: 10). Using story-telling in research not only validates people's experiences, but through deconstructing and reconstructing their experiences, it also opens the narrator/participant to the possibility of self-change, where they may be 'empowered to become more active agents within their social worlds' (Fook unpublished: 4).

Deconstruction

The first meeting with each participant focused on deconstructing her experience. Deconstruction involves identifying and questioning dominant discourses, looking for alternative perspectives and uncovering how different discourses are implicated in supporting the dominant interests (Derrida 1976, 1980, 1988, Rossiter 2005). Dominant discourses are those in which the best interests of the most powerful are maintained. They often infiltrate our thinking and take the form of common sense beliefs or taken-for-granted assumptions that can work against us and our service users. These discourses may operate as unquestionable truths and some of the social arrangements they support may be contrary to our aims as critical practitioners. Exposing assumptions that have been rendered unquestionable automatically presents them for scrutiny. This is an important part of destabilising dominant discourses because their power and dominance lies in the degree to which they remain unquestioned (Fook 2012). Deconstruction examines the implicit values and assumptions in our thinking and action, and aims to highlight our collusion in discourses that can be restrictive or unhelpful to us by limiting our thinking and practice options (Ellermann 1998, Fook 2012, Taylor and White 2000), thus problematising 'taken-for-granted assumptions and day to day reasoning' (White 2001: 102). As Mezirow (1990: 1) explains: 'What we perceive and fail to perceive and what we think and fail to think are powerfully influenced by habits of expectation that constitute our frame of reference, that is, a set of assumptions that structure the way we interpret our experiences.'

In this research, deconstruction involved identifying particular discourses that informed the participants' critical incident or case. Processes for analysing and deconstructing discourse have been comprehensively developed by social researchers (Denzin and Lincoln 2000, Kellehear 1993, Reason and Bradbury 2001). Deconstruction has strong similarities to discourse analysis. For Foucault, discourse is the blending of 'power, language and institutional practice [...] at historically specific times, in order to produce particular ways of thinking: "regimes of truth", which are inextricably bound up with forms of domination' (cited in Ellermann 1998: 36). D'Cruz and Jones (2004) define discourse analysis as the analysis of language as a social structure that connects knowledge and power. It involves examining the construction of the text and identifying which discourses are dominant and which have been relegated to the margins (Jones 1990), or pulling apart the construction of particular phenomena in an attempt to uncover its implicit and hidden meanings (Ife 1997).

We also utilised deconstruction to scrutinise the language participants used to describe their situations. This directed attention to the words that they had chosen to label their experiences as these convey and privilege certain meanings and often indicate the construction of certain implicit hierarchies (Fook 2012). This unearthed, for example, how and why participants had chosen to construct the incidents and cases in a particular way, and revealed hidden meanings that were often not conscious. Importantly, participants were informed prior to agreeing to participate in the study that the purpose of the research was not to represent their incidents or case studies as truths, but to analyse them using deconstruction and reconstruction with a view to developing new thinking and practice. Using critical reflection in this way can potentially liberate us to recast structural problems in a way that emphasises our own personal capacity to respond to them (Fook 2012, Morley 2013b). Alberti refers to this capacity as 'freedom and greater creativity in the way problems are addressed' (Alberti 2000: 47). According to Fook (2002: 90), 'unsettling or destabilizing commonly held or accepted beliefs is potentially one of the most powerful sets of strategies which arise from a postmodern and critical understanding'.

Once the discourses that were operating in participants' accounts were identified and made explicit, participants were asked to examine 'what is left out?' (Rossiter 2005: 5). This included examining what was distorted, missing or hidden from their accounts (Fook 2012). Subjugated discourses are significant because they indicate some of the ways we construct our meanings to preserve dominant practices or structures (Fook 2012). We worked together to uncover how particular discourses constructed participants' identities in particular ways and how they positioned them in relation to their service users, the legal system and its personnel. Such a practice enabled practitioners 'to stand back from the scope of their practice in order to understand its construction within a particular discursive space' (Rossiter 2005: 5). This deconstructive process was facilitated by critically reflective questions that aimed to assist participants to deconstruct their practice. While the questions I used were tailored to each participant's individual story, they were largely based on Fook's (2002: 92–3, later revised 2012: 121–2) model of critical reflection, an adaptation of which appears in Appendix 1. Some of the common questions I asked each participant in relation to the issue of power, for example, were:

- What are your assumptions about power?
- Does that indicate that you have constructed power as a commodity which others have, and that you and/or the victim/survivor do not have?
- What are the implications/limitations for your practice in thinking about power in this way? Does it lead you to feel disempowered?
- Was it your intention to further disempower yourself and the victim/survivor?
- Who benefits from you seeing yourself and the service user as powerless? What might be some other was to interpret power relations in this scenario which lead you to feel more empowered?

Having deconstructed the participants' practice at our first meeting following completion of the interviews, I transcribed the data from each interview then sifted through the stories to analyse the material independently. Guided by critical postmodern theoretical perspectives, I particularly looked for modernist constructions of power as a material entity or commodity; identity as something that is singular and fixed; and the construction of artificial dichotomies that limit pluralised understandings and multiple possible interpretations of the same situation (see for example Ellermann 1998, Fook 2012, Sands and Nuccio 1992). This analysis was then discussed with the participants in the second interview in relation to their own practice scenario, which assisted in identifying the macro-themes that ultimately emerged from the research.

Including Data from My Own Practice Experience

Consistent with the other participants, I selected a case that represented a critical incident that encapsulated some of my concerns with the legal response to sexual assault. The particular case I chose had been troubling for me for two years, and I wanted to learn more about how I might have responded differently to produce a better outcome for the victim/survivor. I made some brief notes about the case and then engaged in a process of interviewing by asking myself a series of questions based on Fook's (2002) model of deconstruction and reconstruction (updated 2012). The questions I posed were similar to those I asked of the other participants during their interviews. Reproducing the research process that I carried out with the other participants, I tape recorded the questions and my responses, and transcribed the data verbatim before attempting to analyse it.

Rigour

Quality criteria for critical and constructivist research are based on notions of historical situatedness for critical theory, and trustworthiness and authenticity for constructivism (Denzin and Lincoln 2000). Rigour is thus constructed in terms of moral, political and ideological value commitments that go beyond 'merely a set of methods for gathering and treating data' (Ratcliffe and Gondalez-del-Valle 1988: 388 cited in Koch and Harrington 1998: 886). In order to promote the trustworthiness of the data in this research, each transcript was sent out to participants for review after both the deconstruction and reconstruction meetings. From their recollection, participants were invited to comment on the accuracy of what I had recorded and encouraged to make amendments to the transcriptions if they felt it necessary. However, none of the participants did so. To ensure the authenticity of my analyses, I shared my analysis of their transcribed interview with each participant. Using more than one person to analyse the material provided a more comprehensive and holistic analysis given that critical reflection relies to some degree on the generation of multiple perspectives. While authenticity and trustworthiness do not attempt to ensure the objectivist standards of rigour including reliability and validity, given the epistemological location of critical research, 'there is no logical requirement for [this research] to conform to the rules of a different (positivist) paradigm' (Webb 1992: 749). In fact, 'qualitative studies are based upon an entirely different and, in fact mutually exclusive set of assumptions, [while] the use of evaluation criteria derived from the quantitative paradigm is totally inappropriate and therefore different benchmarks must be developed' (Nolan and Behi 1995: 588).

Reconstruction

The second stage of the research involved a follow up meeting with participants to work with them to reconstruct their critical incident or case in ways that opened up different possibilities for practise with the legal system. Reconstruction is 'the process of making a new or revised interpretation of the meaning of an experience, which guides subsequent understanding, appreciation and action' (see also Habermas 1979, Mezirow 1990: 1). The reconstruction of participants' accounts was facilitated by drawing on critical postmodern ideas that transcend modernist constructions of the problem (Fook 2012). The postmodernist contention that there are multiple constructed truths instead of a singular, objective view of reality, positioned the practitioner's description of their practice as one possible interpretation among many. This mirrors Rossiter's practice of using discourse analysis as part of critical reflection: 'The sense of "multiple stories" at play helped relocate the notion of experience as brute reality carrying authority by virtue of being "real" to a notion of experience as being constructed, contingent and always interpreted' (Rossiter 2005: 12). Creating this reflective stance enabled participants to accept responsibility as to how they had chosen to construct their narrative, examine why they privileged one account over others, to reject unhelpful assumptions, and to look for other interpretations which led to other possibilities for action. This process paints the participants into their own picture and connects them with the means of change, enabling them to rewrite or reconstruct their account in ways that created different possibilities for change. Part of this process, Rossiter (2005: 9) explains, is uncovering the oppositions or competing discourses; '[i]t is important to understand how the opposition itself locks out practice opportunities'. In constructing two mutually exclusive black and white options, the grey areas in between that also inhere various options are rendered invisible by the dominant discourses. Hence reconstruction is about recovering and revaluing these subjugated discourses in order to conceptualise the situations in more complex and sophisticated ways than binary thinking allows. According to Fook (2012: 111) reconstruction involves 'formulating new discourses and structures'. Bringing in other discourses from the margins that had been hidden allowed us to build on these and create new, more empowering and enabling discourses. This involved coining new terms, developing different discursive ways to construct and talk about particular phenomena, modelling new practices and creating new structures which enabled the new discourses to evolve and become accepted (Fook 2012).

Once participants had determined which discourses maintained power relations in the situations they were reflecting on, it became possible for them to recognise and resist their own participation. While I played a strategic role in engaging participants in dialogue as a basis for shared learning, the process of developing these alternative narratives enabled mutual understandings and an awareness of our capacities to achieve change. This stage of consciousness involves resistance to 'participating in aspects of dominant discourses which work to disempower, or perhaps render a situation unworkable' (Fook 2002: 95). Again, drawing on postmodernism, power is theorised here as something that can be exercised through control of discourse, rather than existing exclusively as a commodity that resides in social structure or is possessed (Fook 2012, Healy 2000, Smith 2008).

This challenged practitioners' initial assumptions about their own powerlessness to act and find alternative ways to construct their subject positions in relation to the legal system and its personnel.

Connected to this, the postmodern construction of identity as relative and changing, depending on context, reconstructs people as embodying multiple subject positions or identities. The suggestion that particular aspects of identity are emphasised at particular points in time, and for particular purposes (Sands 1996), enabled practitioners to reflect on how they have subjectively positioned themselves within certain contexts and discourses, and in relation to social structure. This facilitated a reconstruction of their identities, and that of their service users, in more enabling and empowering terms (Fook 2012, Sands 1996). In this way, it was possible for participants to liberate themselves from thinking about the issues in ways that were oppressing them and restricting their options (Fook unpublished). This resonates with Alfrero's (1972) notion of a conscientisation process in which people move from a fatalistic understanding of being dominated by external factors, to action.

At the conclusion of the reconstruction interviews, I transcribed the data and wrote separate reconstructions of the material, independently from the participants, to generate and develop new theory from reflecting on practice (Fook 1996). This necessitated a critical engagement with postmodern ideas to reconstruct the material with a view to formulating different constructions of the problem and new strategies with which to respond (Fook 1996, 2002).

The critically reflective questions I used to assist in both my separate analysis and during the second interview with participants were based on Fook's (2002: 101, later revised 2012: 123) model for reconstruction, an adaptation of which is presented in the list of questions in Appendix 2. In examining the issue of power, for example, some of the specific questions I asked most participants included:

- What would need to change from your initial interpretation of the situation for you to feel like a more active participant in this situation?
- How might your construction of the case study and your capacity to exercise agency change if you viewed power as something that you could use to facilitate a more socially just outcome for the victim/survivor?
- What are the exceptions to viewing your role in powerless terms? Tell me about some times where you felt powerful and effective in your role?
- How do these changes in the way that you perceive power assist you to rethink your practice?

These questions aimed to facilitate practitioners' sense of agency to construct their stories in more enabling terms, and change their own internal constructions of their situation. This enhanced their capacities to respond in ways not previously considered. When participants reconstructed their self-identities in relation to social structures, they developed new understandings of their cases or incidents. This new understanding of how particular ideas create, reinforce and maintain the existing social order, through reflection and critical analysis of social interactions, exposed the operations of dominant discourses and enabled practitioners to change their inadvertent participation in unhelpful and restrictive discourses (Fook 2004, 2012). In this process, transformative change is almost inevitable because as White (2001: 111) explains, '[o]nce routinised forms of thought have been destabilised in this way, it becomes extraordinarily difficult to continue to think as usual'.

Conclusion

In summary, this chapter has outlined the contribution that postmodernism and critical postmodernism make to expanding feminist thinking about change, and how the inclusion of these ideas have the potential to reduce practitioners' sense of powerlessness and bring about change by assisting them to formulate new practice options. Critical reflection, a method of inquiry that harnesses the emancipatory potential of critical postmodern theorising to be put into practice, was discussed in terms of its capacity to create possibilities for change in practitioners' thinking about change in the legal system. I have argued that that critical reflection, based on critical postmodernism, can assist practitioners to envision possibilities to address the structural problems of the legal system at the level of their everyday practice. The overall design of the research project was presented, emphasising the central processes of deconstruction and reconstruction as integral to the transformative learning processes in which the practitioners who participated in this research engaged.

The next chapter will present the participants' accounts of their practice in detail. Each practitioner's critical incident is summarised, explicating the individual deconstruction and reconstruction journey in which they engaged as part of the transformative learning they undertook during the research process.

Chapter 6
Stories from Front-line Practice

Introduction

This chapter presents the stories of the six counsellors/advocates who participated in this research. These case studies provide the foundation for the remainder of this book. Here, you will first be introduced to a brief demographic overview of each practitioner, and a short account of their narrative about their practice. Each narrative involved a critical incident that captures the frustrations and difficulties they routinely faced in their practice whilst supporting victims/survivors of sexual assault through the legal process. The presentation of these narratives demonstrates the transformative learning processes that each participant engaged in as part of the critical reflection research process. This includes the deconstruction of their accounts, which indicated a range of ways that they had unwittingly contributed to their own sense of powerlessness, and at times, to the further disempowerment of their service users. It also includes the reconstruction of their thinking and practice. This highlights the process of how participants were able to formulate new ways to challenge and change inequitable and unjust power relations and structures, and resist participating in the discourses that sanction the legal system's unjust responses to victims/survivors of sexual assault. Each practitioner's narrative is presented here separately because each participant had her own individual journey and reflection. Whilst there are many commonalities between their experiences, each story contributes something unique and original to our knowledge about practices of power, and resistance within the legal system.

Barbara

At the time of the first interview Barbara was a 33-year-old Australian woman who had worked as an after-hours counsellor/advocate at a regional Victorian CASA for almost three years. Barbara had a background of working in human resources roles, with an emphasis on mediation. She is a qualified social worker and had predominately worked for the Department of Education in school social work roles with primary and secondary students. Barbara chose this incident because even though it had occurred more than 12 months earlier, she was still thinking about it and wondering how her practice might have been different.

Summary of Barbara's Story

Barbara described a situation where a man with an intellectual disability was referred to her after-hours service after being sexually assaulted by an older male who lived in the vicinity of the residential care institution in which the victim/survivor lived. Barbara's main concerns at the time were that the police seemed to respond with hostility towards the victim/survivor and attempted to undermine the crisis care unit process by rushing the victim/survivor, and complaining about his decision to have a forensic examination. Barbara felt conflicted about managing the needs of the victim/survivor, whilst resisting the pressure of the police. 'I felt like I wanted to spend the time with him, but I also felt quite pressured by the police to actually move things along. Therefore I felt in conflict' (Barbara, Interview 1).

The personal distress this incident caused for Barbara was evident throughout her account. It was also clear from Barbara's account that the victim/survivor did not feel validated, supported or heard by the police.

Despite Barbara's observations of inappropriate police conduct, and her stated position that in her role as a school social worker, she would ordinarily challenge people in authority, her practice did not match her espoused theory in this situation, as she did not challenge the police about their behaviour in this instance. 'I was sort of annoyed with myself that I didn't do that because ordinarily I would' (Barbara, Interview 1). She reflected that she would have liked to have done this in hindsight, but presented the following reasons that prevented her from challenging the police at the time:

- There was confusion and a mix-up about the meeting place that occurred at the beginning of the crisis care unit. Barbara felt responsible for this, which inhibited her willingness to challenge the police;
- Barbara experienced a lack of confidence to challenge the police. She stated she felt confused and uncertain about doing this because incidents of conflict with the police had not previously been discussed at CASA staff meetings or training;
- Barbara indicated she did not think it was not necessary to challenge the police during the crisis care unit because she understood that the after-hours co-ordinator of the service would formally raise any issues with the police after an incident;
- Barbara had a sense that there would be both personal consequences for herself and the service user, and a detrimental impact for the service if she challenged the police;
- Barbara felt she lacked sufficient knowledge of police processes and philosophies, and also lacked a suitable opportunity to learn about these;
- She had a fear of potentially 'unknown' consequences of challenging the police;
- And finally, Barbara held a deep belief that the authority of the police should not be challenged.

Implicit Assumptions in Barbara's Narrative

Presented above are Barbara's espoused primary reasons for not being able to challenge the police during the crisis care unit process. Deconstruction of Barbara's narrative revealed a number of additional, more implicit assumptions, which also contributed to her inability to challenge the police at the time. Some of these are outlined below:

- The reasons provided by Barbara for not challenging the police were objective facts;
- Given that Barbara felt she was responsible for the mix up around the meeting place, she should not do anything to further antagonise the police;
- Challenging the police about their behaviour would necessarily be confrontational, and involve negative consequences;
- Conflict should only be entered into when it is safe to challenge and should only happen in private, and in a context where all variables can be predicted and controlled;
- Knowledge, information and preparation brings power, control and comfort (and that Barbara did not have the knowledge, information, preparation or power that she needed in order to challenge the police);
- Power is a commodity that the police had (and that Barbara did not) and that greater police presence equates with greater police power;
- The after-hours co-ordinator had more power than Barbara and therefore should assume responsibility for challenging inappropriate police conduct;
- Police and counsellors/advocates need to share the same philosophy in order to work together harmoniously;
- Challenging the police may have been possible, provided that information that was impossible to obtain, could have been obtained, prior to questioning the police;
- There was something so fundamentally different about her role as a CASA counsellor/advocate, from her role as a school social worker that it prevented her from practising how she 'normally' would;
- A good crisis care unit is one that runs smoothly and is without conflict, (and that Barbara's role is to 'fix things' if there is the possibility of conflict);
- Once you lose control of a situation, you cannot regain it;
- The 'unknown' is problematic and something to fear, and should be eliminated with knowledge and preparation.

Summary of Barbara's Deconstruction

Deconstruction focused on making explicit the above implicit assumptions, recognising their implications for her practice, and the ways that many of them were operating contrary to her intended practice. The following provides some details of Barbara's deconstruction process:

- Barbara realised that she had accepted the terms of reference of the police (for example, that she was at fault for the initial mix-up with regard to the meeting place);
- Barbara acknowledged that she had unwittingly bolstered the position of the police in relation to herself through her willingness to question her own conduct, whilst the possibility that the police were waiting in the wrong department remained a hidden discourse;
- She considered that there might have been other ways to interpret this mix-up. For example, that she was not responsible; that the police were, or it was simply a misunderstanding;
- She recognised her complicit embrace of dominant power relations, including her internalisation of dominant police discourses and language;
- Barbara recognised that in defining herself, her philosophies and that of CASA, by their difference to the police, she constructed two mutually exclusive positions;
- She also realised that her account of the incident positions the police as the dominant players in her narrative, and that defining herself by her difference to the dominant construction, potentially exacerbated her sense of powerlessness and ultimate perception that she could not challenge the police;
- She developed an understanding that how she interpreted the situation influenced her perception that she could not challenge, and therefore led to her inaction;
- She realised that these aspects of her thinking potentially worked against herself and the victim/survivor;
- She realised that her perception about the reasons for, and consequences of challenging the police, were not objective, external issues, but internally constructed assumptions and interpretations that also led to her inaction;
- She realised that her decision not to challenge the police potentially held greater consequences for herself, the service and especially the victim/survivor than challenging them could have had;
- She recognised that the ways that she constructed the situation may have contributed to her sense of chaos, lack of confidence, uncertainty and disempowerment;
- And finally, Barbara acknowledged her emotional response in relation to the incident led her to emphasise the confusion and uncertainty she privileged in her original account.

Summary of Barbara's Reconstruction

Having deconstructed her implicit assumptions, and critically evaluated their implications for her espoused practice, Barbara reconstructed much of her initial thinking and practice. Reconstructed aspects of Barbara's account are presented below:

- Barbara resisted discourses that blamed her about the meeting place mix-up in exploring other possible ways to interpret the situation;
- Barbara rejected the terms of reference of the police that situated her actions as 'bungled' in developing a more enabling discourse, which emphasised different aspects of her arrival;
- She recognised that by resisting this discourse, she transferred responsibility back to the police for their part of the mix up and repositioned the victim/survivor as central and dominant in the discourse – in line with her intended practice;
- Barbara realised that by privileging the co-ordinator's formal channel of redress to make a complaint against police, she limited her capacity to informally advocate for the service user during the crisis care unit process;
- She recognised that her actions did not have to be legitimated by the after-hours co-ordinator in that she was able to validate her own standpoint position in relation to the incident;
- She challenged her dichotomous understanding of the differences between her role as school social worker, and role as after-hours counsellor/advocate in recognising that:
  - conflict is potentially a part of both roles;
  - that the proximity of other colleagues in her school role is not really what enables her to raise issues; and
  - that uncertainty and 'the unknown' are just as much a part of her work at the school as they are in her after-hours role.
- Barbara reconstructed her notion of 'the unknown' from problematic, to something she recognises that she can and does manage;
- Barbara transcended the dichotomy she had created between CASA and the police by positing a new discourse, which located difference within the construction of a 'multi-disciplinary team';
- She reflected on strategies that she had used, and could continue to use to resist internalising the discourses and adopting the language used by the police;
- She identified naming problematic behaviour as a way of exercising power and influencing the discourse;
- She rejected the assumption that once control is lost from of a situation, that it cannot be regained. She privileged different aspects of her account to reconstruct her participation in the incident;
- She reconstructed her identity in more empowered terms, which emphasised her capacity to challenge the police where necessary to meet the needs of the victim/survivor;
- Barbara reconstructed her assumption about needing a private space to challenge the police by reinterpreting the potential positive implications of the victim/survivor witnessing her advocacy;
- She gave herself permission to challenge the police by reconstructing her assumption that challenge would inevitably lead to negative consequences,

by reinterpreting the sharing of her expectations with the police as an opportunity to educate them. Barbara subsequently reconstructed conflict in the after-hours role from rare and unusual to an understandable or potentially expected part of her work in this role;
- She reconstructed her lack of confidence by re-authoring a more empowering narrative about her capabilities;
- And finally, Barbara rejected the assumption that a greater amount of police representation equates with less power for the counsellor/advocate by recognising multiple ways to exercise power.

Ultimately, the process of critically reflecting on Barbara's story enabled her to develop alternative thinking and practices that would have potentially improved the victim/survivor's experience with the police. Barbara's original construction of the situation was limiting and held negative consequences for both her and the victim/survivor. Her reconstructed thinking and practices contributed to her gaining greater clarity around her role and feeling more confident and empowered about challenging the police when she observes inappropriate conduct, where previously she had felt unable to do this.

Rose

Rose is a qualified social worker who, at the time of the first interview, had worked at a regional CASA for two years. Prior to this, Rose had worked for 17 years as a counsellor with victims/survivors of torture and trauma. Rose was in her mid-forties and described herself as an Australian migrant with a multicultural heritage. Rose chose this incident because it was still troubling her. She felt powerless and ultimately ineffective in her role. It also represented the issues that are encapsulated in many other cases that Rose was continuing to work with, and therefore typically expressed the difficulties that she was experiencing in her work in the context of the legal system.

Summary of Rose's Story

Rose described a situation where she was working with the mother of a two-year-old child, who had separated from the father of the child. During access visits the mother believed, because of the behavioural indicators displayed by the child, that the father was sexually assaulting the child. Rose described how the legal system had failed to intervene to protect this child from sexual abuse perpetrated by her father. The child protection unit of the Department of Human Services (DHS), failed to obtain a disclosure from the child suitable for the purposes of court, and the mother was repeatedly forced to relinquish the child for access visits, with inadequate supervision, in which she believed the child was continually being abused. A sense of powerlessness was the overwhelming theme conveyed in this narrative, in that Rose felt there was nothing she could do for the mother, and that there was nothing more that the mother could do to protect her child, yet the abuse was ongoing. The hopelessness of this situation had led Rose to feel she needed to terminate her working relationship with the mother at the time of our first meeting because, as she stated: 'What's the point?' (Rose, Interview 1).

Implicit Assumptions in Rose's Account

A number of implicit assumptions were embedded in Rose's account. Some of these are outlined below:

- Rose's account was an objective description of reality, rather than her construction;
- Rose's impact on this situation was contained within her espoused construction of her support role;
- Power was a commodity that can be possessed or taken;
- Rose, the mother, and the child were unequivocally powerless;
- These powerless identities were fixed and unchanging;
- Rose's identity (powerless and lacking agency) is tied with the mother's powerless identity;
- The problems were entirely legal, related to the inadequacies of structural institutions, and external from Rose;
- Rose had no agency in this situation;
- For change to be meaningful, it must be structural change within the legal system; any other strategies would be 'pointless';
- If Rose was unable to create structural change in the legal system, then she would be unable to assist the mother and child at all and should discontinue her work with them;
- Rose cannot access the means of change;
- The possibilities for change were unlikely so the situation was hopeless;
- Advocacy involves two oppositional protagonists and Rose's role in advocating is to represent the interests of the powerless to those who are powerful – although this would be useless without structural change in the legal system;
- The legal system and lawyers are completely separate from Rose; there were two dichotomous sides in the situation (Rose versus the legal system);
- CASA practitioners cannot provide specialised assessments for child sexual abuse as this practice requires investigation, and investigation is diametrically opposed to a philosophical position of believing that counsellors/advocates universally adopt;
- That the woman nominated to supervise the access between the father and the child was entirely inappropriate and unsatisfactory for the role.

Summary of Rose's Deconstruction

In critically reflecting on her account, Rose deconstructed a number of her assumptions and interrogated their influence on her practice. Some of the deconstruction process in which she engaged is outlined below:

- Rose recognised that constructing power as a commodity, and perceiving herself, the mother and child in powerless terms was potentially unhelpful for all of them;
- In positioning the police, the Department of Human Services (DHS), lawyers, the woman supervising access and other participants as oppositional others, Rose had created two mutually exclusive and opposed positions;
- This dichotomous understanding of the key legal players involved in the situation, and her understanding of advocacy, had produced a dichotomous hierarchy of power relations, where Rose, the mother and the child were located on the powerless side of the dichotomy, which limited Rose's possible practice responses;
- This dichotomous understanding reinforced Rose's sense of powerlessness in working with the mother;
- Rose's sense of fatalism and powerlessness led her not to explore alternative options and practices;
- Rose's dichotomous understanding of the situation, which constructed change only in structural (legal) terms, resulted in her not being able to see or enact other possibilities for challenge or change (including: making a complaint to the supervisor of the police woman who would not take her concerns seriously; using the interaction with the police as an opportunity to raise their awareness; or contacting the woman who has nominated to supervise the child's access visits with the father to discuss Rose and the mother's concerns);
- Rose considered that she, the mother and the child, may occupy multiple and changing subject positions – rather than just one: powerlessness;
- Rose's account of the situation was socially constructed, and that other interpretations may therefore be possible;
- By constructing her work in the dichotomous terms of achieving structural change or disengaging with the mother, Rose significantly limited her practice options, and devalued and marginalised other positive aspects of her engagement with the mother;
- The assumption that conducting specialised children's assessment is investigative, and diametrically opposed to CASA's philosophical position of believing, is an artificial dichotomy that may hold limiting implications for Rose's practice, including limiting Rose's capacity to have input into how evidence of child sexual assault is collected and presented in court;
- There were a number of disadvantages for Rose's participation in 'entering into unhelpful' (Rose, interview 1) patterns of thinking;

- Rose's singular 'truth' about the situation was limiting her capacity to identify alternative interpretations and therefore her practice possibilities;
- Rose's impact on the situation is much broader and consequential than her espoused description of her support role;
- Participating in a discourse that asserts 'we're not funded for that' (Rose, interview 1) may result in a loss of opportunity to educate others who may significantly impact on the experiences of her service users, and a loss of opportunity to exercise power in having some input into the discourses which inform people's thinking about child sexual assault.

Summary of Rose's Reconstruction

Having deconstructed her implicit assumptions, Rose was able to reconstruct her thinking and her practice possibilities for change. The following points provide some details of Rose's reconstructed thinking and practice:

- Rose revised her modernist constructions of power to reimagine power as something that can also be exercised, through for example, her contestation and re-authoring of the discourse;
- Rose created alternative practice possibilities such as arranging to be subpoenaed to give evidence as an expert witness in court, or offering input to support child protection as a way of exercising power, and reframing the discourse, while counteracting Rose's overwhelming sense of structural powerlessness;
- Rose rejected the self-imposed boundaries she had placed on her role that limited her capacity to explore change-promoting practices;
- Rose reconstructed a view of herself as powerful by constructing discourses about her personal agency to effect change;
- Rose developed a discourse that was more affirming of her work;
- She reconstructed the mother's identity in more empowering terms;
- She reconstructed the identity of the child by uncovering hidden aspects of the discourse surrounding the child's resistance;
- She transformed her dichotomous thinking by recognising that practitioners can maintain their believing stance, whilst also being able to conduct specialised children's assessments and reinterpreting CASA practitioners as being well-placed to conduct specialised assessments;
- Rose reconstructed her sense of agency by seeing the children's assessments as an opportunity to exercise power through discourse by disseminating knowledge and influencing issues concerning how children's disclosures of sexual assault are understood.

Ultimately, Rose reconstructed her modernist notions of power and identity, and the dichotomous notions in her original thinking, which were devaluing and limiting her practice. She was able to unearth a number of practice possibilities that promote options for change, through critically reflecting on her practice, that she hadn't previously considered. These possibilities may potentially enhance Rose's capacity to envision agency to challenge the legal system in ways that were rendered invisible by her initial discourses, which were informed purely by a modernist structural analysis.

Bella

Bella is a woman of Eastern European decent, aged in her early forties at the time of the first interview. She worked as a senior counsellor at a regional Victorian CASA. She had extensive experience, working as a counsellor/advocate in the field of sexual assault, and had worked in both regional and metropolitan CASAs for 11 years. Academically, Bella held a Master of Social Work by research and was a Doctor of Philosophy (PhD) candidate. Bella chose this incident because she felt powerless to assist the mother she was working with to obtain a more satisfactory response from child protection and the legal system. She also states that situations like this one, which epitomise how, 'our institutions operate and how contradictory their operation is to their purpose …' (Bella, Interview 1), are common in her practice.

Summary of Bella's Story

Similar to Rose's practice example, Bella described a situation where she was working with the mother of a young child (aged 3 or 4 years). The mother had separated from the child's father, but he still saw the child during access visits. The child was displaying behavioural indicators of sexual abuse, and the mother believed that the child's father was assaulting the child during access visits. Despite the mother's attempts to protect her daughter, both the police and child protection failed to appropriately intervene. This meant the allegations of child sexual assault were unsubstantiated, and so the situation was referred to the Family Court. Bella explained her concerns with this:

> … it becomes an access and residence issue rather than a child protection issue. The protective issues are minimised and myths regarding the motivation of the non-offending parent dominate the conceptualisation of the issues. (Cited in statement made in preparation for interview 1)

> … So, what was frustrating for me, was to see … the mother … feeling very powerless to be able to do anything to help her. (Bella, Interview 1)

Implicit Assumptions in Bella's Account

A number of implicit assumptions were embedded in Bella's account. Some of these are presented below:

- Bella believed her account of the situation was objective and factual and existed independently of her construction of it;
- The problem was external to Bella and resided in abstract, systemic, inaccessible structures such as child protection and the legal system;
- For change to be achieved that is valuable and effective, it would have to be structural in nature;
- Change is something that counsellors/advocates witness, rather than actively influence or engage in;
- Law reform is the ultimate goal in terms of achieving effective, structural change in this situation;
- The problems in this situation were exclusively legal problems, and therefore required legal solutions;
- Legal practitioners are better placed to assist women in this mother's situation;
- Bella's role and knowledge base is completely separate from the lawyers;
- Counselling as a practice is ineffective in responding to these types of structural issues;
- Macro social change is entirely separate from and more important than individual casework;
- The situation was hopeless;
- Bella was powerless and alienated from the means of change;
- Within her role, Bella had no capacity to respond in any way that would make a difference to the process or the outcome;
- Power is a commodity that is held by people in structural positions and equates with professional status;
- Others who do not hold formal power (structural or professional positions of power) cannot access power;
- The mother was powerless;
- Advocacy involves two mutually exclusive and opposed protagonists, and aims to represent the interests of the least powerful (the mother and the child) to the more powerful side (child protection and the legal system);
- There were only two possible ways to understand the situation: Bella's account of the story, or its direct opposite;
- A clear disclosure from a child is the only way to access legal justice in the current system;
- The child protection system and the police were 'unable' to intervene because of structural problems in the system.

Summary of Bella's Deconstruction

Bella was able to deconstruct some of her implicit assumptions and recognise some of the problems they created for her intended practice. Some of her deconstructed thinking is outlined below:

- By accepting the discourse that the police and child protection were 'unable' to elicit a disclosure from the child, suitable for the purposes to take action to protect the child, Bella had taken on the broader system's dominant discourse – which was unhelpful both in terms of how she saw the situation, and her role to support the mother and child within it;
- Assuming that a clear disclosure from the child is the only way to access legal justice, Bella accepts the terms of the dominant discourse which was operating contrary to the interests of both Bella and the mother;
- Constructing the 'contentious nature of the disclosure' (Bella, Interview 1) as the main difficulty, justified the limited and inadequate response of the police and child protection system;
- Bella's initial account of the situation took on a bureaucratic discourse that may implicitly have limited her role;
- Bella realised that she had constructed the problem in a way that exclusively located the cause and solution within the formal structures of the legal system, and that this may have left her feeling limited to be able to effect change;
- Using a structural analysis exclusively to understand the difficulties experienced by the mother may have operated to encourage Bella to feel righteous about what changes should have occurred, but powerless to be able to have implemented them;
- By privileging the role of legal practitioners over her own role, she had implicitly created an artificial dichotomous construction between herself and the legal practitioners in a way that devalued and invalidated her own skills and knowledge base;
- Constructing her role in insignificant and marginalised terms may further have alienated Bella from the means of change and have exacerbated her sense of powerlessness;
- This dichotomous construction between herself and legal professionals served to 'other' counselling in favour of law reform;
- By privileging structural change such as law reform and legal solutions as the ultimate change strategies, Bella may have inadvertently rendered the everyday forms of change and resistance that counsellors/advocates engage in, as insignificant/invisible;
- Bella's binary, structural conceptions of power, positioned her as powerless and increased her hopelessness around enacting any legal change;

- By constructing the mother and child as powerless, Bella unwittingly reinforced their sense of powerlessness, and denied the acts of resistance exercised by the mother;
- The dichotomous positioning of herself and her client as powerless in the context of challenging the police and child protection institutions, operated to distance Bella from her internal agency to reconstruct the scenario in more empowering or enabling terms and be an effectual agent of change;
- The dominant discourses about there being little opportunity to challenge and change the legal system, relies on individuals collectively to accept and participate in it so that change is prevented;
- And finally, Bella recognised it is possible that the 'sinking feeling' (Bella, Interview 2) she experienced each time before she met with the mother, was more related to her construction of what was useful or valuable about her practice, rather than how the mother experienced it.

My separate analysis included:

- Bella's exclusive use of structural theory may have been limiting for her practice and at times, led to fatalism and feelings of powerlessness;
- By constructing advocacy in modernist binary terms, Bella may have limited more collaborative options to effect change;
- By seeing there were only two dichotomous and opposing ways to see the situation (Bella's perspective or the complete opposite), other less extreme conceptualisations of these issues, which might have offered different practice possibilities, were potentially rendered invisible.

Summary of Bella's Reconstruction:

A summary of the main changes in Bella's thinking and practices based on the reconstruction process undertook as part of the research process are presented below:

- Bella revised her notion of power to be more fluid and contextual;
- Bella developed an understanding that power may be exercised through the control of discourse, and that she was able to do this, for example, in the way she presented the story to the lawyer;
- Bella rejected the notion that for her contact to be useful for the mother, she must change social structures to revalue these aspects of individual counselling that were previously silenced by the dominant discourse that only values structural change;
- Reconstruction enabled Bella to value other aspects of her individual counselling work in its own right, rather than defining it by its difference to macro social change orientated practice;

- Bella changed her interpretation of how the mother experienced the counselling, to recognise the she did actually benefit from their work together;
- Bella reconstructed the mother's subjectivity in more empowered and enabled terms;
- Finally, Bella began to see her practice as more situated, and became more aware of the impact of context.

Ultimately, deconstructing Bella's account assisted her to see some of the unintended consequences of using a structural analysis of the problem in isolation. Bella had difficulty reconstructing her account comprehensively, but she was able to see that other interpretations of the situation, which may have had equal legitimacy, may have provided Bella with some alternative practice options, hence lessening her overwhelming sense of powerlessness.

Andrea

Andrea is an Australian woman who was in her late thirties when we met about the research. She was a working mother and had a degree in rural social welfare. She had an extensive history of working in the primary education sector in schools for children with disabilities and special needs. Andrea also worked as a counsellor/advocate at a number of rural and metropolitan CASAs across Victoria, and as an on-call worker at CASA House on the Sexual Assault Crisis Line. Andrea indicated she chose this particular incident for critical reflection 'because it's fresh. Because it's a crisis care unit. It's been a long time since I had done one, and just the response of the police' (Andrea, Interview 1).

The presentation of Andrea's data is incomplete because I only met with her once during the research, rather than twice as I did with the other participants. Unfortunately, Andrea was only able to engage in the first interview due the impact of chronic illness, yet she made some valuable contributions during this meeting. This summary therefore reports on the first stage of the research, rather than the entire process, and outlines some of the directions the process may have taken if the second interview had been held.

Summary of Andrea's Story

Andrea described a duty call where a woman was brought into the hospital in an ambulance due to physical injuries sustained through a sexual assault. The women had been raped by an unknown intruder that had broken into her home. As she explains:

> It was a stranger ... On the morning of the assault she said that she was at the back of the house in the laundry. She turned around to open the door to take the

> washing out to hang it out, and an unknown male, with his face covered with a balaclava burst in through the house and assaulted her. He raped her. And her belief is that he had cut her, although she didn't have a clear memory of it happening. (Andrea, Interview 1)

The woman also had a serious health history of brain aneurysms and the physical assault the woman endured during the rape exacerbated the level of risk to her health.

> She had a huge headache from a blow that she received to the head. On top of that she's actually got a neurological disorder. She's had brain aneurysms and had nine of them clipped. So, she was very distressed about her level of pain and the fact that receiving a blow to the head could make one of the aneurysms burst, and that, you know, could possibly kill her. So her medical stuff was the major concern. (Andrea, Interview 1)

Despite this, it did not seem possible to access appropriate health care for the victim/survivor in the hospital. The victim/survivor was worried about her health and also scared that the stranger would return. He had threatened her, and she was fearful about the possibility of being attacked again. In addition to these concerns, the conduct of the police in this situation was in breach of the practice protocols. The police inappropriately pressured the woman to hurry and to make a statement. The police also intervened to ensure the woman did not have access to the support of her husband and a female friend. According to Andrea, the interaction between the police and the Forensic Medical Officer (FMO) also appeared to have a major influence on the poor police response, as the FMO indicated that she believed the woman's wounds were self-inflicted. The 'suggestion by a neighbour that she was seen kissing a man on the front step' (Andrea, Interview 1) also appeared to compound a negative response by the police and FMO, resulting ultimately in the decision by the police to charge the woman with a making a false complaint. Andrea felt this situation was incredibly unjust and felt powerless to help the victim/survivor.

Implicit Assumptions in Andrea's Account

Some of the implicit assumptions embedded in Andrea's account that she uncovered through deconstruction are presented in the points below:

- The crisis care unit process was either going to focus on the woman's physical injuries, or interaction with the police;
- The woman's medical condition was the most paramount concern in this situation;
- The victim/survivor was vulnerable, fearful and overwhelmingly powerless;
- The victim/survivor was overwhelmed and devastated by the police;

- Andrea accepted the service user's view that she was a powerless victim who should take responsibility for not upsetting her family;
- The victim/survivor was disempowered because she was not professional or educated and that her powerless identity was fixed and unchanging and automatically linked with disadvantaged social categories;
- Power therefore accords professional status and education;
- Power is a possession, or commodity that Andrea possessed, but did not use;
- The police had more power to influence the situation than she did;
- The police were strong, powerful and numerous;
- The role and approach of the police was completely different and separate from Andrea's role and approach;
- Andrea needed to separate the service user from the police;
- The victim/survivor needed protection from the police;
- Andrea's role, as a counsellor/advocate, was to model desirable behaviour for victims/survivors to elicit the more favourable response from the police;
- When the police breached protocol, Andrea's role was to 'observe' and conform to preserve dominant power relations;
- The problems lay exclusively with the FMO and the police and were therefore external from herself;
- The FMO had the power to influence the police and was therefore the most powerful and influential person in the situation, who could not be challenged;
- The situation was hopeless so there was no point in challenging;
- The culture of CASAs impacts on how counsellors/advocates conduct their practice;
- There was no opportunity to critically reflect during practice;
- The only other possible way to see the situation was the direct opposite of Andrea's interpretation;
- And finally, Andrea's assumptions are the 'truth' about the situation, rather than her interpretations.

Summary of Deconstruction of Andreas's Account

I didn't have the opportunity to meet with Andrea a second time, and hence her opportunity to engage in a full deconstruction of her account was limited. However, there were a number of interesting points that emerged from my separate discourse analysis of her account after the first interview. Some of my observations are outlined below:

- Constructing critical reflection as an impossibility during practice may have limited Andrea's opportunities for learning and improvement;
- Seeing that there are only two polarised, oppositional interpretations of the situation, prevents alternative views from emerging and renders possibilities for alternative practices as invisible;

- Andrea had constructed oppositional power relations between herself, and the police and FMO;
- Andrea had aligned herself with the victim/survivor on the powerless side of the dichotomy in relation to the police and the FMO;
- Constructing the police and their role in dichotomous terms may have served to enhance Andrea's feelings of powerlessness;
- The way Andrea positioned the FMO in her narrative of this situation constructs challenging the FMO as an impossibility;
- In assuming that a complaint would have been made against Andrea by the FMO if she had challenged her, Andrea had accepted the dominant frame of reference, which was disadvantageous to both herself and the victim/survivor;
- Constructing the situation as hopeless led to fatalistic thinking and inaction, despite marginal discourses, which indicated that there might have been opportunities to challenge;
- The assumption that Andrea was an observer and that the problems are external to her may have positioned her outside of the means to change them;
- The assumption that the police were mutually exclusive/the enemy, and the assumption that the victim/survivor needed protection from them, meant Andrea's actions may have contributed to an adversarial situation with the police;
- Prioritising the woman's medical issues accepts the mystique of medical knowledge and its associated powers; and that repeated references to the possibility of the aneurysms 'bursting' and the potential for the sudden death of the victim/survivor reinforced Andrea's construction of the woman as extremely powerless and vulnerable;
- This construction of the woman as a powerless victim, on her own, being re-victimised again by the legal system, is juxtaposed against Andrea's construction of the police who are presented as strong, powerful and numerous;
- In constructing the identity of the woman in dichotomous terms from the professionals involved in the situation, Andrea inadvertently reinforced the woman's powerlessness;
- Constructing the victim/survivor as vulnerable and powerless further contributed to a sense of disempowerment for her service user;
- There are gaps, missing discourses, and exceptions to the dominant discourse surrounding the woman as powerless victim in a hopeless situation, which suggest that there are alternative ways to understand and locate her in this story;
- Andrea constructed the 'observer role' in separate and dichotomous terms from the 'participant role', and that this at times benefited the police and FMO;

- Andrea's perception that she and the police were mutually exclusive, combined with the discourses that position the police as in control, may have served to alienate Andrea from the means of change;
- Despite explicitly locating herself in an 'observer role', there were a number of ways in which Andrea 'participated' that may have unwittingly acted contrary to the interests of herself and the victim/survivor;
- And finally, there might have been a number of ways in which Andrea had opportunities to 'participate' more fully in the processes of this crisis care unit, but chose instead to 'observe'.

Summary of Reconstruction of Andrea's Account

Without the occurrence of a second meeting, we did not have the opportunity to reconstruct Andrea's thinking and practice. However, from the narrative she presented in the first interview and my discourse analysis of this there was one obvious aspect of Andrea's account that could be reconstructed. For example, if Andrea recognized that identity can also be interpreted as an evolving construction that can change from one context to another, this may have promoted opportunities to emphasise different aspects of the victim/survivor's identity to construct her in more empowered and enabled terms. Marginalised in Andrea's account were some other narratives that indicated the ways the victim/survivor exercised choice by how she engaged in the crisis care process, and therefore has had influence the over the process.

Olivia

At the time of the research interviews, Olivia was a 35-year-old Australian woman who had worked in both metropolitan and regional CASAs for 14 years. She had experience and qualifications as a community development worker, and was training as a probationary psychologist undertaking a Master's degree. Olivia specialises in therapeutic counselling for children who have been sexually assaulted, and chose this incident because it typified her experience of working with 'the issues about the legal system in terms of children as witnesses' (Olivia, Interview 1).

Summary of Olivia's Story

Olivia described a situation where she worked with a 7-year-old child who was sexually assaulted by an 18-year-old neighbour. Another young girl who lived nearby had made similar allegations against the same perpetrator, about a particularly violent assault that resonated with the dominant mythology surrounding the issues of sexual assault: (for example, the perpetrator was a stranger, the assault was violent involving a masked assailant with a weapon, and, there were multiple victims in separate, single incidents). The perpetrator was charged and Olivia observed that the police and legal system were more responsive to this situation than in relation to other cases that are less consistent with the social mythology. Olivia was hopeful about a conviction, but the ways in which the legal process unfolded resulted in the perpetrator being ultimately acquitted. Olivia felt powerless to change anything, as the technical, legal requirements seemed to work against the child she was supporting. Olivia believed the legal process and outcome exacerbated the child's level of trauma.

Implicit Assumptions in Olivia's Account

There were a number of implicit assumptions embedded in Olivia's initial account of this incident. These are captured in the points listed below:

- Olivia assumed that the police responded more favourably than they ordinarily would because the case resonated with some of the dominant social mythology surrounding sexual assault;
- She believed there was an obvious 'mismatch' (Olivia, Interview 1) between the requirements of evidence that a court stipulates, and the capacity of the child witness to provide this;
- She saw the problems as external to her, in terms of being located in the legal system and its personnel;
- She assumed the legal system was inappropriate for child witnesses;
- Olivia believed that her developmental knowledge about children was a subjugated discourse in the context of the social myths being dominant in a court setting;
- She felt that the ways in which credibility is decided by legal personnel are contentious;
- Olivia assumed that victims/survivors and counsellors/advocates are excluded from legal processes and positioned outside and separate from those who decide whom or what is considered credible;
- Power is a commodity that people possess and is inherent in formal structures;
- That power is inherently 'bad' (Olivia, Interview 1);
- She assumed that aiming to equalise power relations with service users leads to a reduction in power for practitioners;
- The legal system was operating to disadvantage the child witness;
- Olivia was powerless due to her inexperience;
- The legal personnel were far more powerful and important in this context than she was and that legal personnel were too busy to bother;
- Olivia assumed she needed to follow legal rules and conform to preserve dominant power relations;
- Individual counselling work with victims/survivors cannot be effective in challenging structural issues;

- Injustices for victims/survivors in the context of the legal system are due to 'fate' (Olivia, Interview 1);
- For change to occur in the legal system that is valuable, it must be structural in nature;
- Olivia's practice did not have much of an impact on the situation for the child;
- That exercising power by influencing the discourse through, for example, testifying as an expert witness in court is possible, but 'outrageous' (Olivia, Interview, 1);
- And finally, Olivia held the belief that developing alternative approaches to challenging the legal system is too time consuming.

Summary of Olivia's Deconstruction

Through critically reflecting on her account, Olivia factored herself into her construction of this narrative, recognised the implications of a number of her implicit assumptions, and began to deconstruct these. The details of her deconstructed thinking and practices are outlined below:

- Olivia acknowledged that by constructing the problem as external, she alienated herself from the means of change;
- In emphasizing the differences between herself and the legal personnel, Olivia created two mutually exclusive positions, between those who judge and investigate, and those who believe;
- Olivia recognised that there were a number of other dichotomies in her initial account that were socially constructed;
- That these dichotomies may be limiting or unhelpful for her practice;
- Olivia was operating on a number of taken-for-granted truths that are embedded in the culture of CASAs, and that these may be unhelpful in facilitating practitioner empowerment to work towards change;
- Olivia considered the notion that her construction of an 'anti-professional culture' (Olivia, Interview 2) may contribute to her sense of inadequacy when negotiating with legal professionals and perpetuate the belief that she must conform to preserve dominant power relations with the legal system;
- Olivia recognized that her assumption that power is 'bad' (Olivia, Interview 1) may result in her neglecting opportunities to exercise power productively for change;
- Olivia had located herself on the 'victim's side' against the legal system, which exacerbated her sense of powerless (Olivia, Interview 2);
- Olivia's initial sense of being excluded from the legal process might actually be 'self-imposed' (Olivia, Interview 2);
- Olivia constructed her own identity in powerless terms by emphasising her inexperience over other aspects of her experience/expertise;

- Olivia contrasted this construction of herself as inexperienced against the legal personnel who she constructed in far more powerful terms;
- Assuming counselling is ineffective for addressing structural issues devalues counselling as a mode of practice and resistance;
- Olivia's sense of fatalism may lead to inaction in her practice;
- The assumption that Olivia's practice didn't have an impact on the child's experience was not the only interpretation;
- And finally, Olivia recognised that her assumptions about exploring alternative practice possibilities being 'too time consuming' (Olivia, Interview 1) may act as impediments for creating practice possibilities for change.

Summary of Olivia's Reconstruction

Having deconstructed a number of assumptions in her account and evaluated their limiting effects on her practice, Olivia began to reconstruct the possibilities for more critical practice to challenge the legal system. Her reconstructed thinking and practices included some of the following changes:

- Olivia began to see her knowledge base and perspective as different and valuable, rather that oppositional and marginalised;
- This enabled her to see professional differences between herself and legal personnel in ways that valued rather than polarised the various roles;
- Olivia challenged her emphasis on inexperience in working with children to privilege a discourse that instead acknowledged her many years of experience as a sexual assault counsellor/advocate;
- Olivia rejected the assumption that counsellors/advocates are less important than legal personnel, and instead valued the professional status and contribution of counsellors/advocates;
- Olivia rejected the assumption that the legal personnel were too busy to be interrupted, and recognised the importance of regular contact in order to keep the victims/survivor informed of developments;
- Olivia developed a more valued and empowered subject position for herself and her role;
- She reconstructed specific practices by reinterpreting the success of the Office of Public Prosecutions (OPP) to a gain that was achieved through her own actions;
- Olivia discarded the assumption that to be effective, counsellors/advocates have to be confrontational with legal professionals to imagine more collaborative ways of working;
- Olivia recognised that by participation in dichotomous and adversarial aspects of CASA culture, she missed opportunities to engage more critically with some of the unintended consequences of this analysis;

- Olivia rejected the assumption that egalitarianism is associated with a reduction of power to reimagine using power in different ways in different contexts;
- She challenged her assumption that power is 'bad' to recognise that it can also be productive;
- She revised the assumptions that counsellors/advocates should conform to preserve dominant power relations, and developed some new creative ways to work towards change (further details presented below);
- Olivia transcended the initial dichotomy she had constructed between herself and the OPP by creating a new discourse which emphasised teamwork, collaboration and points of commonality rather than difference;
- This enabled her to overcome her construction of hierarchical power relations between counsellors/advocates and legal professionals;
- Olivia identified and rejected fatalistic thinking that may potentially prevent critical practice possibilities;
- She challenged her initial assumptions about enacting new practice possibilities as being too difficult or time consuming, to see these efforts as potentially time saving;
- Olivia rethought the assumption that counselling cannot address structural issues by factoring herself into her narrative in a more active role, which created possibilities to advocate with legal personnel;
- She rejected the assumptions about potential change practices being 'outrageous', to create concrete possibilities for action;
- Olivia reconstructed opportunities to exercise power by participating in discourses, which contribute to victims/survivors' testimonies of sexual assault being perceived as more credible;
- And finally, Olivia reconstructed possibilities to prepare the victim/survivor for the court process quite differently in ways that bolster their position.

Whilst there is no guarantee that changing Olivia's thinking and practices in these ways will alter the ultimate legal outcome of the cases, or the experience of the legal process for the child victim/survivor witnesses, her reconstructed account creates clear possibilities for envisioning change. Her reconstructed account creates uncertainty, whereas previously, the certainty was that there were no possibilities for agency or change. This reconstruction imagines it possible for counsellors/advocates to ensure that different perspectives, such as the one that Olivia was positing about how children give evidence are heard. If they are heard and even become part of the dominant legal narratives, then it may be possible for counsellors/advocates to change the way the legal system understands and responds to victims/survivors.

Christine

At the time of undertaking this research, I was a 33-year-old Australian woman. I had worked as a lecturer in social work for about 10 years. I had a Bachelor of Social Work degree with Honours. Prior to working in academia, I had practised in a number of regional CASAs, working predominantly with adult women, except during an 18-month period when I worked in a youth outreach service for young people (aged 12–25) who were victims/survivors of sexual assault and who were identified as particularly marginalised. I had also worked as an after-hours counsellor/advocate for seven years. I chose this incident for critical reflection because of the disturbing impact it had on me personally. I also wanted to learn more about my practice, particularly in relation to how I advocate and respond to conflict.

Summary of My Incident

I described an incident that occurred in the context of my after-hours crisis care practice, in which a 20-year-old woman (who I have referred to as Lee), had been forced into a car, driven to a secluded area, and then violently sexually assaulted by three male strangers in a cemetery. Due to the nature of the assault, a number of police units from different regions were involved. The major difficulties for me arose in relation to one of the detectives from the Melbourne rape squad. He was demanding that the victim/survivor go to the crime scene with him immediately to 'help them with their inquiries', but she had already talked to the Sexual Offences and Child Abuse Unit (SOCAU) police, had had a forensic examination, felt traumatised, exhausted and was desperate to go home. Given her reluctance to go to the crime scene, the detective tried to dominate and intimidate Lee into doing what he wanted. I kept advocating for her to be able to leave, and tried to reason with him to commence investigations without her. I believed his response towards both of us had been offensive, aggressive, inappropriate and in breach of the Victorian Police Code of Practice. Amongst other things, he accused Lee of lying, and later tried to force her to make a statement of no further action, when she still had not decided whether to formally report the assault to the police or not.

My interaction with the police was intensely conflictual and lasted for several hours. Ultimately, we were able to resist his bullying, and he ended up going to investigate the crime scene with his team of detectives, whilst Lee went straight home from the hospital. Despite this, I was left feeling disturbed by the process. I felt that I should have been able to contain his impact on the process more satisfactorily. I was particularly concerned about the impact of the detective's conduct on Lee's experience. I felt that during the crisis care unit process, the level of conflict may have contributed to her emotional trauma. I was also disappointed because I believed she probably made the decision to disengage entirely with the legal process based on her experience with the police during the crisis care unit.

Implicit Assumptions in My Account

A number of implicit assumptions were embedded in my account. Some of these are presented below:

- The detective had more power than I did;
- I was completely separate from the police and that my role and the goals of my work were entirely different from the police;
- The wellbeing of the victim/survivor was separate from the investigative and administrative responsibilities of the police;
- The police involvement was unhelpful and problematic;
- I needed to plan an escape for the victim/survivor, so that the police would not force her into actions she had not yet decided to take such as making a statement;
- Planning this escape and arranging transport for the victim/survivor were central to maintaining a sense of control over the process;
- I needed to maintain control over the process in order to be useful to Lee;
- There were two clear sides in this situation: myself and the victim/survivor versus the police;
- The police, and in particular the detective, were the enemy;
- The conflict that we engaged in was entirely the fault of the detective;
- Once I had explained the victim/survivor's experience to the detective, he should have respected her need to go home;
- The process that unfolded in the crisis care unit was disturbing;
- Advocacy was an oppositional process that involved two main protagonists (myself and the detective) and that stronger advocacy is better advocacy;
- The victim/survivor needed to be protected from the police;
- The level of conflict that occurred in the process, did not justify the end result;
- My practice in this situation was not good enough and I should have been able to exercise better control/reduce the detective's impact on the situation in order to protect Lee from further harm;
- The level of conflict between myself and the detective was damaging for Lee;
- Lee would disengage from the legal process following her experience with the detective during the crisis care unit;
- The conflict that occurred was negative, and was linked to practice undermined by modernist assumptions;
- And finally, that the only change that is valuable is structural change.

Summary of My Deconstruction

In critically reflecting on my account, I deconstructed a number of my initial assumptions and scrutinised their implications for my espoused feminist practice. Some of my initial learning is presented below:

- Had I interpreted the situation differently, there may have been other ways to approach the situation;
- My own feelings of exhaustion and sense that I didn't have enough information initially, potentially impacted on my interpretation of the events, and distorted certain aspects of my account (such as how I understood the behaviour of the detective);
- I had interpreted the identity of the police in negative terms and constructed these traits as fixed and unchanging;
- My construction of the detective and other police enabled me to interpret the situation in a way that blamed the police and abdicated my responsibility;
- A consequence of locating blame with the detective is that I have constructed him as being in control and powerful, and effectively positioned the service user and myself as the passive recipients of his actions;
- My first contact with the detective may have contributed to the way he approached the crisis care unit once he arrived;
- At times my responses were oppositional and inflammatory, rather than conciliatory in nature, which departed from my espoused practice aims;
- My interpretation of the detective and his behaviour provided justification for my adversarial approach to practice;
- I had participated in a dichotomous hierarchy of power relations between myself and the police, in which the police were positioned within the discourse as more powerful than myself;
- The assumption that I needed to advocate for Lee depicted her as vulnerable and constructed her as the weaker party in relation to the detective;
- Using a modernist framework for advocacy, that assumed that the detective and myself were the two main protagonists, contributed to oppositional and hierarchical power relations;
- My use of warlike language also contributed to oppositional and adversarial relations between myself and the police;
- And finally, this use of warlike language and imagery prevented me from feeling comfortable with my practice.

Summary of My Reconstruction:

Having deconstructed the implicit assumptions in my account and unmasked their unintended consequences for my practice, I was able to change my thinking and potentially adjust my future practice in a number of ways. Some of these changes are outlined below:

- Reconstruction of the detective's identity in less oppositional terms to acknowledge commonalities (such as both of us wanting to see the perpetrators of the violence brought to justice);
- Reconstruction of oppositional power relations between myself and the police, to recognise ways in which my practice could have been more collaborative and constructive;
- Rejection of the assumption that I was powerless;
- Rejection of the notion that the police were unequivocally problematic and acknowledgment that difference doesn't have to be problematic;
- I discarded the assumption that I needed to control the situation, or take responsibility for containing the impact of the detective's behaviour on the situation;
- I developed different criteria for assessing my practice that does not measure it against the assumption that only structural change is valuable;
- I rejected the assumption that modernist practice inevitably leads to conflict and that conflict is always bad;
- Reconstruction of my sense of feeling disturbed about the situation and my practice;
- Reconsideration of the assumption that the conflict that occurred was damaging to the victim/survivor, and an exploration of alternative interpretations;
- Rethinking the assumption that Lee would decide not to report the police because of the experience that she had endured during the crisis care unit, and rejection of this as a measure for my practice;
- Reconstruction of the language and imagery I used to frame the situation to develop less oppositional and adversarial ways of constructing the situation.

Ultimately, reconstructing my account assisted me to validate my practice on reflection. Reconstruction also assisted me to be clearer about options for more collaborative practice. The learning gained from this will assist me to resist feeling disempowered by adversarial power relations, particularly in acknowledging that I have a key part in maintaining or challenging them.

Conclusion

This chapter has grounded the critical reflection process in six concrete stories about practice that were offered by each of the counsellors/advocates that participated in the research. Each practice narrative represents different aspects and perspectives about the struggles practitioners have experienced with the legal system. The short accounts of their critical incidents, and a summary of their deconstructed and reconstructed thinking and practices, have been presented here in order to scaffold and contextualise the following chapters. Whilst each story contributes a unique dimension to the research, and practitioners had their own individual critical reflection journey, there were a number of common themes to emerge from their accounts. A critically reflective macro analysis of these common themes provides the basis of the next two chapters.

Chapter 7
Identifying and Challenging Barriers to Change

Introduction

This chapter is the first of two chapters to present the findings of the research and discuss the ways in which critical reflection on practice developed possibilities for change. Participants' narratives are presented here thematically to capture the key issues in the collective deconstruction and reconstruction of their accounts. While each participant's story discussed a unique case, a number of macro themes ran through participants' accounts. The macro themes that will be explored in this chapter relate to:

- objectivity and reflexivity;
- the impact of a structural analysis in reinforcing a sense of powerlessness in practitioners; practitioners' sense of fatalism and agency;
- the construction of victims/survivors as powerless; and
- the ways in which participants' construct their counsellor/advocate role.

Discussion of these themes convincingly demonstrates the possibilities for change that the participants generated from critically reflecting on their practice.[1]

Objectivity and Reflexivity

One of the first themes to emerge concerns the ways in which practitioners, who originally believed that their representation of their situation was a factual and objective account, moved to a reconstructed understanding of their experience as socially constructed. This demonstrates a process in which they gained awareness of the part that they had played in actively constructing their stories.

---

[1] Despite my own practice being included in the participants' accounts, which are presented here as part of the macro themes, except where I am specifically referring to my own practice, I have used the language of participant's/their learning/their practice/ their accounts for the purposes of grammatical coherence. Hence, in the writing up of the macro themes chapter and the discussion of these in the following discussion chapter, I have needed to privilege the position of myself as a researcher over my identity as research participant in order to avoid grammatical confusion.

Participants' accounts revealed that dichotomous thinking played an important role in perpetuating the view that their stories were objective. Initially, participants were only able to consider either their version or its direct opposite. Hence, the final issue to be discussed as part of this theme is about the reconstruction of more complex understandings of participants' accounts, including transcending the dichotomy they had created between their initial ostensibly objective version and its opposite, and a more reflexive awareness of how they influenced the construction of their accounts. Discussion of this first theme is organised around the following issues:

- participants' perceptions that they were presenting an objective view of their stories;
- deconstructing participants' initial sense of objectivity;
- understanding how dichotomous thinking preserved assumptions about objectivity; deconstructing participants' dichotomous constructions of their situations;
- participants' objective version versus its polarised opposite; and
- reconstructing objectivity: becoming reflexive.

Participants' Perception of an Objective Story

Initially, all participants believed their accounts of their stories to be an objective description of facts, which were assumed to exist independently and externally to them. For each person, this initial lack of reflexivity was expressed in different ways. For example, for Rose, it was explicitly about not being able to conceptualise the situation in any other terms. As she stated, 'I can't see any other interpretations' (Rose, Interview 1). Rose believed that her impact on the situation she presented was confined to her support role: 'The only way I feel I might have influenced the situation is in my advice and assistance to the women' (Rose, Interview 1). Similarly, Bella explained her difficulty in acknowledging her own impact on the construction of her story: 'I would find it really difficult I think to see it [the situation] in any other terms than what I've perceived it to be' (Bella, Interview 2). Andrea, too, had difficulty seeing other potential interpretations of her story. When asked about other perspectives, she replied: 'I've got no idea. I can't think' (Andrea, Interview 1).

Participants' perception that their view of their situation was the *only* view hid an implicit assumption that their construction of the story was an objective, factual representation of the situation. The deconstruction of participants' perception of objectivity is discussed next.

Deconstruction of Participants' Initial Sense of Objectivity

In the process of deconstructing the assumptions about the ostensibly objectively described situations, participants began to realise that their accounts of the situations were actually not objective representations, but socially constructed versions, interpreted through their own social, cultural and political lens, and mediated by their own biography and social positioning. Barbara, for example, realised that her reasons for not challenging the police and the consequences she anticipated were not an objective reality, but a series of internally constructed interpretations that ultimately led to her inaction. In reflecting on this she acknowledged it was 'my interpretation of the situation, more so than actually what was happening … So maybe if I had of [sic] interpreted things differently, internally, it probably would have made me react differently' (Barbara, Interview 2). Barbara also acknowledged that her emotional state at the time of the incident led her to emphasise the confusion and uncertainty she described in her original account: 'I suppose because I did see myself on the back foot, I've emphasised the confusion that I felt' (Barbara, Interview 1).

Similarly, Rose recognised that her impact on the situation was much broader than the description of her support role that she initially described and also included the limitations she imposed on this role. As she states: 'We are so bound by the boundaries we set up. How much should I extend my role? How far does it actually go? And I think that actually often gives us an excuse to stop us because [we believe] it's too hard, or it will become too encompassing' (Rose, Interview 2). When she began to locate herself in the construction of the story, Rose discussed the need to 'think about the common themes in this particular incident and how they stood out, and thinking about those critically, and my role in it; how you can actually influence change' (Rose, Interview 2).

For me, reflexivity was about acknowledging how my feelings of exhaustion and the sense that I didn't have enough information initially, potentially affected my interpretation of the events. As I explained, 'I received a call … [at] about 2:15 in the morning, and I was told by the worker from the crisis line … that I needed to immediately go to the hospital … to meet with a young woman who had been assaulted by a stranger. So she [the worker] didn't give me much more information than that … I guess I was feeling some of her [the victim/survivor's] exhaustion and frustration in some ways because I had already attended another crisis care unit earlier that night, had worked all day, and I was tired. Because of the nature of the assault, this was a particularly long crisis care unit and we all thought that it was nearly over, and then the next minute, it's hours of battling really just to be able to leave' (Christine, Reflection 1).

Deconstructing this commentary suggested that my emotional response to the incident may have coloured how I interpreted things at the time, such as the behaviour of the detective. As I stated: 'I was obviously feeling quite irritated and frustrated at this point' (Christine, Reflection 1). In addition, I recognised that my repeated reference to the crisis care unit as 'this tiny, little space' and being 'stuck … trapped in this small room' juxtaposed against the image of 'the team of about five detectives' (Christine, Reflection, 1) connotes a sense of invasion or of being overwhelmed, which again may have distorted aspects of my account of the situation.

Deconstructing participants' initial notions of objectivity also uncovered the ways in which their thinking had produced a dichotomous view of the situations they presented. This is further elaborated in the following section.

Dichotomous Thinking and the Preservation of Assumptions about Objectivity

Confirming participants' initial sense that there was only one correct way to view their scenario entailed an implicit understanding of the situation in dichotomous terms. When trying to imagine other possible understandings of the situation, participants were often only able to see their own view of the situation, or the direct opposite of their version. For example, when Bella presented her story about the inadequacies of the child protection system and the police response in obtaining a clear disclosure of sexual assault from the child, the only other possible interpretation Bella could imagine was the antithesis of her perspective. When asked if she could imagine other interpretations, she stated: 'Yes, that the child wasn't being sexually abused ... that all those agencies involved; those institutions may have had a point. And that the mother was interpreting herself things that weren't really what she was saying they were' (Bella, Interview 1).

Similarly, when Andrea talked about her unequivocal belief in the story of the victim/survivor who was being threatened with false reporting, the only other interpretation of the situation that she could imagine was that the woman was lying. Understandably, this was a perspective that Andrea was not prepared to accept, yet this construction of the situation supported the assumption that her interpretation of the situation was the only legitimate one: 'I will always go to the side of believing. And really in my role, I don't go into a crisis care unit thinking, oh this is another woman telling lies' (Andrea, Interview 1).

Deconstructing Participants' Objective Version versus Its Polarised Opposite

Deconstructing the dichotomous thinking of participants' initial versions of their stories highlighted how such constructions may have rendered other possible conceptualisations, and therefore other possible practice options, invisible. Bella, for example, discussed how initially assuming that there were only two opposing ways to see the situation meant that other, less extreme conceptualisations, which might have offered different practice possibilities, were potentially hidden from her consideration. This shows that she began to view her experience as socially constructed. Bella was also able to connect her personal experience with the broader social and political contexts, yet, overwhelmed by dominant discourses at the time, found it difficult to envisage alternatives. Her logocentric thinking could not transcend her dichotomous construction: 'So how else could you conceptualise it?' (Bella, Interview 2).

Alternatively, Rose, shifting from her initial construction, referred to the processes embedded in her original thinking as casting the means of change 'out of reach' (Rose, Interview 2). In starting to deconstruct her initial view, she said, 'life is full of contradictions and just because it's the law or you are dealing with a lawyer or a doctor or whoever they are, it doesn't mean that everything is watertight, and I guess there are always gaps in everything' (Rose, Interview 1). Understanding that her experience was socially constructed, Rose began to ask what alternative practice possibilities may be inherent in the contradictions and other multiple interpretations of her story.

Reconstructing Objectivity: Becoming Reflexive

The reconstruction of participants' stories created opportunities to change and rewrite aspects of their narratives through consideration of alternative interpretations and privileging different aspects of the discourse. There were numerous examples of practitioners developing reflexivity, and these will be largely discussed as part of other themes, of which they are also representative. Here I focus on two, small examples that demonstrate this point.

Olivia first described a situation in which she was powerless to do anything to support the child victim/survivor she was working with for legal reasons. Reconstruction of her initial, external account to include herself in the narrative in a more active role, however, created possibilities of advocating with legal personnel at the time of the trial, and implied that these interactions could be an important site for producing more immediate and 'tangible' change. As she said: 'the opportunities were there to talk to the OPP [Office of Public Prosecutions] and before that, meet the prosecutor … At the trial, she met the barrister who was going to be prosecuting on the morning of the trial … but whether perhaps I missed opportunities to advocate more for those sort of things?' (Olivia, Interview 2). Here, Olivia indicates how reconstructing her thinking highlighted different practice possibilities that were hidden to her at the time because of the way she had constructed her original account. These reconstructed practices will now be available to her for consideration the next time she is working in a similar situation.

For Bella, developing an understanding of her influence on the construction of the story can be seen in relation to how she initially constructed the usefulness of the counselling she provided to the mother with whom she was working. Initially, she berated herself for believing that the counselling was not very useful or valuable. 'I remember having this sinking feeling every time I was going to see her because I just thought, this poor person. And why is she coming, you know? … I just didn't think that it [the counselling] contributed towards her child being able to be safe, and I thought that was the main problem in the situation. And I didn't think that I was really helping' (Bella, Interview 2). Reconstructing this perception, Bella recognised that it was possible that the 'sinking feeling' was related more to her notion of what was useful or valuable about her practice, rather than how the mother experienced it. Reflecting on this, she said: 'Yes, that's an interesting point' (Bella, Interview 2). She also began to see and evaluate her practice in a more situated way and became more aware of the impact of context in which she was making the assessment: 'And I already do start to think more contextually. I already have started to think that way' (Bella, Interview 2).

Given an initial lack of reflexivity, which originally led Bella to construct her situation in dichotomous terms, she indicated that reconstructing aspects of her practice to transcend binary conceptualisations of the issues was an empowering experience: 'And it's sort of a bit liberating in a way … I like to be reflective, and that's what I think you need to be … And it's liberating because the world is so complex, and I don't see things [in] black and white' (Bella, Interview 2). We return to Bella's reconstruction of the value of her practice later in the chapter.

A Structural Analysis: Contributing to Practitioner Powerlessness

This second macro theme highlights the ways in which practitioners used a structural analysis to inform their thinking about their practice, and some of the unintended and unfortunate implications of this. Some of the consequences included practitioners feeling overwhelmed by the structural flaws of the legal system and hence powerless. Discussion of this theme is organised under the following headings:

- assuming the problem is structural and confined to the legal system;
- deconstructing the implications of using a structural analysis in isolation; and
- the assumption that practitioners are disempowered by the structural context.

Assuming the Problem Is Structural and Confined to the Legal System

As demonstrated in the presentation of the first macro theme above, practitioners' initial accounts adhered to a belief that their story was an independent, objective construction of the situation. This was often implicitly expressed through their presentation of the problems and issues in purely external and structural terms. All participants at some stage during the interviews talked about the problems they experienced with the legal system in a way that characterised them as structural and external. Bella, for example discussed how the difficulties in the situation she described resided in the operation of abstract, systemic, inaccessible structures such as child protection and the legal system. She described how 'current protocols for investigations of sexual crimes do not incorporate or cater for the nuances and complexity of a young child as a witness. Therefore usually there is no criminal investigation', and asserted her belief that 'often children's welfare is not properly assessed' (Bella, Interview 1). Affirming her structural analysis, she stated, 'the problems as I saw them were really quite massive in terms of the operations I've just explained; those institutions' (Bella, Interview 1). She referred to these systems as 'nameless, faceless entities' (Bella, Interview 2). In addition, she locates the problem in macro structures more broadly: 'I don't … think that our society is really set up to address that issue [of child sexual assault]' (Bella, Interview 2).

Olivia similarly saw the source of the problems in structural and external terms, referring to the obvious 'mismatch' between the court's requirements of evidence and 'how that doesn't fit with how a child might provide that' (Olivia, Interview, 1), as well as identifying external factors that disadvantage the child. As she explains: 'I could see how her evidence could be undermined in that process, and that she wasn't able to give consistent details' (Olivia, Interview 1). In addition, in relation to the child's ability to provide well-articulated, consistent testimony, Olivia indicated: 'there were other factors that were constraining her' (Olivia, Interview, 1).

Central to Olivia's initial construction of the story was an implicit assumption that the current legal system is inappropriate for child witnesses. As she explains: 'she was seven at the time, so her ability to recall and her ability to provide evidence in a kind of narrative framework that a court might require, like giving detailed statements from the start of an event to the end of an event, as opposed to how she might have done it, which would be rambling … highlighted to me, developmentally, that children aren't suited to being credible witnesses' (Olivia, Interview 1). Reinforcing her structural analysis that the current legal system is problematic and disadvantages the child witness, she stated: 'I think it is about balancing the principles that the legal system operates within, with the needs of like [sic] a child witness in this case. And I think that the balance there erred on the side of the legal system' (Olivia, Interview 1).

Deconstructing the Implications of Using a Structural Analysis in Isolation

Drawing on a structural analysis exclusively to understand the problems with the legal response, and practitioners' positioning and agency in relation to them, appeared to have a number of unintended and disempowering consequences for practitioners and victims/survivors. Bella, for example, recognised that the way she had framed her initial account of the situation took on a bureaucratic discourse which may have implicitly limited her perception of her own role: 'Me having the bureaucratic discourse? Like saying the only solution would be the systems acknowledged what had happened? Yes. That's probably right … Well, then we would both be stuck' (Bella, Interview 2). She also recognised that the universal statements that cast the problems as solely structural and external could also have fuelled her feelings of 'frustration' and 'powerless[ness]' and perception of the situation as 'really hard' and 'difficult' (Bella, Interview 1).

As well as leaving Bella feeling 'stuck', locating the causes and solutions of the mother's difficulties only within the formal structures of the legal system may have resulted in Bella feeling righteous about what changes should occur, but powerless to implement them. She articulated these limitations in the following statement:

> What it [a structural analysis of the legal system] does is really objectify the problem to the point where you can't have a solution ... So, it is limiting. I can see how it is limiting, because it objectifies the problem in a way that puts you as a counsellor or social worker in a binary position where you're either helpful or not helpful because there's the system, and there's you – powerless and on the outside of it. There needs to be changes in order for positive outcomes to happen, and if you feel you can't contribute to that process, as a counsellor, it can make you feel like you're not really being helpful, and there's nothing really you can do. So it puts you in this powerless position. (Bella, Interview 2)

Similarly, Olivia talked about a sense of powerlessness that emerged for her because she used a macro, structural analysis in isolation, casting the problem as external and alienating her from the means of change. As she explained: 'when I was re-reading over my account [I realised that] I was ... operating from that assumption that the legal system has all the power and we don't have any, and it's kind of almost [as if] you can't effect any different way of it being responded to' (Olivia, Interview 2).

The Assumption that Practitioners Are Disempowered by the Structural Context

For most participants, the sense of powerlessness they experienced was reinforced by their reliance on a structural analysis of the legal system. For nearly all the participants, at least initially, a sense of disempowerment was palpable. Bella articulates this clearly:

> those various systems seemed to operate in a certain way and to me it seemed like there was no way that we could really intervene and change any of that. That said, for example, if the police decided that they're not going to investigate, no investigation would take place. If the department decided, well there was no child protection issue, then there is no child protection issue! (Bella, Interview 1)

This illustrates Bella's strong sense that she was alienated from the means of change. Confirming this, she stated: 'So, looking at possibilities, and I think, is there much I can do? I don't think so' (Bella, Interview 1).

Rose similarly constructed the problems in her scenario as external from herself, entirely legal, and related to the inadequacies of structural institutions, which led her to feel powerless: 'We were so locked by the legal process, we couldn't really proceed' (Rose, Interview, 1).

Another aspect of disempowerment that emerged from participants' stories of how they positioned themselves in relation to the legal system, was a sense of being excluded. This was particularly evident in Olivia's account when she discussed the contentious nature of how credibility is decided. Implicit in her commentary was an assumption that victims/survivors and their supporters/advocates are excluded from the legal process, or positioned outside and separate from those who decide whom or what is credible:

> the legal system predetermines credibility … There's lots of suggestive impressions and assumptions that influence how credibility is determined … Myths are the social constructions that … act as a filter for it all; how much they like the look of somebody, or whether they fit into their expectations of how the victim [should look]. (Olivia, Interview 2)

She extended this analysis to legal processes and personnel more generally: '[Do I feel] excluded [from how the legal system makes decisions]? Yes, to a large extent' (Olivia, Interview 2).

Fatalism and Agency

Intimately related to the previous macro theme concerning participants' overwhelming sense of powerlessness, is the impact of participants' fatalistic beliefs and their capacity to envisage agency. Discussion of this theme is organised under the following headings:

- fatalism;
- deconstructing fatalistic beliefs;
- and reconstructing practitioner hope, agency and power.

Fatalism

Prior to reconstructing this aspect of their accounts, a strong sense of fatalism was evident in practitioners' narratives. This was manifested in the assumption that it was pointless to challenge or do anything different in the face of the insurmountable structural obstacles that exist for victims/survivors accessing the legal system and the practitioners who aim to support them. Olivia, for example, referred to the injustices for victims/survivors in the context of the legal system as 'not really fair', but 'just the way it is'. She lamented: 'it's a system which has developed over a long period of time, and that's just the way perhaps that it goes' (Olivia, Interview 1).

Rose also contended that the possibilities for change were remote and unlikely, that the situation was hopeless and could even deteriorate if counsellors/advocates tried to mount challenges:

> We should somehow have an opportunity to go out there and fight. You know, let the community know that this is occurring … but we know that that's not going to achieve her much either because again, you go back to that legal perspective, and she might be even worse off in the end. (Rose, Interview 1)

This sense of hopelessness was also evident in Bella's account at times. In relation to her counselling, she said: 'Sometimes I would just be explaining to her why it was impossible to do anything about the situation, and that was really hard' (Bella, Interview 1). For Andrea, this sense that challenge is pointless was encapsulated in her decision not to question the Forensic Medical Officer (FMO): 'I don't think it would have been appropriate. I didn't feel the need to do it. I don't think that I would be listened to. I don't think that anything I had to say would be taken on board' (Andrea, Interview 1).

Deconstructing Fatalistic Beliefs

Deconstructing these fatalistic beliefs highlighted the implications of them for practitioners in potentially overlooking opportunities to create change in their daily practice. Deconstruction also elucidated other possible interpretations potentially more hopeful and enabling. In Andrea's case, for example, her decision to remain silent and not challenge the FMO guaranteed she would not be heard. In this situation, her perspective remained a subjugated discourse. Even though the result may have been the same if she had spoken up, voicing some of her concerns at the time of her attendance at the crisis care unit at least ensures that the issues are named and creates the possibility that they may be heard. Fatalistic beliefs that construct the situation as hopeless may have led to Andrea missing opportunities to challenge what was happening because the way that she had viewed the situation had rendered them invisible to her, or pointless.

Bella's account is also implicated in increasing her sense of hopelessness about enacting any change in the legal system because of the binary, structural conceptions of power she used to understand the situation that fatalistically positioned her as powerless. Deconstructing her assumptions clarified this for her. When asked about the implications, she stated: 'I'd sort of resigned myself to the fact at that point in time that … there was nothing I could do to advocate on her behalf' (Bella, Interview 2). Similarly, Olivia acknowledged that positioning herself on the powerless side of the dichotomy in relation to the legal system exacerbated her own experience of powerlessness and reduced the possibilities she felt she had available to her for challenging the legal system. As she explains: 'The implications are [that I would] probably be a little bit fatalistic about the short term, and maybe not being particularly hopeful about the potential for [the future]' (Olivia, Interview 2). This sense of fatalism, compounded other assumptions that were initially informing her thinking, such as: counselling is ineffective at addressing structural issues; that only structural change is valuable; and that she and the family were powerless in relation to the legal system that has structural power. This combination of assumptions exacerbated her sense of powerlessness and led to paralysis and inaction in her practice. As she explains: 'Probably that by interpreting that certain things may have been *un fait accompli;* that I felt I couldn't necessarily do anything to change them' (Olivia, Interview 1).

Reconstructing Practitioner Hope, Agency and Power

Reconstructing modernist notions of power to explore the ways in which it can be exercised, freed up practitioners to reimagine themselves as more empowered agents in relation to the legal system and other professionals involved in the legal process. This also enabled them to conceptualise other change practices that can parallel broader commitments to structural change. The new practices are potentially just as effective as structural change in terms of creating more hopeful and positive experiences for victims/survivors, but are more tangible and accessible in the immediate future. Such repositioning and reconstructed change practices, combined with a deconstruction of the implications of fatalistic thinking, permitted practitioners to reject the fatalism that initially characterised their thinking and practice.

Rose, for example, rejected her fatalistic thinking and reconstructed alternative practice opportunities to engage in education and change that were previously rendered hidden or pointless. Initially, protesting against the supervision arrangements for a child she thought was being re-abused at access, Rose was dismissed, and accepted that there was nothing more that she could do. However, reconstruction of her narrative created the possibility for her to envisage other options: 'Well, I think that going beyond – you know, the woman who I said wasn't willing to change her opinion – going beyond her, and above her and seek an opportunity to inform them' (Rose, Interview 2). Deconstructing the boundaries Rose herself had imposed on her role, she was able to challenge the assumptions that led her to believe that it was pointless to contact the person who had been designated to supervise access. As she explained, 'I might have got in contact with that woman and said where I was from. I might have found out that her motivations to do the supervision were completely different [from my assumptions about this]' (Rose, Interview 2).

Rose further reconstructed alternative understandings that enabled her to exercise different courses of action: 'I think also, making decisions, and weighing up, and making choices [such as] I'm not going in there at this point, because this will be a long road for what I want to achieve. But maybe I can pursue other avenues, where I can … It's about weighing it up, rather than seeing all this [the options], in black and white' (Rose, Interview 2). In addition, Rose reconstructed discourses about her personal capacity to affect change: 'I think that … first and foremost, there is a way I can change my thinking about how and when I take things further, and also influence my organization to look at things and make decisions before we go out there … By merely persisting, and bringing the dimension of organization, and the organization taking actions to extend that further, I think that could make a difference' (Rose, Interview 2).

Olivia similarly acknowledged that her fatalistic thinking initially limited her approach and that reconstructing this created other practice possibilities: 'I suppose I've probably been operating from that fatalistic notion of it's not going to work, so why bother trying? Because I guess the other way to think about it would be well, if you can't come here, then we'll come to you; perhaps having a little bit more of a collaborative approach to it' (Olivia, Interview 2). Transcending the dichotomy between counsellors/advocates and other professionals, and thereby upending dominant power relations, Olivia thereby proposed a proactive and collaborative approach as a way of overcoming her initial sense of powerlessness.

The Construction of Service Users as Powerless

Discussion of this fourth macro theme begins by concentrating on the ways participants unwittingly constructed their service users as powerless. Secondly, it shows how participants were able to recognise the unintended, disempowering consequences of those assumptions through deconstruction. The final issue explored in this section outlines participants' reconstruction of the identities of service users in more empowered and enabled terms. Commentary about this theme is organised in the following way:

- the assumption that service users are powerless;
- deconstruction of the view that service users are powerless; and
- reconstruction of service users in more empowered terms.

The Assumption That Service Users Are Powerless

The sense of powerlessness and exclusion that practitioners felt about their own roles also informed the ways in which they understood their positioning of the service users. Initially, without exception, service users were unequivocally constructed as powerless. Most of the participants assumed that the service users' identity was static and permanent, and saw them as being powerless vis-à-vis the legal system and its personnel; another unintended feature of using a structural analysis. A number of participants assumed, for example, that those who do not hold structural or professional positions of power, have no power at all. Bella described children, for example, as having 'very little voice' (Bella, Interview 1). Rose's view was the same: 'this 2-year-old, she doesn't have a voice' and 'Young children like that have got no power; like what they feel or express or say, has got no value' (Rose, Interview 1). In relation to the mother that she was working with, Rose said: 'The mother doesn't have a voice' and 'she is totally paralysed. She just can't do anything' (Rose, Interview 1).

Olivia similarly constructed the victim/survivor as relatively powerless and marginalised, polarising her experience as a child witness against that of an adult. In reflecting on her work with the child, Olivia stated:

> I don't think she could understand what people's roles were, and why a lawyer would get to ask her questions and I wouldn't get to ask him questions. Like, it just didn't make sense to her and it just didn't seem fair ... And how do you

> explain that in a way that's preparing her, but also being able to acknowledge the inadequacies? Whereas maybe with an adult, you can do things differently, because you might be able to explain it in a way that it's not so personalised. Like I think it was very personal for her … like she couldn't understand it was about the system. She thought it [the failure of the legal system] was about her. (Olivia, Interview 1)

Andrea similarly assumed that the victim/survivor she was working with was vulnerable, fearful and powerless: 'This woman, the victim, was absolutely powerless' (Andrea, Interview 1). Her narrative emphasised the precarious nature of her situation: 'Absolutely, she was in fear. I could see that she was scared. She was told that it was a warning [by the perpetrator]; that there would be more' (Andrea, Interview 1). She further elaborated:

> This is a woman who had just been traumatised; that had just, in her experience, come within an inch of her life and had just been threatened that if she did talk she would be killed … So then to learn that this was possibly going down the line of a false report, her big concern, apart from being charged, was are they still looking for the perpetrator? She was in fear of her life, and she was of the belief that they had halted the investigation; nothing was going to happen, and she was going to be the one in trouble … It was overwhelming for her, and very unnecessary … It was far too overwhelming for her … I could see she was intimidated. (Andrea, Interview 1)

In addition, perhaps inadvertently reaffirming the service user's powerlessness, Andrea also seemed to accept the woman's view that she should take responsibility for not upsetting the family:

> She was in fear of his [her husband's] reaction, and didn't want her kids to hear of the rape, and because of her extensive medical history there were many, many times where she felt that responsibility of upsetting her family and this was just going to be like the straw that broke the camel's back; that it was just going to be too hard for her children to deal with. (Andrea, Interview 1)

Deconstruction of the View That Service Users Are Powerless

In deconstructing the participants' presentations of their service users as powerless, it was useful to explore some of the implications of these constructions. One of the main consequences was participants' fear of contributing further to a sense of disempowerment for both themselves and their service users. For Andrea, the prioritising of the medical issues in her account confirms the mystique of medical knowledge and its associated powers. This, combined with the repeated references about the possibility of the aneurysms 'bursting' and the potential for the 'sudden death' of the victim/survivor, reinforced Andrea's construction of the woman as extremely vulnerable (Andrea, Interview 1). This construction of the woman as a powerless victim, on her own, being re-victimised again by the legal system, is juxtaposed against Andrea's construction of the police who are presented as strong, powerful and numerous. These factors collectively act to reinforce the powerlessness of the victim/survivor. In addition, there are gaps, missing discourses and exceptions to the dominant discourse surrounding the woman as a powerless victim in a hopeless situation, which suggest that there are alternative ways to understand and locate her in her story.

Similarly, in deconstructing my own account, I became aware that I had assumed that I needed to advocate for the victim/survivor I was working with, which hid an implicit assumption that she is vulnerable and in need of protection. This also unwittingly positioned the service user as the weaker party in relation to the detective: 'I became really protective in that way. I felt I needed to situate myself as a buffer between her and the police to try and protect her' (Christine, Reflection 1).

This theme matched Bella's experience. She realised that constructing the mother and child as powerless may have reinforced their sense of powerlessness and denied the acts of resistance exercised by the mother, which were positioned as a marginal discourse in her initial presentation of the story. Bella recognised that the dichotomous positioning of herself and her client as powerless to challenge the police and child protection institutions may well have distanced Bella from her capacity to reconstruct the scenario in more empowering or enabling terms, and to be an effective agent of change. Her initial construction was 'sort of not helpful though. As you were talking, I was thinking, well I didn't want to construct her in a way that indicated that she was powerless, or even myself, but unintentionally though, that's probably one of the consequences of thinking that way' (Bella, Interview 2).

Reconstruction of Service Users in More Empowered Terms

Recognising that identity can evolve and change from one context to another promoted opportunities to emphasise different aspects of the service users' identities, thus reconstructing them in more empowered and enabled terms. Privileging different aspects of the participants' descriptions enabled a more holistic narrative about the service users' to emerge that enabled participants to discursively relocate their service users within the discourses. As Barbara explains: 'you're not static, so you can just change' (Barbara, Interview 2). Marginalised in Andrea's initial account, for example, were narratives that emphasised the ways the victim/survivor had chosen how she engaged in the crisis care process; thus demonstrating some influence she had over the process. For example, in relation to the forensic examination, Andrea stated: 'she was clear about the process and the reasons, what swabs were taken, and she was consenting to part of the examination, and was very clear about what she didn't want to happen' (Andrea, Interview 1). In addition, Andrea describes the woman's response as being, 'very much about self-preservation' (Andrea, Interview 1), providing a different insight into the degree of agency she was exercising, rather than just being a recipient of all her experiences, which is how Andrea had originally constructed her.

Similarly, Bella was able to reconstruct the subjectivity of the mother she was working with from a woman who was powerless to protect her child in the face of an unresponsive legal system, to a more empowered and enabled identity, by emphasising the mother's active engagement with the legal system and the positive outcomes that she managed to achieve:

> She was able to get some successful outcomes in terms of calling into question the conduct of certain stakeholders in the whole scenario … The capacity she had to advocate on her own behalf … I think she thought of the idea of what she was going to do; how she was going to redress something that she saw was wrong in terms of the process, and she did it and it actually had a good outcome. (Bella, Interview 1)

She added: 'I thought that somehow, someone has to hear what she is saying, because what she is saying is very important and so there must be a way. You can't just be silenced like that … I did see that she had power' (Bella, Interview 2).

Rose, too, was able to reconstruct the identity of the mother with whom she was working in more empowering terms by accentuating different aspects of her story that emphasised the mother's courage, strength and resilience in responding to the legal system. As she states: the 'mother … did everything she needed to do. She actually took the child to the doctor. She took her to a psychologist … She managed to get access stopped; did all of these things' (Rose, Interview 1). Further uncovering these narratives during the second interview, Rose stated: 'Well, it worked out that after I saw you, I think I saw her again, and she told me she was able to change access, get the supervisor of access changed because she hired a private detective, and I thought, "great!"' (Rose, Interview 2). Reconstructing her original assessment of this woman as 'totally paralysed', Rose arrived at quite a different conclusion: 'I actually think she's a lot more powerful than I gave her credit for because she's got that oomph in her and that determination' (Rose, Interview 2). Rose acknowledged that this more empowered construction of the mother also helped her to feel more hopeful and personally empowered in working with her: 'I think I look at the whole situation and the players within it quite a bit differently now … I've thought a lot about this, other ways in which we can move with things a lot more towards positive outcomes and not feel so stuck' (Rose, Interview 2).

Rose also reconstructed the identity of the child by uncovering hidden aspects of the discourse about her identity. Moving from the construction of 'this two-year-old, she doesn't have a voice … young children like that have got no power', Rose reconstructed the child in much more empowered terms including: 'the child fought not to see her father … and … she was able to report back to her Mum, and she was able to identify and speak up about what she wasn't happy about … Yeah, and I think that as she grew older, he wouldn't be able to get away with what he is doing' (Rose, Interview 2).

These reconstructions suggest that by privileging different aspects of the discourse, practitioners were able to reimagine the identities of people who were originally constructed as most powerless, and least able to facilitate change in the context of the legal system as well as to be active agents who have exercised power to force significant changes. Extending this theme, I had also constructed the victim/survivor in my account as someone in need of protection from the detective. I unintentionally portrayed her in relatively weak terms, assuming that the conflict that occurred during the crisis care unit between the detective and myself was damaging for her. In reconstructing this, however, I was able to highlight different aspects of my narrative that suggest other, more empowering interpretations may be just as legitimate. Given that:

> I had been resistant to him … Lee actually started to take on some of that as well. He [the detective] was saying, "We have to ask the hard questions" and "It's your role to help the police with their enquiries". And she was saying things like, "I thought the police were supposed to be here to help me", which I thought was quite a legitimate … way of looking at the situation. (Christine, Reflection 1)

Similarly, re-evaluating the impact of the crisis care unit process on the service user, I stated:

> I talk about the impact for Lee as a negative thing potentially, but in emphasising different aspects of my account and my experience of working with Lee, there were actually times when she started to model some of that resistance for herself, so in some ways, it gave her a process [by] which she too could also resist, which could also be interpreted as quite empowering. (Christine, Reflection 2)

Prior to reconstructing these narratives, a strong sense of powerlessness permeated the participants' commentary in relation to both service users and practitioners. This may be another unintended consequence of using a structural analysis in isolation to theorise the inadequacies of the legal system.

Participants' Construction of Their Counsellor/Advocate Role

This macro theme focuses on how participants saw their own roles as counsellors/ advocates, particularly in relation to others. The discussion begins with the acknowledgement that participants' initial accounts were imbued with a sense of powerlessness that linked their identities to the experiences of the victims/ survivors. Perpetuating this construction, participants clearly differentiated themselves (often in oppositional terms) from other professionals whom they used as scapegoats to personally represent the structural faults and failures of the legal system. Deconstruction of these assumptions revealed that constructing oppositional power relations with other professionals had a number of unintended disempowering consequences for both participants and their service users. These are presented, as are participants' deconstruction processes, in ways that demonstrate how participants reclaimed responsibility for the construction of their identities in relation to others. Finally, participants begin to reconstruct more practical possibilities for collaboration by transcending the binary oppositional constructions between themselves and other professionals that characterised their initial accounts. Discussion of this theme is organised in the following way:

- counsellors/advocates alignment with victims/survivors;
- locating the problem with legal personnel;
- counsellors/advocates as separate and different from other professionals;
- deconstructing dichotomous power relations between counsellors/advocates and other professionals;
- participants' acknowledgement of self in their construction of others; and
- reconstruction: transcending the dichotomy between counsellors/advocates and other professionals involved in the legal process.

Counsellors/Advocates Alignment with Victims/Survivors

Evident in practitioners' original accounts was the notion that as practitioners, they often aligned themselves with their service users. Building on some of the unintended consequences of relying on a structural analysis in isolation, participants often indicated that they viewed their situation through a number of dichotomous constructions. They were hence faced with aligning themselves either with other professionals involved in the legal process, who can be seen as oppressing service users, or with victims/survivors, whom they are committed to supporting. Participants' stories indicate that counsellors/advocates chose to side with the victim/survivor, which through this dichotomous lens, is assumed to be in opposition to the legal and medical professionals. As Olivia stated: 'it's been kind of like, you're on the victim's side, and then there's the legal system on the other side – the side that has the power' (Olivia, Interview 2).

This was evident in my own account as, 'I felt I needed to situate myself as a buffer between her [the victim/survivor] and the police, to try and protect her' (Christine, Reflection 1). Here, there is an implicit assumption about two dichotomous and mutually exclusive sides, in which I was united with the victim/survivor, in opposition to the police.

This was also a feature of Andrea's story. Deconstruction of her interview indicated that she had aligned herself with the victim/survivor on the powerless side of the dichotomy in relation to the police and the FMO: 'I guess, as the process in the crisis care unit unfolded, I became a bit more protective of the victim/survivor' (Andrea, Interview 1).

The assumption that victims/survivors need the protection of practitioners aligns counsellors/advocates with victims/survivors and ties the two identity group together. As Olivia explains: 'probably a part of the work entails some identification with victims' (Olivia, Interview 2). While this construction unites practitioners with victims/survivors, it does so in opposition against seemingly powerful structural forces, which practitioners perceive as inaccessible and impervious to change, reinforcing the powerlessness of both themselves and victims/survivors. This can lead to a position that Rose articulated clearly: 'I feel quite hopeless, like them' (Rose, Interview 1). Olivia described how this identification with victims and experiences of helplessness and victimisation 'kind of influences how you operate ... You're kind of identifying with that victim position, and not necessarily at a really conscious level' (Olivia, Interview 2). She talked about this dichotomous discourse putting practitioners in 'a marginalised position' (Olivia, Interview 2). Highlighting practitioners' participation in this unhelpful discourse, she defines it as 'self-imposed marginalisation, in some respects' (Olivia, Interview 2).

Locating the Problem with Legal Personnel

This construction also exacerbated a sense that people working in the legal system, including magistrates, police, lawyers, barristers and forensic medical doctors are menacing. This was often expressed by participants through locating blame with other professionals for the difficulties that arose in the situations they described, almost as if they personified the failures of the legal system. For example, Olivia's account indicated that the lawyers, the magistrate and the police had the power to intervene to determine the outcome that unfolded for the child witness she was working with, but they did not have the expertise or insight needed to exercise their discretion fairly. As she explained: 'They [the legal personnel] were taking it very much on face value, what she [the child witness] said, and whether or not that fitted with what they would expect from a credible witness' (Olivia, Interview 2).

The tendency to cast the problem as external and locate responsibility with other legal professionals was also a feature of a number of other participants' stories. Andrea's account, for example, indicated a belief that the problems resided exclusively with the FMO and the police, and therefore were external to her. The following quote captures this sentiment, particularly in relation to the police:

> My hope is eventually that police officers will get a conscience and gain some kind of empathy ... They see their role as just finding the truth, whatever they interpret the truth to be. It's about punching down and getting to the facts, but they've forgotten about, you know, people, and the impacts; not only the trauma of a sexual assault, but also them and their influence on people. (Andrea, Interview 1)

Similarly, in the situation that I described, I initially found it much easier to place blame on the detective, rather than examine how my own behaviour and practice may have contributed to the conflict: 'I just felt like this person [the detective] had come in, and completely shattered any sense of safety and calm for her that I had worked hard to create' (Christine, Reflection, 1). I emphasised how the detective had:

> attacked both Lee and myself for several hours. He was saying things like, you know, "why are you still here? Your job is done. Your job is welfare. Her welfare has been taken care of. I'm the legal person. I need to ask the difficult questions". And just kept pushing her. (Christine, Reflection 1)

I also discussed the police involvement in a way that assumed it was unhelpful and problematic. I stated, for example, that:

> I was concerned about police pressure for her to be making statements and going to the crime scene that night ... I was very concerned about his insensitivity, his bullying behaviour ... denying her control over her choices: that he was just reproducing all the characteristics of the perpetrator that she had had to endure earlier in the evening. (Christine, Reflection 1)

So initially, from my perspective, the problems during the crisis care unit lay solely with the main detective, and everything that he represented structurally: white, professional, middle-class, male power and privilege.

Bella similarly assumed that the problem lay with the people working in the legal system. She talks about the obstacles that these people represent for children trying to obtain safety, protection and justice from the legal system:

> Any family reports that are ordered by the family court are done by an independent person who may see the family and parents once or twice. In this case, [the psychologist] saw the child for probably half an hour and made some fairly sweeping generalisations about the personality of the mother, the personality of the father, and the nature of the disclosure of the child. In fact, took the mindset that the child was totally making this up and that that was a common thing. (Bella, Interview 1)

Rose, in making what Bella refers to as 'some fairly sweeping generalisations' similarly affirms this view of the legal system and its personnel as problematic, ironically by remarking that 'the legal system especially, they don't think reflectively. There's only one way of doing things and that's it' (Rose, Interview 1).

Counsellors/advocates as Separate and Different from Other Professionals

Since the other professionals involved in the participants' scenarios were assumed to be responsible for the structural flaws in the legal system, participants needed to differentiate themselves from these problematic others. All of the participants defined their roles and approaches to their practice as completely separate from those of other professionals. They often chose also to define themselves by virtue of their difference to the other professionals involved. Barbara, for example, highlighted the differences she saw between her approach to practice and that of the police: 'my empowerment versus their control of the situation at all times really. So [our approaches] are totally at different ends of the spectrum. I see them as real black and white, and yet we're trying to work together' (Barbara, Interview 1). She implicitly assumes that in order to work effectively or collaboratively with the police, they must have the same philosophy as CASA workers. Difference in this sense is also assumed to be problematic: 'So that's how I felt at the time and it makes it really, really difficult' (Barbara, Interview 1)

Rose made a similar assumption about the legal system and lawyers being completely separate and different from her. In her account, there are two clearly delineated sides: Rose versus the legal people: 'lawyers and so on … They are not interested in the person the way we are' (Rose, Interview 1). Bella also saw her role and knowledge as completely separate from the lawyers. When I suggested that she had valuable skills and expertise to offer the mother she was working with, she responded: 'Except legal advice' (Bella, Interview 1). Andrea, too, assumed that the role and approach of the police was completely different and separate from hers: 'It was believing: me in my role believing this woman, and it really felt like the police were not believing, and [they were] really supported by the FMO' (Andrea, Interview 1).

This assumption was also clearly embedded in my account in which I had constructed the police, particularly the main detective, as the enemy: 'He was standing up and often towering over us. It seemed like he was yelling at us; being really loud; being really dominant, and essentially trying his hardest to intimidate us' (Christine, Reflection 1). I further elaborated: 'So I will call this rape squad detective John … because he reminded me of John Wayne, of some kind of cowboy who was going to come in and take over, and show us all how it should be done' (Christine, Reflection 1). For me, there were two clearly demarcated dichotomous and oppositional sides: myself and the victim/survivor, versus the police. This was epitomised in the following quote: 'Surely if he was the best detective and evidence collector in the world, who had to "ask all the difficult questions" as he kept saying, then he would understand the importance of supporting the victim/survivor; having her on his side' (Christine, Reflection 1).

Deconstructing Dichotomous Power Relations between Counsellors/Advocates and Other Professionals

Deconstructing the embedded assumptions in the divisions that participants had constructed between themselves and other professionals, Olivia stated:

> And I think it is something quite unique to CASAs … I was probably more operating in that framework then, than I would now, but you're always sort of

> at loggerheads with systems. We're trying to change them so you've always got that sense that you sort of have to be enemies with them or something. And that you'd be betraying [other workers and victims/survivors] if you weren't operating in that very confrontational way. (Olivia, Interview 2)

My deconstructed commentary supports this. I realised that my use of warlike language such as 'battling', 'threat' and 'enemy' contributed to perhaps unnecessary, oppositional and adversarial relations between me and the police: 'I guess referring to him as a cowboy, and seeing him as a bully, and adversarial and aggressive and all those kinds of things are not particularly respectful of him and his role, and not probably consistent with the anti-oppressive practice ethics that I aspire to' (Christine, Reflection 1).

Expanding on the reflection on the impact of CASA culture, Olivia explained one of the ways that dichotomous power relations are maintained within this environment: 'there's this culture of kind of talking about these terrible things that they [the police] have done, and "Oh the police did this"' (Olivia, Interview 2). She described how this unites workers in opposition to the police, but 'in a marginalised position' (Olivia, Interview 2). Earlier references to her perception of being excluded by the legal system were also deconstructed at this point. As she explains: 'People in my position might sometimes exclude themselves, more than they really are excluded by others' (Olivia, Interview 2).

The ways in which practitioners conceptualised and practised the advocacy component of their roles was also indicative of perpetuating this dichotomy. For almost all of the participants, advocacy was assumed to involve two mutually exclusive and opposed protagonists, and aims to represent the interests of the least powerful person or group to the more powerful side. With Bella, for example, it was:

> offering to speak with whoever it was, whether it be the lawyer, the department or the police, to clarify their reasons for not proceeding, or clarify what their understanding was of the situation, and to introduce other perspectives for them, [which] might give more information that hasn't been previously considered. (Bella, Interview 1)

Later, Bella stated: 'I had very clear ideas about what advocacy should entail. To me it does mean acting on or behalf of someone else or an issue' (Bella, Interview 2).

Similarly, Rose talked about her dilemmas in advocating with the police in a way that assumed dichotomous power relations:

> I think that the way we work with the police is hard … The philosophy that we have and the philosophy that they have, and the level of knowledge that we sit with, as opposed to what the police sit with creates problems … It's a constant

> battle because they are supposed to be the protectors, but they don't have the knowledge that we have … This is what it is: the opposites. (Rose, Interview, 1)

Compounding this, Olivia said that operating collaboratively or co-operatively with police and legal personnel may be seen by other counsellors/advocates as: 'almost as though you're doing the wrong thing … You're kind of selling out or something' (Olivia, Interview 2).

Deconstructing these assumptions highlights how all of the participants had created artificial dichotomies between professionals involved in the legal process, and themselves, and/or the service users with whom they were working. For some participants, as previously noted, this was about casting blame on others. Yet deconstruction suggests that one of the consequences of this is that each time practitioners construct themselves as separate from other professionals and apportion blame to them, they contribute to their own sense of powerlessness. My location of blame with the detective, for example, constructed him as in control and powerful, and myself and the service user as the passive recipients of his actions. As I stated: 'even though I tried to advocate strongly and protect her, I couldn't do much to prevent what transpired, so I probably felt a bit powerless at times' (Christine, Reflection 1). Reflecting on this later, I recognised that, 'seeing it as socially constructed, I can acknowledge that this is an interpretation which constructs the detective as having too much influence over the situation and exerting too much power' (Christine, Reflection 2). What I had effectively done was to dichotomise a hierarchy of power relations between myself and the police, in which the police were more powerful than I: 'I have really positioned myself on Lee's side against the police, so I have constructed those two mutually exclusive positions … which actually contributed to our sense of powerlessness, rather than us feeling more enabled or empowered' (Christine, Reflection 2). Further outlining the unintended consequences of my original account, I realised that 'one of the implications in deconstructing that further is that the police are constructed as the enemy, so again just perpetuating that notion there are sides and that they are mutually exclusive and oppositional' (Christine, Reflection 2).

Similarly, Andrea constructed the police and the FMO in a way that emphasised their difference from her approach to working with the victim/survivor. Deconstruction highlighted that this, combined with the discourses that positioned the police in the dominant role, may have served to alienate Andrea from any means of change and ultimately enhanced her feelings of powerlessness. In addition, her assumption that the approach of the police was mutually exclusive to that of her own, combined with her belief that the victim/survivor needed protection, may have contributed to Andrea's adversarial response towards the police.

Rose made similar acknowledgements. She became aware that in positioning the police, the Department of Human Services, the lawyers, the woman supervising access, as oppositional others, she had also created two mutually exclusive and opposed positions:

> I've made judgements … we judge them by their profession, and what we know of their profession or what we had previous experiences of. We don't actually give them a chance. They were very much preconceived ideas and you know: oh well, that's how all police are, and we'll be reacting. Oh that's their understanding, and the lawyer? Yes, I know all about him. But I've never actually met that lawyer. I don't know anything about him. (Rose, Interview 2)

Rose also made a related assumption when she asserted that conducting specialised children's assessments involves investigative processes and are therefore diametrically opposed to CASA's philosophical position of believing.

Olivia similarly created two mutually exclusive positions when she emphasised the differences between herself and the legal personnel by making a distinction between those who judge and investigate, and those who believe: 'my role with her [the victim/survivor] was to operate from a position of believing and accepting what she was saying … whereas a judge is in the position of needing to make a judgement about whether or not something happened' (Olivia, Interview 2). More significantly, Olivia constructed herself in powerless terms by emphasising her inexperience over other aspects of her experience: 'I hadn't been working with children for very long' (Olivia, Interview 1). Juxtaposing this construction of herself as inexperienced against the more powerful legal personnel arguably contributed to her sense of powerlessness and perpetuated an unhelpful hierarchy of power relations between the herself and the legal system. In describing the barrister in her practice scenario, she stated: 'the … barrister was this woman [who] kind of swept up in her gown and was very busy and officious and you felt that you should be a bit grateful if she spoke to you for five minutes' (Olivia, Interview 1). Deconstructing this, when asked who benefited from this discourse, she replied, 'Well, they do' (Olivia, Interview 1).

For Barbara, deconstruction helped her to recognise that in defining herself, her philosophies and that of CASA by their difference from the police, she had participated in oppositional power relations that operated contrary to her interests. Initially, she said, 'I felt like we were running on two different trains really; different philosophies of how to approach this. And I was like, well I don't know about your background and training, but it feels like it's totally different to mine' (Barbara, Interview 1). However, she realised that her account of the incident positions the police as the dominant construction in her narrative, and that defining herself by her difference, she potentially exacerbated her sense of powerlessness and her ultimate perception that she could not challenge the police. When asked what the implications might be for her, of participating in this binary oppositional relationship, she acknowledged that this construction left her, '[n]owhere. Powerless' (Barbara, Interview 2). She also recognised that constructing herself as 'powerless', 'flustered', 'confused', 'vulnerable', and 'on the back foot' (Barbara, Interview 1), may have contributed to the sense of chaos, lack of confidence, uncertainty and disempowerment she experienced during her interaction with the police.

Participants' Acknowledgement of Self in their Construction of Others

The construction of the police, lawyers, FMOs as oppositional 'others', combined with apportioning blame solely on them while exonerating ourselves, reinforced a sense of hopelessness and powerlessness for practitioners. Hence, the participants began to factor themselves into accounts by taking responsibility for how they constructed the people working in the legal system, the assumptions they made about them and their behaviour towards them. Rose recognised, for example, that in viewing the police, the DHS, lawyers and the woman supervising access as oppositional others, she had created two mutually exclusive and opposed positions: her and them. As she explained on reflection about the arrangements for supervision of access: 'I've made judgements like, she [the woman nominated to supervise access] has got a business, and he [the father suspected of sexually abusing his child] goes there on a regular basis, and she's got a vested interest in making everything easy for him' (Rose, Interview 2).

Similarly, in deconstructing my assumptions about the detective, I acknowledged that 'my initial account constructs him as quite an evil character, when there could have been a number of different interpretations [of] his behaviour' (Christine, Reflection 2). I had interpreted the detective as unreasonable, bullying, dominating and aggressive and had constructed these traits as fixed, unchanging and unequivocal. Through deconstructing my assumptions, I became aware that the conflict that had developed between the detective and myself during the crisis care unit was not only his responsibility, but that my behaviour also contributed. As I explained: 'initially I didn't look at how I had contributed to the adversarial situation that had emerged. When he would say, "I'm sorry, what's your name again?" and I would respond "My name is still Christine!" I'm aware that in hindsight that might not have been the most helpful response to defuse the situation' (Christine, Reflection 1).

Through deconstructing my account, I was also able to acknowledge that by seeing the detective and other police in oppositional terms, I had interpreted the situation in a way that solely blamed the police and abdicated my own responsibility: 'The assumptions implied in my account, I guess, are that the adversarial nature of the contact was his fault because he came in and caused the disturbance' (Christine, Reflection, 1). I later recognised that my first contact with the detective over the telephone may have actually contributed to the way he approached the unit when he arrived:

> when I spoke to him on the phone initially, I was of the opinion that she [Lee] was going home, that I'd arranged transport, that the unit was virtually complete. And that he was going to have to hurry and if her was going to catch her, but that she wasn't going to go to the crime scene; that she wasn't going to make a statement that night. (Christine, Reflection 1)

Deconstruction of the implicit assumptions in my account also highlighted how my interpretation of the detective and his behaviour at the time justified my adversarial practice. The notion that he 'attacked both myself and Lee for several hours' for example, created a discourse that legitimised my defensiveness in response (Christine, Reflection 1). Similarly, the use of forceful language about him 'burst[ing] in', being 'aggressive', 'intimidating', 'dominating', 'bullying', and a 'cowboy' allowed me to avoid questioning myself about why I had stated that 'I just kept interrupting him' (Christine, Reflection 1). Initially, it also enabled me to dismiss any credibility to his suggestion that I had been 'so obstructive' (Christine, Reflection 1) as this was located as a marginal discourse in my initial account of the incident.

Painting myself into the picture in this way suggests that had I interpreted the situation differently, there might have been other ways to approach it as I acknowledged during my preliminary reflections:

> So … maybe there was a possibility that there was a different way to address those issues with him. Perhaps in a more collaborative way, so that he might not have come in with such a determined agenda … In hindsight there [were] ways that I could have … talked to him before he came in, to position him as an ally; to almost put us in his power to try and get him to support her needs, so that we weren't working oppositionally, but working towards the same goals. (Christine Interview 1)

This attempt to transcend some of the perceived artificial dichotomies that participants initially constructed between themselves and other professionals involved in the legal process is significant. As counsellors/advocates simultaneously emphasised their difference from others, they also constructed other professionals as having more power, thus contributing to their own sense of powerlessness.

Reconstruction: Transcending the Dichotomy between Counsellors/Advocates and Other Professionals Involved in the Legal Process

Prior to being able to reconstruct their identities as practitioners in more empowered terms, participants needed to reconstruct the dichotomous hierarchy they had constructed between themselves and other professionals. In so doing, they began to acknowledge some of the points of commonality between the roles. In reconstructing my own account, for example, I reinterpreted the detective's behaviour as possibly wanting to assist the victim/survivor (albeit in a different way from me) by securing the best possible legal process for her in terms of collecting evidence. As I stated, 'this could be reinterpreted [to mean that] that they [the detectives] are also trying to assist her and help her and facilitate her access to recourses in their own way' (Christine, Reflection, 2). This new discourse describes us as coming from slightly different angles yet working towards the same aim of supporting the victim/survivor. Reconstructing this dichotomy and relocating the detective as an ally rather than an enemy creates possibilities for more collaborative practice that were excluded by my original account. As I explained: 'constructing it in a way which perhaps situates us as a team where we can work together in that we offer different things, but might be working towards similar goals … emphasising our shared purposes, can find some mutuality' (Christine, Reflection 1). I further elaborated:

> For example, talking to the detective about Lee's circumstances and wishes, and asking him what we are going to do about this situation, given that she's so tired would bring him in as part of the solution, rather that constructing him as the problem, and in oppositional terms. Then we're actually all working on the same side. (Christine, Reflection, 2)

Here, instead of trying to contain or block the impact of the police, my role becomes more about:

> engaging the police to act in her interests, to relate to them in ways in which it is expected that they will be there to support her … and … creating a less dichotomous stance in relation to the police, and a less dichotomous understanding of their role, and seeing us more in terms of being a team. (Christine, Reflection, 2)

This becomes an important point later, too, when I talk about my initial need to try to control the situation. Perhaps most significantly, this reconstruction overcomes the oppositional power relations between the police and myself. As I explained: 'looking at the commonalities that we have, actually transcends that dichotomy which therefore removes me out of a position of feeling a bit powerless in relation to the police' (Christine, Reflection 2).

Barbara also adopted the team analogy in reconstructing the dichotomy she had created between CASA and the police. She proposed a new discourse that locates difference within the construction of a 'multi-disciplinary team' (Barbara, Interview 2). She rejected her initial contention that the police would need to have the same philosophy as counsellors/advocates in order to work collaboratively, to instead acknowledge some points of convergence between herself and the police: 'even just the basic: that we're there for the victim/survivor' (Barbara, Interview 2).

Olivia also reconstructed the dichotomy between herself and the OPP (Office of Public Prosecutions) by creating a new discourse that emphasised teamwork, collaboration and points of commonality rather than difference: 'maybe it's been about saying, you know, "we're all the professionals involved in supporting this person and getting the best outcome for the victim"' (Olivia, Interview 2). In addition, Olivia reconstructed the internal hierarchy she had created between her knowledge and that of the legal personnel by presenting her knowledge as different and valuable, rather than oppositional and marginalised: 'those who are involved in the legal process … they have all of this knowledge, and you have none of that process, but perhaps not recognising the knowledge that you might have about the impact of trauma, and her development and crisis' (Olivia, Interview 2). She further reconstructed her understanding as valuable without devaluing it by dichotomously comparing it to legal knowledge. She explained that it is 'a discourse that's probably informed by a different theoretical position … I knew her [the client]. I had an ongoing relationship with her and so [I] had maybe a bit more of the contextualising information, and how she presented' (Olivia, Interview 2). This effectively reconstructs her professional differences in ways that value rather than marginalise her role. Olivia also highlighted the implications of this reconstruction for her practice: 'maybe approaching it from the assumption that you're all operating as equals, like all professionals who are there for this person, rather than feeling like you're asking for information and you should be quite apologetic' (Olivia, Interview 2).

Conclusion

Overall, this chapter has outlined some of the most significant macro themes to emerge from participants' critical reflection on their practice. Some of the key issues presented here included participants' initial construction of their narrative as objective and factual, and their development of a more reflexive stance. This involved participants being able to acknowledge the ways that their own values, assumptions and interpretations had influenced their construction of their story, themselves, others in their scenarios, their sense of power and powerlessness and ultimately their capacity to act in ways that might make a difference for victims/survivors' experiences of the legal process. This was fleshed out further through deconstructing the implications of practitioners' use of a structural analysis in isolation to inform their work, which had the effect of reinforcing their sense of powerlessness, fatalism and lack of agency. The deconstruction of practitioners' narratives demonstrated how their participation in various unhelpful discourses had led them to perceive the victims/survivors they were working with as powerless; and ultimately on the disempowered ways that had constructed their own counsellor/advocate roles. Reconstruction of these themes to create alternative understandings demonstrates the ways that practitioners were able to use the critical reflection process to generate new knowledge, and new ways to think about their practice from the reflexive analysis of their critical incident. The next chapter will continue to fill out the details of the transformative learning processes that participants engaged in as part of the research in order to develop new possibilities to work towards change.

Chapter 8
Finding Alternative Paths: Resisting Further Obstacles to Change

Introduction

This chapter continues to report on the key findings of the research and discusses the ways in which critical reflection on practice developed possibilities for change. Again the macro themes to emerge from participants' narration of their practice are presented in the collective deconstruction and reconstruction of their accounts. The macro themes that will be discussed in this chapter relate to:

- professionalism, hierarchy and oppositional power relations;
- power;
- the questioning of macro social change as the ultimate change strategy and a revaluing of the contribution that counselling might make to change practices;
- identifying and challenging practitioners' participation in unhelpful dominant discourses; and
- uncovering and changing other unhelpful discourses.

The chapter concludes with a summary of these themes, which showcase the possibilities for change that the participants generated from critically reflecting on their practice.

Professionalism, Hierarchy and Oppositional Power Relations

This macro theme, concerning participants' hierarchical constructions of professionalism, adds another dimension to the previously deconstructed oppositional power relations that were discussed in Chapter 7. This extra dimension, which involved a sense of inferiority on the part of participants in relation to other professionals, also resulted in the broader devaluing of social work. These assumptions, along with the perceptions that other professionals were more powerful, were deconstructed with reconstruction providing opportunities for practitioners to value their differences from other professionals. This reconstruction of participants' own professional identity enabled them to feel more empowered in their roles and able to conceptualise new thought and practice. This collection of sub-themes is organised under the following headings:

- the assumption that other professionals have more power;
- the devaluing of social work;
- deconstruction of the assumption that other professionals are more powerful; and
- reconstruction of participants' own professional identities to transcend oppositional power relations.

The Assumption that Other Professionals Have More Power

As explored in the preceding chapter, most participants were ultimately successful in reconstructing the dichotomy between themselves and other legal professionals by focusing on points of commonality rather than difference. However, another related theme in participants' original narratives was an overwhelming sense that other professionals have more power than they do. Olivia, for example, assumed that legal personnel are much more powerful and important than her. As she described it: 'those who operate in the legal system, like the police and lawyers, have a particular sense of authority. You know, socially sanctioned authority, as well as their own kind of internal self-importance, which is a bit intimidating' (Olivia, Interview 1). In invoking hierarchical notions of professionalism, she explicitly contended: 'they're more important' (Olivia, Interview 2). Emphasising this importance, she assumed that they were too busy to bother and indicated the implications for her practice: 'I don't know that I had a lot of contact with the police or the OPP because you know, they are hard to get on to and they're busy' (Olivia, Interview 1).

Similarly, Andrea assumed the FMO had more power to influence the situation than she did. As she explained:

> On leaving the crisis care unit, my belief [was] that [the victim/survivor] was going to see her GP [General Practitioner]; that the police were actually going to take her to see her GP because the phone call had been made in the crisis care unit. But what actually happened … what I learned happened, was that they took her back to the station. She made a report and the next day, they put it to her that the forensic evidence didn't match up with her story and that she could possibly be charged with false reporting, which was devastating to her. (Andrea, Interview 1)

In Andrea's account, the FMO is the most powerful and influential person in the situation:

> Initially it felt like the police, the SOCAU [Sexual Offences and Child Abuse Unit] officers were supportive of this woman and her story [but] the turning point was the forensic evidence at the scene and what the forensic medical officer had to say in relation to the wounds that she had received … the forensic medical officer … her assuming that the wound was self-inflicted and you know,

the raised eyebrow about not having the vaginal swab. Certainly her opinion influenced the way other people were looking at it, especially the police. (Andrea, Interview 1)

Rose, too, positioned other professionals in more powerful positions. In relation to providing specialised assessments for child sexual abuse, she stated: 'the courts are asking why don't we [CASA] provide a specialised assessment, but we are not in a position to make that assessment … It's DHS that can provide that specialised assessment. They're the ones who can order it' (Rose, Interview 1).

The Devaluing of Social Work

The assumption that other professionals have more power also seemed to lead to a devaluing of social work for some participants. For Bella, the consequences of creating an artificial and dichotomous construction between herself and the legal practitioners caused her to reflect on her social work role more broadly. It was the privileging of the role of legal practitioners over her own role that exacerbated the devaluation and invalidation of her own skills and knowledge base:

> I did my undergraduate degree in the early eighties and that was very much what was taught. And even subjects about social work research, it was all … almost all the literature started off with this preamble about how, you know, social work doesn't sit anywhere, and it doesn't have legitimacy because it's not scientific. It's not sort of, [legitimate] you know, almost an apology, and we need to really validate what we do and what we say. And that was really indoctrinated. (Bella, Interview 2)

Barbara and Olivia also referred to a broader devaluing of social work, particularly when contrasted with other professionals. Barbara said, for example, in reflecting on the perception of social work in her school:

> even looking at the status of social work on a wider scale … when you say we have expertise and stuff, I think you hear so much in the social work field that, you know, teachers will say, "I do social work, or someone else can do social work" … Or "oh, you're a social worker?" [disapprovingly] "Oh you're not a psychologist" [disappointedly] "You're just a social worker". So I don't know whether that's subconsciously ingrained a little bit because I went away and thought about that a bit too. (Barbara, Interview 2)

Olivia talks about the devaluing of social work more as an unintended outcome of the CASA culture:

> I think to some extent the way CASAs are set up has contributed to that a little bit. Like, I think that model of [feminist social work practice] … there's lots of valid

> things about it: like not being the expert, and kind of having this power-sharing idea about things, means that you're not working in an environment where you are acculturated to think, I am an expert, and I have special knowledge and skills and that people should listen to me. It [the feminist social work culture] sort of like almost undermines that … I can see how those cultures can really influence … because CASAs have had sort of this anti-professional culture in lots of ways, whilst it's been predominantly social work. (Olivia, Interview 2)

Elaborating on this as a psychologist, she said:

> I have to also say … the part of me that thinks about that [professionalism] differently, or that expresses that differently, is becoming more acculturated with psychology, which I think is probably better at [professionalising as a discipline] … almost similar to the legal system in portraying that prestige, and "we know stuff" and "we're the experts", and "we do research". (Olivia, Interview 2)

Deconstruction of the Assumption that Other Professionals Are More Powerful

In deconstructing their accounts, participants began to realise that defining themselves by their difference from other professionals involved in their situations, while simultaneously constructing these professionals as more powerful, was another way in which they contributed to their own sense of powerlessness. It was necessary to deconstruct the assumption that other professionals were more powerful in order to more comprehensively transcend oppositional power relations and uncover practitioner agency to create change. Finding points of commonality helped with this.

Bella initially viewed the training, skills, resources and knowledge of lawyers as more valuable and relevant than her own. Her sense of powerlessness was explicitly expressed when she stated that in her role, she had no capacity to respond in any way that would have made a difference to the process or the outcome: 'I wasn't going to necessarily have any impact as a counsellor for that person' (Bella, Interview 1). Reinforcing this, she stated: 'since that time I have seen other workers who have probably done more than myself … but I can't see that that's necessarily made a difference' (Bella, Interview 1). This explains why she described herself as 'feeling very powerless to be able to do anything' (Bella, Interview 1) and said that 'it is easy to feel powerless and overwhelmed by systemic ignorance. It is difficult to assist women to have a voice and to be hopeful about positive outcomes' (Bella, cited in statement made in preparation for interview 1). Yet, beginning to deconstruct this, Bella recognised that constructing her role in such insignificant and marginalised terms may have further alienated her from the means of change and exacerbated her sense of powerlessness: 'So it made me feel helpless … because [I was] thinking the only solution is that somebody … or some organisation that had authority recognised this, then they could help that person, or if I could get them to help her' (Bella, Interview 1).

For other participants, this comparison between those who have power and counsellors/advocates was made in relation to the ratio of those present. Barbara assumed that greater police presence equates with greater police power: 'I thought, you [the police] have actually got each other to bounce off a bit, and actually create that sense of, you know, power' [whereas] 'here's little old me, and my head and my brain, and there's those two' (Bella, Interview 2). The disempowered language that Barbara used ('little old me') is also significant.

Andrea also assumed that more police equals more police power: 'The police certainly had power and there [was] strength in numbers too' (Andrea, Interview 1). I made a comparable assumption that greater police presence connoted greater police power. As I stated:

> John arrived with a team of about five detectives from the Criminal Investigation Unit. They were all in suits. They were all carrying clipboards and brief cases. They conveyed a sense that they felt they were very important. And they come in in numbers, so at this stage we've got seven police at the hospital in this tiny, little space, and myself and Lee. (Christine, Reflection 1)

For Olivia, some feelings of powerlessness were attributed to her assumptions about her level of inexperience. A number of times in her initial commentary she had made reference to her perception that she 'hadn't been working with children for very long' (Olivia, Interview 1).

There were related assumptions in other participants' accounts, such as when Barbara indicated a belief that knowledge, information and preparation brings power, control and comfort (and that she herself did not have the knowledge, information, preparation or power that she assumed she needed):

> I like to be in a space where I am grounded and ready to go. And for me to be sort of flying by my pants … I even instantly felt like, are they just going to think I'm an absolute idiot? They might think I'm a bit unorganised and everything like that, which I'm totally not, but I just felt that maybe they were thinking that too. (Barbara, Interview 1)

The 'unknown' (Barbara, Interview 1) – in terms of what may eventuate if Barbara had challenged the police – was initially regarded as problematic and something to fear, and to be eliminated with knowledge and preparation, particularly as she attributed both knowledge and power to the police.

Rose, too, recognised that this dichotomous view of the key legal players involved in her critical incident, combined with her oppositional understanding of advocacy, had produced a hierarchy of power relations, where she, the mother and the child she was working with, were on the powerless side of the dichotomy. She acknowledged that such a construction limited her possible practice responses. As she states of the possibility of challenging legal processes or decisions: 'Yeah, you make it very inaccessible. You make it unapproachable' (Rose, Interview, 2).

Reconstruction of Participants' Own Professional Identities: Transcending Oppositional Power Relations

Transcending these oppositional power relations with other legal professionals was integral to counsellors/advocates feeling more empowered and able to conceptualise new thinking and approaches to practice. For example, central to my reconstruction of oppositional power relations with the detective was the exploration of other possible interpretations of his identity. I acknowledged earlier that my initial narrative provided an unbalanced account of him as evil, and deconstructing this highlighted the negative implications for my practice. Reconstructing this to unearth other potential interpretations, I stated:

> There could have been a number of interpretations around his behaviour other than him just being evil: he could have been having a bad day; his boss might have been putting pressure on him. There could have been any number of other interpretations … I can see that he might have really wanted perhaps to go and find these people and bring them to justice, to get statements from them, to make them accountable for their actions. I'm also aware that he was down from Melbourne so possibly hanging around for a few hours while she [the victim/survivor] had a sleep wasn't going to be the most tenable or convenient option for him. Perhaps he was busy and had other things to do as well and was just trying to do his best on this as well as attend to other responsibilities or whatever. So I can kind of see where he was coming from in terms of trying to manage his time, and co-ordinate the investigation, and not have evidence potentially go missing from the crime scene if the investigation down at the crime scene was delayed for a few hours. (Christine, Reflection 2)

Ultimately, I had learned that 'reconstructing my account … has further strengthened my capacity to see other interpretations of the situation and the people within it as legitimate' (Christine, Reflection 2). Drawing on these alternative interpretations also assisted me to reconstruct the notion that the police were unequivocally problematic while acknowledging that difference need not be problematic: 'So in using postmodernism to reconstruct this polarised construction of what the police offer and what I offer, difference doesn't have to be a threat to equity. We can offer different things and that doesn't have to be problematic. In fact it could be beneficial' (Christine, Reflection 2).

For Olivia, reconstructing oppositional power relations was also about transcending binary oppositional constructions and framing the situation differently: '[we're] not on a different side to the OPP because they want a conviction, so if there's any way for you … to increase the possibility of them getting it, then you'd think that you'd be actually really useful and helpful for them' (Olivia, Interview 2).

In addition to reconstructing oppositional power relations through repositioning themselves in relation to the legal system and its personnel, participants also needed to rethink the value of their roles and the contributions that they had made as counsellors/advocates. This involved uncovering more positive narratives about their practices. Olivia, for example, had felt as though she 'lacks entitlement' (Olivia, Interview 2) to approach legal personnel when advocating for her service users. Rethinking this assumption involved Olivia revaluing her own sense of worth and professional status. She subsequently talked about 'positioning [herself] as having knowledge and expertise in terms of trauma and developmental stages for children, and research on children as witnesses' (Olivia, Interview 2). She also reconstructed her initial assumption that the legal personnel were too busy to be interrupted by a mere counsellor/ advocate. Creating a counter-discourse that constructed her as more valued and empowered, Olivia stated: 'Well they probably are busy, but like, so am I' (Olivia, Interview 1). In addition, she rejected her initial emphasis on inexperience working with children and found an alternative discourse that acknowledged her many years of experience of working as a sexual assault counsellor. As she said: 'I've been working in CASAs for about 14 years' (Olivia, Interview 2).

Rose similarly reconstructed her dichotomous view of the key legal players, acknowledging the limitations for her practice and rejecting the construction that made her feel powerless to act: 'There's a lot that can be done there that can change that attitude. I would have a lot of opportunity there to influence that change, if I really wanted to' (Rose, Interview 2). In addition, she reconstructed the value of her practice by transcending the dichotomy she had created between her philosophical position of unquestioning belief and the DHS commitment to investigation. Rose transformed her thinking to recognise that practitioners can maintain their stance of belief while also being able to conduct specialised children's assessments. She explained:

> there's a shift in that too ... Some of the CASAs came across this forensic program that is happening in America at the moment in this area where there is the possibility to actually do this investigative type of work, but without contradicting that philosophical position of belief. (Rose, Interview 2)

Rose recognised that CASA practitioners are well placed to do such assessments; in the alternative discourse that she was building, these assessments present an opportunity to exercise power and influence by disseminating knowledge about how children's disclosures of sexual assault are understood, 'and use the knowledge that we have, that we've gained in the meantime to our advantage in doing this process, and value that knowledge in a way that doesn't compromise it' (Rose, Interview, 2).

Given that power and powerlessness were central themes in all of the participants' accounts, it is worthwhile deconstructing how participants were actually conceptualising power in their original commentaries. This will be discussed next.

Power

Power is one of the most central themes to this research, considering that power is implicated in all of the other themes. Participants' initial accounts indicated they conceptualised power as a tangible commodity or possession that people either have or do not have. They saw the legal system and its personnel as having power, and the participants and victims/survivors being powerless. Power was accorded by professional status or position, and was seen as inhering in formal structures and institutions. Deconstructing these modernist notions of power, participants were able to recognise the disempowering consequences of seeing power in finite, concrete and dichotomous terms. Participants' accounts discuss the ways in which they reconceptualised power in order to experience empowerment. Reconstructing power as relative, contextual, changing and exercised through the influencing of discourse, was a way to rethink the limiting way they had initially viewed power. This macro theme is discussed in relation to the following issues:

- power as a commodity or possession;
- power residing in formal structures;
- power and powerlessness being linked to social status and position;
- deconstruction of modernist notions of power; and
- reconstruction of modernist notions of power by exercising power through discourse.

Power as a Commodity or Possession

For some participants, including Rose, power was seen as a commodity that can be possessed, given or taken. She initially described the woman she was working with as having 'no power to change anything' (Rose, Interview 1). She also said: 'the thing is, in a very hopeless situation that can look very bleak, how do you sort of … [effect change] when you feel all of your power has been taken away from you?' (Rose, Interview 1). Like others, Olivia also conceptualised power as a commodity when she indicated a belief that aiming to equalise power relations between practitioners and service users leads to a reduction in power for practitioners. As she explained:

> that model of … not being the expert, and … having this power sharing idea … means that you're not working in an environment, where you are not acculturated to think "I am an expert, and I have special knowledge and skills and that people should listen to me". It sort of like almost undermines that … sets us up to be not as powerful. (Olivia, Interview 2)

Power, in this sense, was also seen by Olivia to be finite.

Power Resides in Formal Structures

Power was also conceptualised by a number of participants as being inherent in formal structures. Rose, for example, initially commented that 'power is very solid and strong and you can't penetrate that' (Rose, Interview 1). For Olivia, too, power is structural, embedded in systems and hierarchical. As she explains:

> the legal system, whatever that entity might be, had power, and she [the child victim/survivor] didn't. Like in terms of a hierarchy, she had the least. And then maybe her mum and her family were next in terms of feeling the least powerful. And then I felt like I didn't have much. (Rose, Interview 1)

Power and Powerlessness Are Linked to Social Status and Position

For other participants, seeing power as a commodity was expressed through a belief that it inheres in professional and/or educational attainments and equates with professional status. Bella, for example, said: 'the power there accords my position' (Bella, Interview 1). She assumed that the after-hours co-ordinator had more power than she did, 'because of the role she is given' (Bella, Interview 2). Andrea defined power in similar terms: 'It's position' (Andrea, Interview 1). Her account also equated power with professionals, and powerlessness with a lack of structural or professional position. Referring to the victim/survivor she was working with, she said:

> This woman was from a low socio-economic group. She possibly had minimal education and even put herself down in front of the police … she also referred to herself as "nuffy", "nuf-nuf" and that that was her nickname. Certainly she felt that she wasn't important to the police, the FMO, or even to me; that we were all educated people with important jobs. (Andrea, Interview 1)

Deconstruction of Modernist Notions of Power

Implicit in these constructions was an assumption about the powerful and the powerless being two mutually exclusive groups; a person belongs to one group or the other and their identity is defined by their position. In the comment cited above, Andrea assumed the woman was disempowered because she was not professional or educated, and that her powerless identity is fixed and unchanging and automatically linked with social disadvantage.

For nearly all the participants, viewing power as a possession or a commodity had unintended, disempowering outcomes. Beginning to deconstruct this, Olivia said: 'I probably am guilty at times of falling into that all or nothing dichotomy about power: that you either have it or you don't' (Olivia, Interview 2). Rose illustrated this point when she said that conceptualising power as a commodity, while constructing herself and the mother and child as lacking power, may have been unhelpful for all of them. When considering the implications of this construction of power, she said: 'No, it doesn't benefit me and it doesn't benefit the person I am trying to help either' (Rose, Interview 1).

It is interesting to note that while service users were assumed to be powerless in relation to professionals and systems, most counsellors/advocates, despite their professional education and status (which they see as bestowing power), assumed that other professionals had more power than they did. One possible explanation for this is that, as Olivia suggests, there is an assumption that 'power is bad ... because that's what causes sexual assault, and it corrupts' (Olivia, Interview 2). Power was therefore seen by participants as something that counsellors/advocates do not have and would not want to have, because it is 'bad' and associated with 'professionalism' (which CASA practitioners reject). This discourse may actually produce complicity with oppression and create an interest in resisting suggestions that counsellors/advocates can exercise power to work for change. It may ultimately reinforce a sense of powerlessness, hopelessness and victimhood for counsellors/advocates and victims/survivors.

Reconstruction of Modernist Notions of Power: Exercising Power through Discourse

In deconstructing their modernist discourses about power, participants were able to recognise their disempowering consequences. This process pointed to the need to reconceptualise power in different ways in order to experience empowerment. For example, reconstructing my initial assumptions about power existing as a commodity, and transforming these assumptions to understand power as something we exercise through the control of discourse, enabled me to address my sense of powerlessness. As I explain in relation to my interaction with the detective: 'the discourses that I had posited ultimately became dominant in our interaction because they were accepted by him, which is an exercise of power' (Christine, Reflection 2). Further reconstructing my account, I said:

> I actually exercised power in quite a productive way, and this challenges and reconstructs my assumptions about feeling powerless in the situation too. Controlling discourse as a means of resistance ultimately resulted in Lee's wishes being actualised ... He [the detective] left the crisis care unit; he went and investigated the crime scene independently without her, which he wasn't prepared to do initially. (Christine, Reflection 2)
>
> Given this outcome, I ultimately concluded that "I did actually resist those dominant power relations". (Christine, Reflection 2)

Similarly, Barbara found a way potentially to exercise power in her situation despite feeling overpowered by the police at the time. She identified naming problematic behaviour as a way of actively participating in the construction of the discourse. As she stated: 'I'm pretty good at not responding, or even just saying something like, "There's no need for that"' (Barbara, Interview 2), which at the time may have changed her feelings of powerlessness for the better in relation to the police and their inappropriate treatment of the service user. She also rejected the assumption that a greater number of police equates with less power for the counsellor/advocate. Recognising how unhelpful this interpretation had been for her, she said: 'That's not helpful. That leads us to feel powerless' (Barbara, Interview 2). Reconstructing power as something that can also be exercised, she proposed a more enabling discourse: 'Regardless of the numbers, I can still use humour to deflect and some other things that might [challenge the police] regardless of how many of them there were' (Barbara, Interview 2).

Another assumption that Barbara questioned was that power is distributed to people according to their position in a professional hierarchy. She recognised that her actions do not have to be legitimated by the after-hours co-ordinator – she was able to validate her own standpoint position in relation to the incident. In relation to the police misconduct she stated: 'Regardless of whether I did challenge them or not, if I did, I would still follow it [a complaint about the conduct of the police] up at the other end too' (Barbara, Interview 2).

Bella similarly reconsidered her notion of power to see it as fluid and contextual, rather than purely structural:

> I can see how in particular contexts power changes, and even in a sentence or a paragraph of conversation with someone, things can change, and that it isn't necessarily seen in that structural way of someone possessing it, and it can be more fluid; [just] because someone has status, doesn't mean they have power necessarily, and vice versa. (Bella, Interview 2)

Bella also developed some understanding that power can be exercised through the control of discourse, and that she was able to assist the mother to exercise power in how she told her story which she then presented to the lawyer. As she articulates: 'we did talk about how to present her story to her lawyer; how to engage in that process: that family court process' (Bella, Interview 2).

One of the ways that Olivia reconstructed her initial notions of power was to reject the assumption that egalitarianism is associated with a reduction of power. She did this by acknowledging that practitioners can operate differently and use power in various ways in different contexts, and in relation to different people. Doing this, she also changed her initial assumption that power is 'bad' and reconstructed it as simultaneously productive: 'I actually think it's a good thing to have power; it's about the ways that it's exercised that's important, and that it's not abused' (Olivia, Interview 2), thus demonstrating a more complex and nuanced conceptualisation of power.

Rose also changed her assumption about power being simply a commodity or possession, to something that can also be exercised. This freed her to think that regardless of her position within a structure and in relation to the legal system, she could exercise power by participating in the construction of discourse in which children's disclosures of sexual assault are located and understood. As she imagined:

> If it was for instance that I was called to court, you know, for my professional opinion of what I thought of this case; whether this man should have access or not to this child, then that would give me some power because I think that I would voice an opinion. (Rose, Interview 1)

Olivia took this one step further. Reconstructing opportunities to exercise power by influencing the discourse that informs the ways in which victims/survivors' testimonies are heard, so that they are perceived as more credible, she proposed the idea of requesting the prosecution to subpoena her as an expert witness in order to express her understanding of how developmental stages and trauma affect how a child provides evidence in court. She stated that she 'should be saying, "well you should be subpoenaing me as an expert witness and I'll give evidence about that"' (Olivia, Interview 1). 'Maybe at a committal hearing a magistrate may have … more … understanding [about how] to inform a jury. Perhaps if they did hear [the] kind of perspective [that challenges social myths], that might help them to make sense of what they've heard in a different way' (Olivia, Interview 2).

Between them, the participants created alternative practice possibilities such as arranging to be subpoenaed to give evidence as an expert witness in court, or offering input to support child protection as a way of exercising power and control over the discourse. This counteracted their initial sense of structural powerlessness. In affirming this, Rose said: 'you give yourself the power to value your professional opinion and your professional capacity' (Rose, Interview 1).

Macro Social Change as the Ultimate Change Strategy? Revaluing the Contribution of Counselling

This theme begins with identifying the ways in which participants had initially assumed that social change was the only meaningful change strategy. As with most of the research and activism in this field of practice, this had the effect of preoccupying them with law reform, and devaluing much of the individual and counselling work they were engaged in. This commitment to broad social change, which had the effect of artificially separating practitioners from the means of change, was viewed as another consequence of using a structural analysis in isolation. Ultimately, the value of counselling, and the contribution that participants make to their service users, was reinstated as a dominant discourse among the participants. The collection of themes in this section is organised under the following headings:

- the assumption that structural change (including law reform) is the only meaningful change strategy;

- the assumption that counselling (or individual casework) is ineffective in responding to structural issues;
- deconstruction of the assumption that only structural change/macro practice is valuable; and
- reconstructing the value of counselling/individual work: rejecting assumptions that only social change is valuable.

The Assumption that Structural Change (Including Law Reform) is the Only Meaningful Change Strategy

Related to the macro theme that identified the unintended consequences of using a structural analysis in isolation, is the view that structural change is essential to improve victims/survivors' experiences of the legal system. This implicit suggestion was often expressed by participants through their exclusive commitment to law reform and legal solutions. Bella, for example, indicated that one of the main ways counsellors/advocates could participate in meaningful change is 'by having input into the formal processes' (Bella, Interview 1). Change is therefore also understood as something that counsellors/advocates witness, rather than actively influence or engage in: 'I think to myself ... remember back when you started as a social worker: rape in marriage was not illegal at all, and in that time it has become illegal. So ... things do change' (Bella, Interview 1). Law reform is therein seen as the ultimate goal in terms of achieving effective structural change in this situation. As Bella stated: 'With law reform can come cultural and social change' (Bella, Interview 2). Given her perception that the problems are legal in nature, she also believed that they required legal solutions: 'the only way that I thought she [the mother she was working with] may be able to have an outcome that ensured the protection [of] the child was having a good lawyer' (Bella, Interview 1). She also said that 'the most effective, practical solution' was that the mother should have 'a good advocate, a legal advocate' (Bella, Interview 1). Later, she agreed with my observations: 'I probably do have a legalistic framework around significant change. I'd probably agree with that' (Bella, Interview 2).

Similarly, Olivia explicitly expressed the belief that for useful or valuable change to occur in the legal system, it must be structural in nature: 'I suppose at some level my assumptions are that there needs to be structural changes' (Olivia, Interview 1). Rose made the same assumption and felt that if she was unable to create structural changes in the legal system, then she was unable to assist the mother and child that she was working with at all. She rationalised this in the following way: 'It's sort of not helpful for us to stay involved because ultimately that person [the mother] needs to make changes legally for anything to actually really, really change. Otherwise we just keep on sort of maintaining the status quo' (Rose, Interview 1).

The Assumption that Counselling (or Individual Casework) is Ineffective in Responding to Structural Issues

The devaluing of individual work was another broad theme embedded in participants' initial stories, hidden by the commitment to structural intervention. This was evident in my own narrative. Despite successfully advocating for the needs of the victim/survivor to be met, my initial assessment of my practice was simply that is was not good enough.

> The outcome was sort of like a victory at the time, but given how disturbed I felt by the whole process and disempowered I felt, and seeing the impact on Lee as well, of such a negative interaction with the police and my fear that she probably just decided to disengage and not report to the legal system: in that sense, it's hardly a victory. It's hardly something that is worth celebrating. I don't see it as particularly good practice. (Christine, Reflection 1)

Other participants, including Bella, were more explicit about seeing counselling as ineffective in responding to structural issues, and much clearer about seeing social change as entirely separate and more important than individual casework. As Bella stated:

> So from a counselling point of view, I was asking myself, well, what am I doing? What? Despite giving her information about those systems, despite offering to advocate on her behalf ... those various systems seemed to operate in a certain way and to me it seemed like there was no way that we could really intervene and change any of that. (Bella, Interview 1)

Olivia was similarly explicit that individual counselling work with victims/survivors cannot be effective in challenging structural issues. As she explained, 'when you're providing counselling or therapy, you can't address the more structural aspects of it, which made me feel ineffectual' (Olivia, Interview 1). For this reason, she also initially devalued her practice, believing that it had little impact on the situation for the child she was working with, 'aside from the fact that, you know, yes she could give evidence via closed circuit TV and those sorts of things that happened, and probably would have happened regardless' (Olivia, Interview 1).

Deconstruction of the Assumption that Only Structural Change/ Macro Practice is Valuable

Participants deconstructed the assumption that structural change is the only meaningful way to respond to the difficulties that practitioners experience in supporting victims/survivors of sexual assault. Deconstruction highlighted how the macro issues had been artificially separated from micro practices in a way that unnecessarily devalued individual counselling. Rose, for example, in dichotomously constructing her work in terms of achieving structural change *or* disengaging with the mother, arguably limited her own practice possibilities, and unconsciously participated in a discourse that devalued and marginalised the positive aspects of her engagement with the mother. On reflection, she concluded that this approach 'devalues everything all along: it's the agency and her; the child who's disclosed; and myself. Definitely' (Rose, Interview, 2).

Similarly, Bella recognised that this dichotomous construction served to 'other' counselling in favour of law reform and privileged structural change such as legislative solutions as the ultimate strategy for change. This rendered other forms of change and resistance that counsellors/advocates engage in insignificant and invisible:

> Yes, because then I felt really conflicted with what I was doing with her as well … I could see how it was helpful for her, but I didn't think it was very significant because I just didn't think that it contributed towards her child being able to be safe, and I thought that was the main problem in the situation. And I didn't think that [counselling] was really helping. (Bella, Interview 2)

Deconstructing my initial devaluation of the gains made by the advocacy I had engaged in with the detective, I too realised that exclusively using a structural analysis could potentially lead practitioners to 'only value structural change … We think that for change to be valuable, we have to change the whole system' (Christine, Reflection 2). Recognising and rejecting this assumption and its limiting implications enabled me to revalue aspects of my practice that had been devalued by the structural change discourse.

Reconstructing the Value of Counselling/Individual Work: Rejecting Assumptions that Only Social Change is Valuable

The assumption that only structural change will be effective in transforming victims/survivors' experiences of the legal system was another belief that participants revised during the reconstruction stage of this research process. Deconstructing this assumption showed how it alienated practitioners from the means of change and reinforced a sense of powerlessness, whilst at the same time devaluing their casework and counselling by comparing it to social change. However, practitioners felt that social change was something from which they were largely removed. It is interesting to note that of the change practices proposed by practitioners, none were structural in nature and none changed traditional professional hierarchies or altered legislation concerning the formal operations of systems. Despite this, all the proposed new practices have the potential to deliver better processes and outcomes for victims/survivors.

As previously mentioned, Rose suggested that counsellors/advocates are well placed to make specialised children's assessments and to obtain disclosures from children. This is an example of how counsellors/advocates engaging in one-on-one work with victims/survivors can potentially make a difference to the experience of their service users. Expanding on this, Rose also began to reconstruct a discourse that was more affirming of her work: 'you can help someone to feel more powerful if you do provide a different perspective about something; help them to think differently about something' (Rose, Interview 2).

Addressing another aspect of this theme, Bella reconstructed the notion that for her contact with the mother to be useful she needed to change social structures. She was able to revalue aspects of her individual counselling that were previously silenced by the idea that only structural change counts:

> Another thing that I think to myself is don't get caught up in thinking you have to do something that's life changing for this person. You have to also pay attention to the subtlety of what occurs in the interaction between yourself and the person. For example, I know a person had got so much out of coming, and it was only because of the relationship we had. That she trusted, she felt she could tell me things, and that was really beneficial for her; that is important work you've done for that person, even though maybe the situation isn't resolved, or that we didn't actually get a definitive outcome. Something near it might have happened, or circumstances change and so on. (Bella, Interview 2)

Bella also began to validate other components of her individual counselling work, rather than defining them by their distance from social change-orientated practice:

> I've actually engaged in some important counselling practice and some significant work with people at a much deeper level for them, and I know and can see that that has been helpful, and to acknowledge more complexity, and that sometimes when people present around a certain issue that may not even be the major issue, or one of the most important things for them. And to put aside my assumptions [about only social change being valuable] … to travel that journey with them, being open to it changing [has] been helpful. That's been a really good experience … seeing things in a more complex way. (Bella, Interview 2)

Ultimately, Bella was able to reconstruct her interpretation of how the mother experienced the counselling, counter her 'sinking feeling' and see that the mother did benefit from her work.

Similarly, Olivia changed her assumptions that counselling cannot address structural issues: 'I think it depends on the approach you take to counselling or therapy, and there can be structural change … you could work quite systemically if you use a social and political analysis to inform the way you do counselling' (Olivia, Interview 2). She also began to rethink the privileging of macro change practice when discussing some of the valuable aspects of her personal work with the child: 'I certainly think it was probably better having my involvement than having nothing … something she might take from that that was … having one person outside her family who she felt did believe her' (Olivia, Interview 1). Uncovering previously subjugated narratives, she further elaborated:

> I went to court with her to show her the place with the TV, to show her where she would be going; that sort of thing. And the OPP was successful in applying [for me to] be the Independent Third Person, who was with her when she gave the closed circuit TV evidence for the committal hearing. (Olivia, Interview 1)

Embracing the value of micro change practices, Olivia created a number of different possibilities to prepare the victim/survivor for the court process: 'The other thing that I was thinking of was whether knowing more about, what sort of questions … [the defence may ask the child during the cross-examination process]; whether a bit more understanding [of the legal process may have helped the child] … There could have been more scope for preparing her a bit more in the counselling' (Olivia, Interview 1). On the matter of advising about how children 'cope' with the process, she said, '[m]aybe if [I] argued that this is where she is at developmentally, and [that rehearsing testimony] is actually an okay thing to do. [I need] to be clear about why it is okay to do this with a child, rather than being apologetic' (Olivia, Interview 2). Further reconstructing the role of counsellors/ advocates as agents of change, she said:

> There are certain procedures that are supposed to happen, but actually don't in terms of there being the OPP meeting with the family beforehand … And I think because we're regional, it [the meeting with the OPP] actually happens about half an hour before it goes to court, and there's just this acceptance, of "oh that's just the way it is" but I suppose you could just insist that those sort of things are [observed], because I think they are supposed to be … There are some things … that I would force myself to be a little more definite about, what I [think] should happen … at the trial say, being more assertive or forceful with the OPP. (Olivia, Interview 2)

Other local acts of resistance identified by Olivia included presenting the victim/survivor's case more convincingly so that certain aspects of the process could be adjusted, or presenting alternative discourses for legal professionals to consider. Other changes proposed involved working more collaboratively with legal personnel and encouraging them to play a more active support role. As Olivia suggests, 'maybe the police or the OPP could have been more involved in preparing her, given that they probably would have more of an understanding of what might unfold' (Olivia, Interview 2). Describing a reconstructed collaborative practice, she said: 'Maybe what I should have done differently was advocate for her to be supported in that process, but not necessarily by me' (Olivia, Interview 1). Further rethinking her initial assumption that only structural change is valuable, she also suggested:

> It is about enlisting those people [legal professionals] rather than having an oppositional position [in relation to them]. So maybe that if you made a real point connecting with them, like in a particular case of developing a relationship with the lawyer – that might affect some change in individual cases and the ways that they are handled, which, in little things, big things might grow. (Olivia, Interview 1)

Reconstructing the same assumption that was evident in my original construction of my practice incident, I stated:

> I don't know what I was expecting was possible when I decided that this wasn't very good practice. It's probably not realistic to expect that he [the detective] is going to suddenly see things completely from my point of view and apologise, and make himself available at a later time, and put in for recommendations for change around the internal operational police processes that put pressure on police to put pressure on victims/survivors! Obviously these kinds of things are not going to evolve in one interaction, but it doesn't mean that we can't value what was achieved by smaller, local acts of resistance. So, reconstructing this incident has enabled me to value aspects of my practice that I was initially quite critical of and disappointed with. (Christine, Reflection 2)

Identifying and Challenging Unhelpful Dominant Discourses

This theme concentrates on participants' indulgence in a number of dominant discourses that were operating contrary to their interests and the interests of their service users. This includes discourses about conflict with police and other legal personnel being undesirable and problematic. It also includes discourses about counsellors/advocates having to conform to unjust social arrangements in order to preserve dominant power relations. Deconstruction of participants' accounts revealed an important implicit dichotomy between collaboration and challenge. Ultimately, in addressing these issues, reconstruction aimed to create possibilities to practice in ways that are simultaneously collaborative and challenging (if necessary). The themes in this section are presented in the following order:

- the perception that loss of control equates with loss of power;
- conflict as bad;
- conforming to preserve dominant power relations;
- deconstruction of the assumptions that conflict is bad and counsellors/advocates should conform; and
- reconstruction: creating opportunities for challenge whilst practicing collaboratively.

The Perception that Loss of Control Relates to a Loss Of Power

Prior to deconstructing practitioner's accounts of their incidents, overwhelmingly, practitioners felt they were powerless to do anything, and that what was being done was ineffectual or not good enough. Some initial accounts indicated that this was linked to a need for control. My own account, for example, suggested that I felt that I needed to maintain control over the process. This was evident in a considerable amount of my commentary being devoted to planning an escape for the victim/survivor so that she could get away from the police. As I stated: 'Planning an escape for Lee felt central to maintaining a sense of control over the process, which is why such emphasis was given to arranging transport' (Christine, Reflection 1). While I was trying to hold on tightly to a sense of control, Barbara, who felt that she had lost control, had a sense that once you lose control of a situation, you cannot regain it. As she explained:

> I got off on the back foot and that made me feel a bit flustered, I suppose ... talking to the police, it just made me feel uncomfortable. Then I was sort of questioning myself I suppose. And then also, I wanted to [challenge the police] and I wasn't too sure. Yeah, it just made me feel probably a bit vulnerable and a bit confused I suppose at times. (Barbara, Interview 1)

She further elaborated: 'It could have been totally different if I had ... been there [at the crisis care unit] before them [the police] and just been waiting for them. It could have been totally different' (Barbara, Interview 1). In relation to this she later said 'initially I probably actually interpreted [the situation in a way] that led to my demise I suppose, or just sort of set me into a bit of spin, or on a particular path' (Barbara, Interview 2).

Conflict as Bad

The initial feelings of needing to have control had particular implications for Barbara because consequently, she felt as though she could not challenge the police. This was linked to a broader assumption by other participants about conflict or confrontation with police and other professionals in positions of authority, such as FMOs, being bad or invoking negative consequences.

Barbara made an assumption that raising issues with the police would be necessarily conflictual or confrontational and would have undesirable consequences: 'Oooh, I don't want to do that; they [they police] are going to come and hunt me down with their guns [laughs] ... Yeah. I did make an assumption there that that wouldn't be a good idea' (Barbara, Interview 1). She also referred to expected negative consequences for herself and the service: 'I just thought, oh, there could be some repercussions ... for me personally, but also for CASA.' She also assumed there would be adverse consequences for the service user: 'To be honest, I was worried about what they [the police] would say or then start getting into it about this person [the service user]' (Barbara, Interview 1). Barbara also believed that conflict should only be entered into when it is safe to challenge and should only happen in private, and in a context where all variables can be predicted and controlled. As she explains: 'we were out in the foyer and … in that context, maybe I thought, ooh, this is not a good thing for things to get heated out here, and the fact that the victim/survivor was nearby as well at that stage …' (Barbara, Interview 1).

The reluctance to engage in conflict or, in my case, regret at having been too embroiled in it, was expressed in terms of feeling that it did not justify the result: 'Even though I advocated strongly and her needs were ultimately negotiated and successfully met, I think the process had been so awful that it really negated the outcome' (Christine, Reflection 2). I also assumed that the level of conflict between the detective and myself was damaging for the victim/survivor and that, because of it, she would disengage from the legal process. This again highlighted an unconscious value that conflict should be avoided:

> I suspect her indecision [about] reporting was probably resolved by her interaction with that detective. I suspect that despite the fact that she'd been assaulted and that there was a process which would potentially assist her in court, … despite going through that whole process, having the forensic [examination] and everything, that she probably chose not to report [because] she had found her experience with them to be so abhorrent that she just didn't want to engage with them any further. She felt like she had been treated as the criminal. She felt disbelieved, dismissed … unsupported and re-victimised, so I could understand if that ultimately was her decision. (Christine, Reflection 1)

Because I had resisted the detective during the crisis care and then regretted my actions, I later recognised my implicit assumption that conflict is negative: 'I had an implicit assumption that modernism is problematic: that modernist advocacy is flawed … because it leads to conflict' (Christine, Reflection 2).

Conforming to Preserve Dominant Power Relations

Related to the assumption that conflict is bad and to be avoided is the belief that 'good' practice is without conflict and that counsellors/advocates should therefore try to defuse it. This is particularly clear in Barbara's account when she explains her decision to avoid conflict even when that meant not raising legitimate concerns with the police about their inappropriate conduct: 'I'd be worried about that [engaging in conflict with the police] … I think maybe too, I didn't know what I was going to get in response and then I thought, this probably shouldn't be happening when we're trying to support this person' (Barbara, Interview 1). In addition, we obtain a strong sense from Barbara's account that she wanted to avoid upsetting the police thereby maintaining the status quo. She felt responsible for the mix-up about the initial meeting place with the police and the victim/survivor, and felt that because of this, that she should do nothing further to antagonise the police such as questioning their conduct and treatment of the victim/survivor. As she explains: 'So there was an issue at the start ... They weren't sort of in a great mood I suppose by the time I got there ... Not feeling like I could challenge them [resulted from] a combination of their manner and how we started things off' (Barbara, Interview 1).

The initial impulse to conform in order to preserve dominant power relations with the police and other professionals was also evident in Olivia's account. This was conveyed, for example, through her quite accidental challenge of legal rules that she later realised did not conform to established legal protocols. Despite the effectiveness of this challenge, having realised her practice transgressed standard procedure, she stated she would not repeat it again. As she explained about gaining permission to be the Independent Third Person: 'Yeah, I requested it ... I was successful in my request to be the Independent Third Person ... I didn't realise it was a very unusual request, whereas now, I wouldn't even consider that [making the request again] as a possibility' (Olivia, Interview 2).

Andrea similarly constructed herself in a way that preserved dominant power relations – as an observer. When she was working with the woman who had just been raped by a stranger, and the police intervened to prevent the woman being supported by her husband and female friend, Andrea indicated that she

> informed them that I would be letting her know that [the police sent her support people away], which was absolutely devastating to her. She felt that her husband and her friend didn't want to speak to her. So I worked a lot at that point on supporting her and letting her know that they actually did come to the hospital to support her, to speak to her, and that it was the police's decision, and not mine. (Andrea, Interview 1)

While I did not have the opportunity to meet with Andrea on a second occasion, during our first meeting there was no evidence that she had criticised the police intervention as inappropriate. This is despite describing this intervention as 'devastating' for the victim/survivor (Andrea, Interview 1). This is consistent with Andrea's espoused role of 'trying to promote calmness and serenity ... taking on an observer role and not a participant role' (Andrea, Interview 1). Her role, she said, was 'setting an example to the victim/survivor ... If you play the police's game, if you don't get extreme in your responses, they will deal with you on a civil level' (Andrea, Interview 1). This construction of the counsellor/advocate role arguably invokes a number of inadvertent implications for her practice that may be interpreted as disadvantageous for herself and the victim/survivor. Her commentary clearly paints the police as having the ultimate power and dictating the terms of reference while it is the role of the counsellor/advocate to assist the victim/survivor to conform to their expectations.

Another way in which Andrea affirmed dominant power relations was in her construction of the situation in a way that reinforced her assumption that the FMO could not be challenged, again justifying her compliance:

> It was more about opportunity. She [the FMO] was pretty much in and then out. It was a pass of comment, out the door. And on her way out the door she said to the police she felt the wounds were self-inflicted, and then she was off to another job. And in my role as a counsellor/advocate, you know, we just don't get involved with the FMOs. You know, they think they are above everyone else, and if I had prevented her from moving onto the next job, I probably would have had a complaint made against me. (Andrea, Interview 1)

Andrea also made other statements in her first interview that I would have liked to have had the opportunity to explore with her further. One was: 'I certainly had power. I had the ability to ask the police to leave. Although it didn't sort of come about' (Andrea, Interview 1). I would have liked to talk to Andrea about how she had understood this. Was this another opportunity for her to participate, where instead she opted to observe? She also made reference to the visibility of the weapons that the police carry, and the insensitivity of this for the victim/survivor who had just been attacked by a stranger. This was one of a number of instances when Andrea described a situation that would ordinarily call for her intervention, but she offered no details of her response, creating the impression that she was again observing rather than participating. Had there been a second interview, I would have liked to delve into the possibilities for her to request that the police hide their weapons.

Deconstruction of the Assumptions that Conflict is Bad and Counsellors/Advocates Should Conform

This construction of the counsellor/advocate role that avoids or defuses conflict, or conforms to preserve dominant power relations, apparently contradicts earlier views of counsellors/advocates being 'at loggerheads' with other professionals and systems, while creating adversarial and confrontational practice responses through perpetuating dichotomous power relations. There appears to be an implication that if practitioners operate in a collaborative way with other professionals involved in the legal process then they must be conforming, because challenge would necessarily be confrontational or conflictual. Deconstructing my own account, I acknowledged that my use of combative language and imagery prevented me from feeling comfortable with my practice, rather than feeling uncomfortable about the challenge *per se*:

> even though Lee's needs were … met because of my resistance of the detective, I didn't want to see this situation as a victory … On reflection, I think part of the problem is that I was using an image that doesn't really fit with the scenario

> or my espoused practice. It's not an accurate image, or one that I find useful. I don't like war. I don't want to associate my practice with war, even though I did want to advocate strongly for the ... service user against someone who was attempting to exercise power through controlling discourse as much as me, even if that meant engaging in conflict. I initially felt uncomfortable valuing this practice because I framed it in terms of winning a battle, whereas there must be other ways to frame it, that don't have that same connotation. (Christine, Reflection 2)

For others, further deconstruction of the assumption that divides collaboration and challenge, and leads to counsellors/advocates practising in conformist ways, highlighted the implications for practitioners whose role it is to support and advocate for victims/survivors. Barbara, for example, acknowledged that her decision not to challenge the police potentially held greater consequences for herself, the service and especially the victim/survivor, than not challenging: 'And he [the victim/survivor] actually said to me at one stage, he felt the police didn't want to speak to him' (Barbara, Interview 1). She analysed how her perception of a lack of agency to challenge the police was in some ways self-imposed. One of the ways she did this was to explore other possible interpretations of the situation, particularly in relation to the mix-up about the meeting place, for which she initially assumed responsibility: 'It might not have had absolutely anything to do with me bungling up. It could be all to do with the fact that they'd known this victim/survivor ... or whatever' (Barbara, Interview 2). She began to realise that these aspects of her thinking and initial construction of the story potentially worked against her and the victim/survivor: 'I can see it totally clearly ... how much all of that [assumption that she could not challenge the police] was in my head, you know, and how I was constructing that for myself, without them doing that for me' (Barbara, Interview 2).

Analysis of Andrea's account also highlighted the way she positioned the FMO in her narrative, seeing her as someone who simply could not be challenged. In addition, in assuming that a complaint would have been made against her by the FMO if she had challenged her, Andrea had accepted the dominant frame of reference that was disadvantageous to both her and the victim/survivor. Despite explicitly locating herself in an 'observer role', there were a number of ways in which Andrea 'participated' that may have unintentionally been contrary to her interests and those of the victim/survivor. There may also have been occasions on which Andrea had opportunities to 'participate' more fully in the processes of this crisis care unit, but she chose instead to 'observe'.

Reconstruction: Creating Opportunities for Challenge Whilst Practising Collaboratively

Some practitioners initially assumed that challenging legal personnel or processes to advocate for victims/survivors would be necessarily confrontational or conflictual. Conflict was seen as having a potential range of negative consequences for the practitioner, the victim/survivor and the service. This explains why on a number of occasions, participants indicated that they had chosen not to engage in conflict and therefore not challenge perceived injustices. In my situation, for example, my decision to challenge the detective may have resulted in my practice being inflammatory or adversarial. For example, 'I asked John to leave the room with me at this point and I spoke to him outside briefly about my need to consider reporting his conduct as constituting a breach of the police code of ethics to his superior' (Christine, Reflection 1). The assumption about conflict being negative resulted in my feeling regretful about my practice. Reconstruction of these assumptions about challenge necessarily involving conflict, and conflict being undesirable, allowed new discourses about challenge and conflict to develop. In reconstructing my account, for example, I stated:

> In some ways on the first reflection I felt quite badly about what I should have done, or what could have been done differently, but in creating a discourse that is valuing of what was achieved, I think that what she [the victim/survivor] wanted to happen, did happen, in terms of leaving the CCU [crisis care unit] and going home without being forced to go to the crime scene … I was there to support and advocate for and with Lee at times, that's how things unfolded, conflictual as it was, and I now feel I can validate that practice. (Christine, Reflection 2)

While throughout the reconstruction of my practice I looked for opportunities for less oppositional practice and will continue to do so in future, I no longer feel I need to devalue my practice because it happened to become conflictual on this occasion.

This re-thinking enabled me to address my initial sense of disturbance when first reflecting on the conflict and my practice:

> What reconstructing this incident has enabled me to do is to feel confident that I did resist appropriately at the time, and that I am now in a better position to validate the practice that I engaged in without constructing it in a way that emphasises the negative or problematic interpretations, and to emphasise the aspects that really did work to benefit the victim/survivor, and the same in relation to the service. (Christine, Reflection 2)

In addition, I rethought my earlier assumption that the crisis care unit process had been so conflictual that Lee would decide not to make a statement to the police:

> the reality is, this is my assumption, a social construction of the situation, and I have no idea about whether she actually decided to go ahead with making a statement or not. Given that I only saw her on that one occasion and the service's commitment to confidentiality means that we usually don't know what happens to a victim/survivor after our initial work with her is completed … Perhaps she

> did make a report to the police, or may still choose to at some stage down the track if she hasn't already. (Christine, Reflection, 2)

Extending this, I deconstructed the assumption that if Lee did choose not report the assault to the police, that this reflected poor practice on my behalf: 'it's not necessarily a negative thing if Lee chooses not to report. Ultimately if she makes an informed decision not to engage with the legal system … then that's entirely her prerogative [and that] needs to be respected' (Christine, Reflection 2).

For other participants, assumptions about challenge leading to conflict, and conflict being bad, were manifested in different ways and reconstructed with different outcomes. Barbara gave herself permission to challenge the police by rethinking her assumptions that challenge would inevitably lead to negative consequences and by reinterpreting the sharing of her expectations with the police as an opportunity to educate them: 'if I turn my thoughts over to that sort of thinking I could actually be assisting them' (Barbara, Interview 2). Barbara changed her view of conflict in the after-hours role from a rare or unusual occurrence to an understandable or potentially expected part of the work: 'These scenarios exist … Let's be real about it' (Barbara, Interview 2). She also tackled her lack of confidence by rejecting the discourse that she should take responsibility to make relationships with others in the legal process work amicably: 'letting go of some of that responsibility … to establish relationships with the surrounding people. My sole focus is the victim/survivor' (Barbara, Interview 2).

Similarly, Olivia's critical reflection on her assumptions about challenge and conflict helped her to think differently about the ways in which she could have advocated for the victim/survivor. These involved challenging legal personnel and processes through the means of collaborative practice rather than conflict. Proposing a different way of working with the OPP for example, she said:

> You often ring them [the OPP], and in your mind, you're thinking I'm doing this for the victim and their family, to help them. But if you were doing it [on the assumption that] they [the police] need to know about what are going to be the constraints for her [the victim/survivor] or maybe how she's likely to present, so they need to do some preparation to avoid that. Just thinking about it in that way is quite different. (Olivia, Interview 2)

Similarly, instead of feeling marginalised or excluded from legal processes and meetings, Olivia thought about ways in which to become more active. Again, this was about challenging exclusion, but through inclusive and collaborative means: 'I could just experiment with it I guess … I'm arranging this meeting of the people who are involved, and want to invite you to it' (Olivia, Interview 2). In suggesting this, Olivia, is also inserting herself in the discourse as a more empowered agent. These reconstructed change practices demonstrate a potential exercise of power through influencing the discourse. The following quote provides another example of this in relation to a different aspect of the legal process:

'perhaps there might have been ways that I could have argued more strongly about certain conditions that may have made a difference to the way that she was able to provide that evidence' (Olivia, Interview 2). Directly challenging the assumption that to challenge effectively as a counsellor/advocate you must be adversarial and confrontational with legal professionals, she continued: 'a way of changing might be to offer knowledge in a kind of collaborative way, instead of seeing that you sort of have to be enemies with them or something' (Olivia, Interview 2).

Uncovering and Changing Other Unhelpful Discourses – The Final Pieces

This final theme extends the previous one in identifying and challenging further unhelpful discourses. Those that are addressed include: participants' assumptions that if it were possible to create ideal circumstances, then counsellors/advocates would be able to more effectively contribute to change; and that external factors such as limitations imposed by service funding prevent counsellors/advocates from being proactive about challenging legal injustice. The themes are organised in the following way:

- the need for ideal circumstances;
- deconstruction of practitioners' participation in unhelpful discourses; and
- resisting unhelpful discourses: re-authoring new discourses and constructing alternative opportunities to challenge.

The Need for Ideal Circumstances

Another discourse that was contrary to participants' interests was the suggestion that if it were possible to create idealistic circumstances, then counsellors/advocates would be able to contribute to change. This appeared to contribute to a sense of powerlessness and inaction for participants. Bella illustrated this point when talking about how she would have ensured that the child was protected if she had had more decision-making power 'if I was the magistrate at the Family Court then I could make that decision' (Bella, Interview 2). Another assumption potentially reinforcing Bella's sense of hopelessness was that a clear disclosure from the child was the only way to access legal justice in the current system: 'what was paramount in this situation is that [for] children in that age group … it is very difficult to have a disclosure that is completely clear' (Bella, Interview 1). This perpetuates a sense of fatalism, given that the developmental stage of the child prevented a clear disclosure being obtained, thus leaving no possibility to access justice 'in the current context of what the requirements are' (Bella, Interview 2).

Andrea indicated that such a sense of hopelessness might have shifted if different opportunities had been available to her to challenge the FMO: 'I was one step removed … I didn't actually hear directly from the FMO that she felt that the wound was self-inflicted. It [came] from the police, so the opportunity was not there to grab … by the time [I had heard], she had gone' (Andrea, Interview 1). In Barbara's account, this theme appeared in her assumption that challenging the police may have been possible had information been obtained prior to their questioning: 'if I had more knowledge about what their role was, I could challenge them a lot more about that' (Barbara, Interview 1). Moreover, challenging the police might have been possible if any potential conflict could have been entered into in a safe and private environment where variables would have been more predictable and controllable. As already mentioned, she noted that they were in a public space, the foyer, and she believed that this location was 'not a good thing for things to get heated … but if we had our own space maybe to talk about things that could be different' (Barbara, Interview 1).

A further indication of the assumption that ideal circumstances are required lay in participants' identification of external factors preventing them from being more active in challenging legal injustice. Olivia explained, for example, that developing alternative approaches to challenging the legal system is time-consuming and she often has too many other things to do, which is 'a bit of a disincentive sometimes' (Olivia, Interview 2). Similarly, Andrea talked about the difficulties in critically reflecting during practice: 'I guess when you are thinking on your feet … your responses are very immediate. And there's not that opportunity to really critically reflect on what's going on, or how it's going' (Andrea, Interview 1).

Deconstruction of Practitioners' Participation in Unhelpful Discourses

Analysis of participants' accounts suggested that people had unwittingly participated in many ways in discourses that were unhelpful for their practice. For example, Andrea's statement that critical reflection is impossible during practice might limit her opportunities for learning and improvement. Similarly, Olivia's assumptions that exploring alternative practice possibilities is too time-consuming and her concern about 'getting caught up in how you would actually do that', combined with thoughts like 'oh no, I couldn't do that', might be impediments to creating changes in practice (Olivia, Interview 2). Rose acknowledged that participation in a discourse that says 'we're not funded for that' (Rose, Interview 2) may result in loss of opportunity for her to educate others who could affect the experiences of her service users and for her to have substantial input into the discourses that inform the thinking of people involved in the legal process following child sexual assault.

Barbara's participation in dominant discourses was evident in her complicity in existing power relations, including her internalisation of dominant police discourses and language (referring, for example, to the forensic examination as a 'rigmarole'; or talking about being 'allowed' to speak to the victim/survivor, as if the police need to give permission (Barbara, Interview 1). She was quite shocked when she reflected on this use of language: 'Far out! I'm sounding like them … I may as well go and get my uniform now, and put my badge on' (Barbara, Interview 2). Deconstruction of this internalisation of dominant discourses also highlighted to Barbara that she had accepted the police description of matters such as the initial mix-up about the meeting place. As she stated, 'that's interesting. I'm trying to make everything better … I'm actually trying to fix things up and I've taken responsibility that it was all my fault because I was downstairs' (Barbara, Interview 1). She also acknowledged that she unwittingly bolstered the position of the police in relation to herself through her willingness to question her own conduct, while the possibility that the police were waiting in the wrong department remained hidden: 'I hadn't even considered that it might have been them [the police] waiting in the wrong spot. I just assumed it was my fault. I automatically started to go into justification mode' (Barbara, Interview 1).

Paralleling this, Bella's use of language indicates that she too had accepted the discourse that the police and child protection were 'unable' to elicit a disclosure from the child that would satisfy the requirements to take action to protect her. She had unwittingly taken on the discourse that relies on proving the validity or truth or falsity of claims. In assuming, for example, that a clear disclosure from the child was the only way to access legal justice, she had adopted the dominant discourse that is contrary to her interests and those of the mother and child. Moreover, she had framed the difficulties in terms of the 'contentious nature of the disclosure' (Bella, Interview 1), again inadvertently justifying the limited and inappropriate responses of the police and child protection system.

Resisting Unhelpful Discourses: Re-authoring New Discourses and Constructing Alternative Opportunities to Challenge

Practitioners inadvertently adopted a range of dominant discourses during this research, arguably to the detriment of themselves and the service users with whom they were working. Many of these have already been analysed, but other specific expressions of these discourses are included here because they demonstrate the ways in which practitioners have been drawn into unhelpful discourses. Participation in these discourses ultimately limited their capacity to work towards change. These examples also highlight how practitioners later rejected this participation in their own oppression to reconstruct more empowering discourses and subsequent practices.

For some practitioners, including Olivia, assumptions that enacting new practice possibilities are too difficult or time-consuming were overturned. Although considering different ways of advocating before and during a trial might be more time intensive, it would later conserve time if it results in minimising the negative impacts of the legal process for victims/survivors: 'It's a cliché, isn't it? But [it's about] working smarter rather than harder … there might be times when you could invest a lot more time and energy into things which would have the effect of being preventative' (Olivia, Interview 2). She also resisted her participation in an unhelpful discourse that stunted her options. While initially embracing a discourse that called her input into the court process 'outrageous', she rethought this to create concrete possibilities for action. She replied in the affirmative when I asked her: 'I wonder if challenging those assumptions about being not as professional, not as articulate, not as expert in your role, may actually assist you to feel much more confident to exercise that power and to actually take the stand [in court]' (Olivia, Interview 2). So I made a further proposition: 'if there was a way to present your perspective then that could actually be quite a powerful way of affecting change. That could potentially have implications for changing the way that system makes its decisions?' (Christine as researcher, Interview 2 with Olivia). She replied:

> Yes, absolutely if you were really clear about why ... If you were prepared to give evidence as part of that. Like talking about why perhaps the evidence she presented was the way it was and that sort of thing, and that in a way is privileging the knowledge that you have about her in particular, but also about developing trauma and that sort of thing. (Olivia, Interview 2)

Olivia also rethought her participation in unhelpful, dichotomous and adversarial aspects of CASA culture in order to engage more critically with some of its unintended consequences. When asked about this, she stated: 'I would like to think so' (Olivia, Interview 2). This is also evidenced by the range of collaborative change practices that Olivia developed that have been presented throughout this chapter.

Barbara also resisted unhelpful discourses. In her case, it was a rejection of discourses of self-blame about the meeting place mix-up and an exploration of other ways to interpret the situation. As she states: 'it [the attitude of the police] might not have had absolutely anything to do with me bungling up. It could be all to do with the fact that they'd known this victim/survivor ... or whatever' (Barbara, Interview 2). Barbara refused the police description that she had 'bungled' and developed a more enabling discourse which emphasised different aspects of her arrival: 'I was on time ... I was actually meeting the criteria that we're supposed to meet' (Barbara, Interview 2). She recognised that by resisting this discourse, she was giving responsibility back to the police for their part in the mix-up and repositioning the victim/survivor as central and dominant in the discourse. As she stated in rejecting her self-justifying stance at the time: 'I probably just would have introduced myself and focused on the victim/survivor' (Barbara, Interview 2). She also realised that seeing the options of challenging the police through formal and informal processes as mutually exclusive also limited her capacity to respond. Her reconstruction suggested that in addition to the after-hours co-ordinator raising issues with the police after an incident, she would also be able to do so when they occurred: 'regardless of whether I did challenge them or not, if I did, I would still follow it up at the other end too' (Barbara, Interview 2). In addition, Barbara changed her attitude to 'the unknown', from problematic to something that she can manage: 'Whatever will be, will be, and I'll handle that because I can' (Barbara, Interview 2).

Similarly, Barbara rejected the assumption that once control of a situation is lost, it cannot be regained. She privileged different aspects of her account to reconstruct her participation in the incident: 'in a sense I did regain some [power/control] … because I got on with the forensic [investigation]' (Barbara, Interview 2). She also rethought her identity from someone 'vulnerable' and 'flustered' to someone in control: 'when I was with the victim/survivor, I was with that person, and I did everything that I should be doing' (Barbara, Interview 2). Finally, she changed her assumption that she needed a private space in which to challenge the police, by reinterpreting the implications of the victim/survivor witnessing such a challenge: 'It might have been powerful for him to see that and show him how supportive I was of him … but also maybe would have given him some information about his rights' (Barbara, Interview 2).

Exploring this theme in relation to my own account, I saw that one of the most unhelpful discourses in my commentary located the conflict with the detective in a discourse of battle, of 'intense fighting' (Christine, Reflection 1). Changing the language and imagery I used to describe the situation allowed me to develop more useful discourses:

> I felt uncomfortable valuing this practice because I framed it in terms of winning a battle. And it's not about winning, but perhaps about valuing what smaller changes and acts of resistance do contribute to more positive experiences and outcomes for victims/survivors. And valuing practice that does continue to resist and challenge … The reason I felt disturbed by it … was because the outcome was positive, but I didn't feel like I could validate the practice that I had engaged in because of the way that I'd framed it … So that helps to understand the implications of using some of that language [of] winners and losers, and to find different ways to frame the situation. (Christine, Reflection, 2)

In summarizing my thinking, I stated:

> Perhaps in reconstructing this, it's not even about framing it as points of resistance, but looking at the ways that we could have complemented each other's roles, and how I could have perhaps taken a lead role in facilitating that more collaborative approach. (Christine, Reflection 1)

Conclusion

This chapter has built on Chapter 7 by continuing to present key findings from the research. These past two chapters have presented a critically reflective analysis of the macro and micro themes that I identified from the amalgam of practitioners' experiences. These themes highlight the most prominent, often implicit assumptions common to participants' accounts, and the collective deconstruction and reconstruction of these assumptions, which have enabled the development of new practice possibilities for change.

Specifically, this chapter has explored issues related to participants' constructions of professionalism and hierarchy and they ways this led to the development of oppositional power relations. The central theme of power was particularly emphasised since it underpins the understanding of nearly all the other themes. Macro social change was questioned as the ultimate change strategy and participants began to revalue the contribution that their micro level counsellor/advocate practise might make to change. Identifying and challenging practitioners' participation in unhelpful dominant discourses, and uncovering and changing other unhelpful discourses was also comprehensively explored in this chapter in order to remove obstacles to change that were present in participants' thinking and practice.

The narratives expounded by the participants about their practice provide some clear examples of the ways in which critical reflection enabled them to develop possibilities for change. By tracing the journeys of the participants from their initial constructions of their critical incidents, which clearly expressed feelings of powerlessness, fatalism and disillusionment, these chapters have demonstrated transformative learning in the ways that participants used critical reflection to identify and rethink their original assumptions and retell their stories in ways that positioned them as more enabled and empowered. Through this critical reflection, the participants developed a range of possible new practices in their interactions with the legal system that they had not previously considered. The implications of this are analysed more fully in the following chapter.

Chapter 9
How Does Critical Reflection on Practice Develop Possibilities for Change?

Introduction

This chapter concentrates on the two most significant themes to emerge from participants' accounts. These are: 1) that even in the most disempowering contexts it is possible for practitioners to envisage their own power to bring about change; and 2) that critical reflection is a powerful tool to assist practitioners to connect with this sense of agency. The broader implications of these themes are discussed in connection with relevant literature that assists to contextualise these key findings.

1) That Even in the Most Disempowering Contexts it is Possible for Practitioners to Envisage Power to Bring about Change

I begin this section by defining what I mean by a disempowering context. Secondly, I discuss why working to support victims/survivors through the legal process can be considered a disempowering context. I then explore the potential implications of this analysis, and present an alternative construction of the problem. Thirdly, I outline the reconstructed practices of change and resistance that practitioners developed during this research that demonstrate how they might envisage their own power to bring about change despite the legal context that often disempowers them. Finally, I describe the broader implications of the creation of these change practices, and connect these new practices with possibilities for practitioners to envisage agency in other disempowered contexts.

What is a Disempowering Context?

A disempowering context is characterised by structural, institutional, ideological and interpersonal barriers that prevent practitioners from exercising agency and power to bring about change (Davies and Leonard 2004: ix–xv, Mullaly 2002: 92–121). Disempowering contexts are those that create a sense of powerlessness in critical practitioners and that rigidly constrain practitioners in their daily work, particularly in their pursuit of social justice and other emancipatory ideals. Given that globalisation has resulted in sweeping contextual changes including increased bureaucratic control, reduced resources and technocratic discourses of professionalism that limit critical practice, the context in which most social work and human services practice takes place is constantly changing, chaotic, uncertain and may generally be considered disempowered (Davies and Leonard 2004: ix–xv, Fook 2008: vi, Lehmann 2006: 201). For example, recent commentaries concerning the contexts in which social workers operate continue to highlight practitioners' level of 'disillusion[ment] increasing as a function of business management models being implemented to measure productivity in social care work' (Baker 2013: 120).

Why Are Counsellors/Advocates Disempowered in the Context of the Legal System?

A review of the existing research on the problems with the legal response to sexual assault provided insight into the structural reasons why the legal system does not provide a legally and socially just response to victims/survivors of sexual assault. Feminist literature of the past few decades clearly indicates that the structural context in which counsellors/advocates work operates to disempower practitioners and services users (see for example Brownmiller 1975, Carmody and Carrington 2000, Scutt 1996). These barriers can intersect in a multitude of ways to compound a sense of powerlessness (Astbury 2006: 3–4, Mullaly 2002: 118–21).

Paralleling what has been indicated by the research literature, each participant's story in its original form illustrated the structural problems of the legal response that were assumed by the practitioners to manifest the misogynist norms deeply ingrained in patriarchal society. Participants articulated the impact of the perceived inadequacies of the legal system on victims/survivors and on their practice, and many discussed the barriers for change in ways that highlighted their sense of powerlessness and lack of agency to respond. Most of the practitioners held quite fatalistic views about their practice. Fatalism refers 'broadly to feelings of disempowerment, of lack of agency or ability to act upon and effect change' (Fook 2004: 22). In participants' initial accounts, fatalistic views took the form of believing that it was pointless to try to work towards change even when there appeared to be concrete opportunities to facilitate different outcomes. This is perhaps why fatalism has been defined as 'an antibody, attacking occasional virulent strains of discontent and rebellion' (Heaney and Horton 1990: 86). Writers from other fields, including mental health, have made similar observations about the impact of fatalism, noting that the ways practitioners construct clients 'encourage[s] the view that they are … "beyond help"' (Kicuroski 2008: 71 citing Gregory 2007). More broadly, fatalism has been referred to in conjunction with pessimism as an indicator of practitioners' dwindling hope for emancipatory possibilities in the face of global capitalism (Leonard 2004). This was reflected in the initial stories of practitioners who described their sense of helplessness in the face of the seemingly enigmatic, structural problems of the legal system.

Implications of Retaining a Disempowering Analysis

Whilst this structural/feminist analysis of victims/survivors' experiences of the legal system offers a number of useful functions, including a comprehensive critique of the legal response to victims/survivors of sexual assault, and of the broader patriarchal context and social mythology that sanctions and perpetuates this response, it also had a disempowering effect. Participants' accounts revealed that this construction of the problem compounded their sense of fatalism about change in that they saw the mechanics of the legal system to be unchallengeable. Essentially, the initial constructions located the research problem in external, abstract structures that were assumed to be impervious to human agency.

Consequently, one of the major assumptions embedded in the original construction of the problem was that changes, particularly those seen as external to practitioners such as structural and legislative changes, are necessary to improve the response of the legal system to victims/survivors of sexual assault. However, this construction of change arguably crystallises the idea that practice in this context is strongly permeated by structural disempowerment.

In addition, the initial conditions assumed to be required for practitioners to envisage their agency and bring about change were: 1) that practitioners needed greater access to formal power structures; 2) that participants needed to develop more professional recognition and credibility (which they believed to be linked to having more power); 3) that legislation must be radically changed; and 4) that patriarchal power relations and structures must be dismantled. Deconstruction of participants' narratives, demonstrated that all of these assumptions operated to further reinforce their sense of disempowerment and lack of capacity to work towards change.

Other Constructions?

This research does not claim that any of the changes that were deemed necessary to promote the conditions for better legal processes and outcomes for victims/survivors have occurred. However, participants' accounts do suggest that even in the most disempowering contexts that practitioners were able to envision agency and power to bring about change. This was possible because the changes or solutions originally thought to be necessary conform to the original construction of the problem that renders other change practices and possibilities invisible – a feature of logocentric thinking (Derrida cited in Gregory 2007: 131–47). Changing this construction of the problem and participants' positioning in relation to it enabled different understandings to develop and different practice possibilities to emerge.

Paralleling this, innovative feminist writers are similarly developing alternative constructions of problems, when the original construction represents a barrier to achieving feminist ideals, by reconstructing notions of change (see for example Almeras 2001, Carmody 2003, Carmody and Carrington 2000, Mills 1996,

Thomas and Davies 2005). White (2006) for example, identifies possibilities for resisting the detrimental impact of dominant discourses of managerialism on feminist social work. Consistent with work by Thomas and Davies (2005), she notes that:

> ideas about resistance have been extended beyond a narrow focus on the collective activities of oppressed women towards a wider appreciation of resistance as multifaceted. This opens up a view of resistance that does not have to be synonymous with large-scale transformation, as depicted by the dominant perspective in feminist social work literature, but can encompass a range of challenges by women social workers, working in and against managerialism for more critical forms of practice that seek to engage with furthering women's interests. (White 2006: 144–5)

Presenting a related argument, which reconceptualises modernist notions of power, change and agency, Kenney (2003: 179) contends that we must begin to see change as 'produced by networks of insiders and outsiders rather than exclusively caused by elites in formal positions'. Participants' initial stories tended to confirm much of what was already known about the problems with the legal response to sexual assault and the level of structural disempowerment experiences by both practitioner and victims/survivors. However despite this, practitioners' reconstructed accounts indicate that insights drawn from critical postmodern theory and critical reflection facilitate different, more enabling and empowering interpretations of the situation to be produced.

Fay (1977 cited in Fook and Askeland 2006: 43) argues that the ways in which individuals understand themselves 'is embedded in the social structure and that therefore if choices about social circumstances are revealed, then opportunities for personal control are provided'. In this sense, although the structural conditions within the legal system are seen as determining, practitioners could still create possibilities for change through using critical reflection to develop new understandings; a phenomenon that has been documented about critical reflection in other contexts (Fook and Napier 2000: 223, Gardner 2013, Morley 2004). This accords with the literature that suggests that critical reflection can be used to release practitioners from hegemonic assumptions (Brookfield 2000), particularly in relation to creating possibilities to imagine power and agency through exposing and unsettling 'dominant assumptions with the expressed purpose of challenging and changing dominant power relations' (Fook and Askeland, 2006: 47). In this sense, critical reflection:

> maximises the practitioner's ability to see possibilities for change, and thus maximises (but does not guarantee) their ability to influence change. Change is comprised of many factors, many unpredictable and unknown. Critical reflection simply maximises one aspect – the practitioner's agency and role. By retheorising change and its possibilities, so that the social worker actor is

> located directly within the possibilities, critical reflection can be an enabling and empowering tool. (Fook and Napier 2000: 224)

Participants' accounts essentially demonstrate this process using the prism of the legal system as an example.

Related to this, Almeras (2001: 54) similarly emphasises the agency of individuals, or the efficacy of localised responses for working towards change, drawing on Castoriadis' concepts of radical imagination and the social imaginary (Castoriadis 1998 cited in Almeras 2001). Almeras (2001) argues that individual changes in the attitudes and behaviours of men may create new constructions of masculinity that reject the domination of women and lead to collective change that can challenge discrimination and violence against women. She further explains that violence against women:

> is a historical product of the imaginary constitution of society, its social imaginary. As a primary network of social imaginary significations, patriarchy fabricates individuals in reference to these significations, imposing on society a patriarchal code where violence against women is part of a given symbolic system. (Almeras 2001: 55)

Almeras also argues that 'when men denounce violence against women they are challenging the context of the traditional imagery of power and violence that constitutes the masculine norm. This type of challenge of radical imagination leads to the creation of new forms and is essential for change' (Almeras 2001: 55).

Reconstructed Practices of Agency, Resistance and Change

Arguably, the change practices implied by theorists such as Almeras (2001), Carmody (2003), Carmody and Carrington (2000), Kenney (2003), Lancaster and Lumb (1999), Mills (1996), Thomas and Davies (2005), White (2006) and the practitioners who participated in this research, have clear implications for enabling practitioners to envision power and agency in concrete, tangible and meaningful ways that facilitate the possibility of more satisfactory processes and outcomes for victims/survivors. Participants' accounts suggest that while structural changes were not achieved, structural change is not the only way to achieve the emancipatory aims of feminist practice. They developed a range of creative and critical practice responses to address a variety of ostensibly structural problems that were affecting their service users' experiences. These practices took numerous forms. For example, the problem of not being able to access the public prosecutor until the day of the trial (Mitchell et al. 1995, Townsend 1996) (initially seen as a structural problem due to the hierarchical and inaccessible nature of the legal system and its personnel), was addressed by reconstructing opportunities to advocate for a meeting to occur between the public prosecutor and the victim/survivor prior to the trial.

Similarly, in revaluing micro change practices, participants created possibilities to prepare child witnesses differently for the court process, including arguing more persuasively for particular conditions that might make a difference to the way they are able to provide evidence. This includes encouraging children to rehearse their testimonies prior to giving evidence in court. Despite this practice being described as problematic in legal discourse (see for example Child Safety Services 2009), participants created new discourses that validated this type of preparation as a legitimate and necessary part of the process. The reconstructed discourses privilege understandings of appropriate preparation based on children's developmental stages and the imperative for children to be supported during the legal process.

Other writers, too, are beginning to use critical reflection to make their practice more genuinely responsive to the needs of children (Cosier 2008: 45–59, Tseris 2008: 30–43). Critical reflection enabled one child protection officer, for example, to reconsider her practice of pressuring children to submit to forensic medical examinations. Deconstructing her practice enabled her to acknowledge that she had uncritically adopted dominant legal and medical discourses that defined the child's best interests in terms of compliance. This led her to neglect the emotional impact of such an examination on a child. However, deconstruction enabled her to recognise and resist her assumption that a medical examination was the '"normal" thing to do, and … that being examined by the doctor is "good for" or in the "best interests" of the patient' (Cosier, 2008: 49).

Linking these reflective observations about child protection practice with the participants' accounts from this study highlights the capacity for practitioners to identify dominant discourses and reconstruct alternatives that enable resistance to the pressure for practice to become 'task-focused rather than client-focused' (Cosier 2008: 55), or 'less "forensic" and more "relational"' (Fook and Gardner 2007: 139), particularly in statutory environments that are often viewed as 'more reactive than reflective' (Baker 2012: 118). Because deconstruction involves examining how discourses are implicated in particular ways of thinking (Ellermann 1998, Rossiter 2005), other literature similarly outlines how practitioners are using critical reflection to uncover 'adult-centred' discourses of children's participation within the child protection system that fail to achieve their espoused aim of incorporating the perspectives of children (Tseris 2008: 39). This demonstrates how '[c]ritical discourse analysis gives researchers [and practitioners] 'permission' to 'take sides' and 'actively participate in order to uncover, demystify or otherwise challenge dominance' (van Dijk 1997: 22 cited in Naudi 2006: 118).

Other change practices to emerge from this research include presenting the victim/survivor's case more convincingly so that certain aspects of the process can be favourably adjusted, and presenting alternative discourses for legal professionals to consider. This parallels the work of Philadelphoff-Puren (2004) who explores the implications of drawing on poststructuralist theories of language to reconstruct understandings of women's refusal and consent during sexual assault trials, and Erlich (2001), who has similarly undertaken research that analyses the constitutive role of language in sexual assault cases. Philadelphoff-Puren (2004: 243) suggests that instead of adopting the feminist strategy to enforce the understanding that 'no means no' we should focus on the ways women's refusals are reinterpreted as consent through the 'institutional rewriting of rape as romance'. In this way she expands Stephen's (1994) attempts to reconstruct rape by drawing on feminist critiques of the evidence of phallocentrism within the law. While Stephen (1994: 226) argues that 'we should listen more to what women have to say about the rape experiences and what they understand them to mean', Philadelphoff-Puren draws on Butler (1997) who uses poststructuralist theory to explore the relationship between language and politics, and challenges the contention that women are able to say no and have it interpreted in the manner that they intend by a range of people in different contexts. Given that requiring women to explicitly say 'no' contravenes established cultural norms of expressing refusal or resistance, Philadelphoff-Puren (2004: 244) argues that 'it is counter-productive for feminism (or the law) to require and encourage women to say 'no', when this request ... might actually obscure and delegitimise the real work of refusal that women actually perform in sexually violent situations'. In addition, she argues that feminist approaches that have attempted to legislate 'no means no' are problematic, because of the ways in which 'no' can be reinterpreted as 'yes' in hegemonic patriarchal contexts. She suggests that:

> [t]he principal political problem for women is that their refusal is able to be *recontextualised* within the coordinates of a discourse that will both extinguish the efficacy of that refusal and exonerate the actions of the men who assault in spite of their resistance. (Philadelphoff-Puren 2004: 251)

Also contributing to this linguistic scholarship on sexual assault trials, Erlich (2001:1) has similarly demonstrated that the language used during judicial proceedings serves not only to 'revictimize victims' but has a 'role in defining and delimiting the meanings that came to be attached to the events and subjects under scrutiny'. As she explains: '"Seeing" the events and participants in question was not a transparent process, but one made opaque and partial by a range of culturally – and institutionally-authorized linguistic practices' (Erlich 2001:1). Indeed, she provides empirical substance to support the claims that such discursive practices render victims/survivors' stories 'unrecognisable and imperceptible', highlighting the primacy of analysing and understanding 'discourse in constructing and constituting social realities' (Erlich 2001: 11).

Reconstructed practice is therefore broadened from a narrow focus on the problems of law or the political struggle of women to own how their refusal is interpreted in the trial process, to encompass transforming the '*cultural* texts which stage the unreliability of women's speech' (Philadelphoff-Puren 2004: 254, italics in original). Both Erlich (2001) and Philadelphoff-Puren (2004) demonstrate the capacity for practitioners to reconsider how they might challenge linguistic constructions of concepts like, for example, refusal and sexual consent.

Expanding the range of reconstructed practice, the participants in this research also demonstrated related practice strategies for change involving more collaborative work with legal personnel, such as initiating more active support roles. For example, instead of feeling marginalised or excluded from legal processes and meetings, participants imagined possibilities for challenging their perceived exclusion through developing more inclusive and collaborative means or working such as taking the initiative to arrange meetings and inviting the relevant legal personnel to participate. The process resonates with practitioners from other fields who have described critical reflection as 'crucial in helping me to uncover my own assumptions, how these are challenged, and how I would like to work towards changing them along more empowering lines' (Evans 2008: 13, see also Gardner 2013).

Participants also created agency to respond to the structural issues of dominant mythology and technical rules of evidence in court that are perceived to undermine victims/survivors' testimonies. This was achieved by creating opportunities to exercise power and influence the discourse that informs the ways in which victims/survivors' testimonies of sexual assault are understood. The notion that power can be exercised through re-authoring the discourse (Foucault 1987 cited in Featherstone and Fawcett 1995) has been acknowledged by many writers and used in a variety of different contexts to create change (see for example Alberti 2000, Cosier 2008, Ellermann 1998, Evans 2008, Fook 2012, Healy 2000, Morley 2004, 2009, 2011, 2012, Mullaly 2002: 21–3, Kicuroski 2008, Rossiter, 2005, Taylor and White 2006, Tseris 2008, Wieczorek 2008). The emancipatory potential of this reconstruction is captured by Rubensohn (2008: 90), who states, 'One's choice of discourse can be a profound act of resistance'. This practice potentially creates a capacity for practitioners to increase the credibility of victims/survivors' testimonies in the eyes of police, magistrates and jurors. This discretionary space change was developed in concrete terms with the idea that practitioners request that the prosecution subpoena them as expert witnesses so that they may express their opinions on how children's developmental stages and subsequent trauma affect the ways in which they give evidence in court. This potentially reframes cross-examination as an opportunity to inform the court, including the legal personnel and jury members, and debunk social myths, instead of the practitioner experiencing unequivocal disempowerment as has previously occurred and been comprehensively documented.

Further opportunities for practitioners to bring about change were generated by the research when they reconstructed their views of power and their own position vis-à-vis the police and other legal personnel. Some practitioners, for example, reconstructed their assumptions that challenging dominant power relations would inevitably involve negative consequences, by reinterpreting the sharing of their expectations with the police and other legal professionals as an opportunity to educate them. This reconstructed practitioners with the power and responsibility to challenge inappropriate conduct by professionals involved in the law, while more effectively supporting and advocating for their service users.

Practitioners also envisaged potential opportunities to create change in response to the problem of sexually abused children falling through the well-documented gaps in the system that occur when the police and child protection agencies have failed to obtain disclosures (see for example Sjöberg and Lindblad 2002: 312–14). By transcending the artificial dichotomy that practitioners had created between their philosophical position of belief and the child protection system's commitment to investigation, participants recognised that they could maintain their belief while *also* conducting specialised children's assessments. Further critical reflection enabled practitioners who work as counsellors/advocates to see that they are well placed to conduct the assessments that can provide them with further opportunities to take control of the discourse, disseminate knowledge and influence the contexts and ways in which children's disclosures of sexual assault are understood. This is potentially an active response to a major structural and systemic problem (Child Safety Services 2009, Sjöberg and Lindblad 2002: 312–14), and parallels the assertions of other writers who have referred to the need for practitioners to transcend dichotomous constructions in practice. As one author comments:

> A "child-centred" discourse of participation has the potential to create a more useful interpretation of [the professional] role, because it does not necessarily view the multiple responsibilities of a child protection worker as disconnected from one another, nor does it set them up in a hierarchical fashion … "child-centred" practice implies creating social justice outcomes for children in a broad sense, and can therefore incorporate the responsibility of social workers to pursue both protective and participatory practices. (Tseris 2008: 40)

These examples offer insight into how even in the contexts where service users are subject to clear structural disadvantage and disempowerment, and practitioners' options for envisioning agency and creating discretionary practice space to agitate for change appear to be extremely limited, local acts of resistance in practitioner's day-to-day practices can create significant possibilities for change. This enables practitioners to develop the agency to respond to structural issues that have been previously assumed to only be responsive to broad institutional changes. Todd's (2005: 138) commentary, which draws on Pile's (1997) suggestion that the 'production of "inner spaces", marks out the real break point of political struggle', becomes relevant here. She suggests that instead of focusing exclusively on traditional stereotypical activities associated with social change and social activism, such as large-scale political demonstrations, we should begin to question 'whether resistance may be as much an internal practice as an external one' (Todd 2005: 138). It is instructive that Todd does not oppose external large-scale change to internal resistance and believes that neither should be privileged, 'but rather co-existing and supporting each other' (Todd 2005: 138).

Such reconstructions not only reposition practitioners in the discourse as more empowered responsible agents, but also demonstrate how reconstructing our thinking highlights different practice possibilities for change that had previously been fatalistically constructed as structural in nature and therefore unchangeable (Fook 2007a: 372). This builds on the literature that suggests that the theory and practice of critical reflection can mitigate the forces of fatalism (Fook 2004: 22–6). Furthermore, these reconstructed practices highlight some of the ways that modernist structural analyses, that were initially informing participants' perceptions, unintentionally rendered these change practices as invisible. These changes therefore provide some empirical evidence of the capacity of critical reflection to produce identifiable outcomes in a systematic way, which is still developing in the current research literature (Fook 2008: vii, Fook et al. 2006: 7). The following section will expand this discussion in explaining how critical reflection was integral in assisting practitioners to connect with their sense of agency.

2) Critical Reflection Is a Powerful Tool to Assist Practitioners to Connect With Their Sense of Agency

Participants' accounts provide empirical evidence for the claim that critical reflection can be a useful process for practitioners in a range of contexts (Fook 2004, 2012, Fook and Askeland 2006: 47–57, 2007: 521, Fook and Gardner 2013, Morley 2008b, Napier 2006: 9–15, Pockett and Giles, 2008). Those who participated in this research were able to use critical reflection to develop theory and practice, and ultimately create new possibilities for change. This segment discusses why and how critical reflection enabled practitioners in this project to envisage their capacity to bring about the changes outlined above. In particular, it is argued that critical reflection was able to facilitate practitioners' sense of agency by: i) improving the match between their espoused theory and their practice; ii) enabling practitioners to make their practice more critical; and iii) highlighting practitioners' participation in unhelpful discourses and constructing narratives that emphasised their capacity for resistance and change. In what follows I will summarise some of the benefits of critical reflection as indicated by the changes that occurred in participants' thinking and practice during the processes of deconstruction and reconstruction, and relate these to the literature that discusses some of the broad uses of critical reflection (see for example Fook and Gardner 2007: 139–40).

i) The Capacity for Critical Reflection to Improve Congruence Between Participants' Espoused Theory and Their Actual Practice

For most of the participants critical reflection highlighted a disparity between their espoused intentions and their practice; a phenomenon well documented in reflective approaches to learning (Argyris and Schon 1976, Schon 1983, 1987) and practice (see for example Fook 2012: 45, Fook et al. 2006: 8–13). During the research process, participants used critical reflection to improve congruency between feminist theory or their intended practice, and their actual practice (Morley 2009, 2011, 2012).

Differences between theory and practice in this sense were probably first identified by educationalists Argyris and Schon (1976) and later developed further by Schon (1983, 1987) who proposed a reflective process for uncovering hidden assumptions, particularly in relation to professional learning. Some authors also credit the earlier work of Dewey (1916; 1933) as being formative in the development of our current understanding of uses of reflective practice (Fook et al. 2006: 8, Mezirow and Associates 1990, 2000, Redmond 2004).

The anomalies between participants' theory and practice took numerous forms. For example, most practitioners had the overt intention to empower the victims/survivors they were working with, yet deconstruction of their accounts uncovered a number of ways in which they had unintentionally contributed to a sense of hopelessness and disempowerment in both themselves and the victims/survivors they were working with (Moffat 1999). This was evident in practitioners' narratives through their use of victimised language to describe service users, their construction of dichotomous categories between victims/survivors and the legal system, hence positioning themselves in opposition to dominant power structures and relations.

Some participants revealed this unwitting disempowerment of service users through the omission of their perspective when recounting their story. This disparity between an intention to privilege the voice of the service users on one hand, and a practice that marginalises or excludes their experiences on the other, has been documented by practitioners in other fields. For example, Tseris (2008: 33), a child protection practitioner, observed of her own practice 'that the very process aimed at giving' the child she was working with 'a voice would in fact disempower him further'. Tseris (2008) discovered that her narrative about her practice with the child had privileged her own interpretation and excluded his perspective. This exposed the incongruence between her espoused commitment to genuine collaboration with the service user, and her actual practice. This sort of disparity between theory and practice has also been identified by Kicuroski (2008), a practitioner in mental health who, in the deconstruction of his narrative, used critical reflection in order to reveal how he had neglected to include the perspective of his client, despite aiming to be participatory in his approach. Similar to participants in this research, his deconstruction highlighted the incongruence between his theoretical commitment to empower service users and his practice that had inadvertently disempowered his client and undermined his emancipatory aims. As Kicuroski (2008: 63 citing Napier, 2006) acknowledges, critical reflection exposes the 'difference between espoused theoretical ideas and values, and actual practices'.

Another example of the gap between espoused theoretical intention and practice is clearly documented elsewhere in the literature, with for example, one manager's account of his attempt at enthusiastically introducing critical reflection sessions into his team supervision responsibilities within a statutory context. Despite laudable intentions, he describes struggling to do this in a way that way that was consistent with the emancipatory goals of critical reflection (Baker 2013).

Other writers have similarly identified 'a difference between the theory implicit in action ("theory in use") and the theoretical assumptions ... [that were] consciously articulate[d] ("espoused theory")' (Fook: 1996: 4) This confirms the view that critical reflection can assist practitioners to recognise a multitude of perspectives (see for example Brookfield 1995, Gardner et al. 2006, Griffin 2003: 207–20, Hess 1995: 80), especially those of the client (Redmond 2004, Morley 2008b). The practitioners' accounts from this research additionally confirm a number of other contentions that have been made about critical reflection including that it identifies the gaps between theory and practice, and assists practitioners to devise strategies to address them; that critical reflection can result in increased self-awareness (Tsang 2003), self-discovery (Maich et al. 2000), self-affirmation/directedness (Napier 2006), enhanced self-evaluation (Griffin 2003), increased sense of mastery, control and self-actualisation (Fook and Askeland 2006), and greater acceptance of ambiguity (Grant 2001) and uncertainty (Tsang 2003). Participants who undertook this process of also validated the assertion that critical reflection can result in an increased understanding of reflexivity that allows practitioners to analyse a situation with a heightened appreciation of their involvement within it (Fook 2004, Gardner et al. 2006: 229–31, Morley 2008b).

This was the case for participants who thought that they had exhausted all possibilities for supporting and advocating for victims/survivors, and then were surprised to learn of the many different avenues for practice that critical reflection had exposed. The process of critical reflection opens 'up new ways of understanding and responding, which may not have otherwise been considered' (see also Fook 2007b: 371–2, Tseris 2008: 31). This supports the argument that those who engage in critical reflection develop greater awareness of the options available to them (Fook and Askeland 2006: 48–52) and are able to conceptualise decisions they need to make about practice in broader terms (Fook 2004: 22–6). Deconstruction of the assumptions embedded in participants' narratives highlighted a multitude of practice options that had been rendered invisible or impossible by dominant discourses that practitioners were initially using, or by a sense of fatalism that had made alternative options for practice seem pointless. Fook and Askeland (2006: 51) describe critical reflection as enabling practitioners to develop a greater awareness of available choices:

> moving usually from framing choices in "forced choice" terms to provide multiple choices, and sometimes from a more fatalistic frame ("dilemma") to a more empowered form ("opportunity"). These ways of reframing understandings of practice provide more opportunities for new practices. In this process participants also experience a "liberation" or empowerment, as if freed

> from ways of constructing a situation, which restrict options and ways of doing and being.

So, while critical reflection highlighted a gap between practitioners' theoretical commitment to provide the most effective support possible and their capacity to do this in practice, it also created opportunities for reconstruction. This process further involves an:

> understanding of how individual people might challenge, resist, and remake the ways social structures play out in their lives. Part of this process involves creating an awareness of how hidden assumptions behind our practice may be directly influenced by social contexts or social learning ... Second comes a recognition of how this thinking may be undesirable or restrictive, thus limiting the range of options for practice, and sometimes for self-recognition ... Third comes a reframing of professional practice. (Fook and Askeland 2006: 52)

In this research, part of this reframing of professional practice took the form of creating opportunities to make practice more critical. As Fook and Askeland (2006: 41) explain, '[i]n critical reflection the material that is being reflected upon is filtered through an analysis based on critical theory'. Critical perspectives aim to challenge dominant power structures and relations, including positivistic, exploitative and oppressive understandings of the world (see for example Agger 1998, Brookfield 2001, Fook and Askeland 2006, Rossiter 1996). The capacity for critical reflection to enable practitioners to make their practice more critical will be discussed next.

ii) The Capacity for Critical Reflection to Enable Practitioners to Make Their Practice More Critical

The model of reflective practice developed by Argyris and Schon (1976) and Schon (1983; 1987) to identify and address gaps between theory and practice was later expounded by Fook (1996, 2002, 2007) who used the 'critical incident technique' (Brookfield 1990, Flanagan 1954, Fook and Askeland 2006). Fook (2002, 2012) also draws upon more critical contributions to reflection (Brookfield 1995, 2000, 2012, Mezirow and Associates 1990, 2000) to combine postmodern and critical theories as a basis for critical reflection in social work. A number of theorists have refined our appreciation of critical reflection by contributing to the development of discourse analysis (Ellermann 1998, Taylor and White 2000, White and Stancombe 2003) using postmodern thinking in reflection (Lesnick 2005, Parker 1997), narrative-based approaches to develop interpretive, naturalistic and participative methodologies (Frost 2006: 107), hermeneutic inquiry to develop a deeper understanding of social processes, and reflexivity (Fook 2007b, Fook and Gardner, 2007: 27–30). Expanding on the reflective model that assisted participants in this research to identify and uncover the disparities between their theory and practice, discussion of this theme outlines some of the ways in which practice was improved using critical reflection by aligning it with their espoused intentions.

Fook (2004: 20) suggests that adding a critical dimension to a reflective model of practice contributes 'a broader framework for understanding what critical reflection can and should help achieve'. Some of the specific principles of critical theory include:

- Connecting personal experience with structural issues – including an understanding of how individual experience is socially constructed and influenced by social and political factors. This includes a critical analysis of the intimate relationship between knowledge and power;
- An analysis of how power operates both at structural and personal levels, including an awareness of how individuals can exercise personal power and agency within structurally defined contexts;
- Praxis – and explicit appreciation of the connection between theory and practice;
- A commitment to social transformation, particularly with concern to how our everyday actions might enhance social justice ideals or equally might contribute to dominance of others and the bolstering of our own privilege, despite our intentions to combat harmful power relations;
- An analysis of how people respond to the broader social inequalities that shape their life and how they use critical reflection to reconstruct their identities, opportunities and circumstances;
- An emphasis on questioning taken-for-granted assumptions and developing an openness to a range of different sources of knowledge and alternative perspectives (for example, empirical knowledge and non-positivist, inclusive, subjective ways of knowing);
- An understanding of how the words that we use to label our experiences create (inter)action and power relations; and
- Critical reflexivity on our own beliefs, theory-bases and practice (see for example Allan et al. 2009, Fook 2012, Fook and Askeland 2006, Mullaly 2007).

This broader critical understanding provided a framework to allow practitioners to evaluate their practices and consider their intended purposes. For example, despite participants having a clear commitment to protecting victims/survivors from oppression, some participants occasionally acquiesced when police or other legal and medical professionals acted in hostile and dismissive ways towards victims/survivors. Sometimes the inaction was justified by a belief that resistance would create serious consequences. Fear of 'rocking the boat' was an important motivating force for ensuring participants' compliance with dominant power relations, confirming the argument that emotions such as fear can adversely influence professional practice (see for example Brookfield 1995, Fook and Askeland 2007: 527, Fook and Gardner 2007: 103). As Brookfield (1995: 39) explains, in the process of a practice becoming the 'object of systematic inquiry … any critically reflective journey involves our negotiating feelings of impostorship, lost innocence, and cultural suicide along the way'.

Deconstruction of participants' accounts revealed the ways that these emotions, and a number of implicit values and assumptions were operating contrary to practitioners' theories, their intended practices and the interests of the victim/survivor. Identifying these values, assumptions and emotions, and recognising their consequences for practice enabled participants to change them and to reconstruct their practice in ways that gave them 'permission' to challenge the unfair practices they had witnessed. Developing consistency between participants' feminist frameworks and their practices created change possibilities in the form of challenging the police, other legal professionals and medical professionals in ways that had previously seemed inconceivable.

While the often inappropriate and insensitive responses of the police are well documented (see for example Fileborn 2011, VLRC 2008), a focus on such external factors diverted practitioners' attention from their responsibility to protect the victim/survivor from dominating forces. Critical practice invokes the need to advocate appropriately for victims/survivors and ensure that their rights are respected in the process of their engagement with the police and other professionals.

Using critical reflection to scrutinise practice for the purposes of improving it (Fook et al. 2006: 8–10) enabled participants to recognise the injustices in the interaction between legal professionals and processes, and the victim/survivor. It highlighted the need to advocate for the victim/survivor in order to intervene and challenge unfair processes and responses. This process also enabled practitioners to develop a more contextualised understanding of their situations and located their experiences within the wider socio-political environment; a concept linked with critical reflection elsewhere (Fook and Askeland 2006: 50–52, Gardner 2013, Gardner et al. 2006: 220–31). As Fook (2008: vii) argues, critical reflection creates the possibility 'for professionals to find ways to act more *responsibly* in uncertain environments, by being able to create knowledge which is more directly *responsive* to specific situations deriving directly from their own experience' (italics in original). Hence, critical reflection enabled participants to link critical theory with practice and to generate theory inductively from reflecting on and reconstructing their practice experience, thus developing theory with more personalised meaning (Fook and Gardner 2007: 140).

Highlighting the need for practitioners to interrogate how their practice might depart from their critical intentions, other writers have warned that '[s]ocial workers are not immune to the influences of society, so they need to be constantly assessing and questioning their own views and practices, to ensure that they are not in fact, replicating the very things they so vehemently oppose' (Tseris 2008: 45). This is supported by Cosier (2008: 47) who recognises that 'enthusiasm does not guarantee good practice: even the best intentions can be misguided'. It also resonates with participants' accounts as some practitioners discussed their intention to advocate 'strongly' for victims/survivors, but had overlooked how they had participated in oppositional power relations that worked against those intentions. Such recognition led most participants to rethink the ways in which they had conceptualised their relationships with other professionals and develop more collegial approaches; an outcome of critical reflection that has been acknowledged elsewhere (Fook 2007b: 371, Fook and Gardner 2007: 139, Maich et al. 2000: 309–24).

At other times, practitioners lamented the power and inaccessibility of the legal system, yet actively avoided opportunities to advocate for change, instead choosing to conform to particular processes that preserved dominant power relations. An issue also discussed in the literature by Cosier (2008), for example, cites an example of her practice that oppressed a child who had been sexually assaulted by coaxing her into having a forensic examination. She states: 'at the time I sincerely thought that what I was doing was right, but immediately afterward I began to think that my actions may, in fact, have contradicted the values I claimed to be supporting' (Cosier 2008: 47). This example confirms participants' accounts of how critical reflection can enable them to develop an awareness of their implicit assumptions (Gardner et al. 2006: 229–31), and begin to think and act more critically (Fook and Gardner 2007: 139-40, 194, Maich et al. 2000: 309–24, Morley 2004, 2008b).

Mills (1996: 266) makes similar observations about the legal responses to female victims/survivors of domestic violence. She argues that 'staunch feminist' practitioners may inappropriately impose their expectations on victims/survivors in ways that deny their 'uncertainty and emotional and cultural loyalties' when making decisions about leaving a violent partner. She argues that for women in this situation, 'criminal interventions as they are currently designed may be completely unresponsive to their needs' (Mills 1996: 263). She advocates the use of postmodern informed approaches to guide practice as these ways of knowing recognise that relational notions of justice are non-linear, and validate the subjective and interactive aspects of victims/survivors' experiences. She argues that domestic violence services need to be fluid, responsive to women's needs and to:

> recognise that true empowerment for battered women is achieved not through obedience to the expectations of legal or social work advocates … but through acknowledgement of the woman's need to reconsider and re-evaluate the meaning of the trauma in a flexible time frame and supportive environment. (Mills 1996: 266)

A major catalyst of this capacity to think and act more critically was participants' recognition of how dominant ideologies and discourses had become embedded and reproduced in their own thinking. Developing this awareness created opportunities for them to reconstruct narratives that emphasise their agency for resistance and change. This practice has been discussed elsewhere in other contexts (see for example Alberti 2000, Brown 2012, Gardner et al. 2006: 229–31) and will be the focus of attention in the next section.

iii) The Capacity for Critical Reflection to Create Opportunities for Resistance and Change

A significant element of practitioners being able to conceptualise and enact their practice in more critical terms involved uncovering the ways in which they may have participated in discourses that were unhelpful for their practice. One example is participants' exclusive reliance on structural factors to theorise the situations in which they were working. The emphasis on external aspects of the problem, such as the impact of patriarchy and dominant social mythology on the legal process, along with inadequate legislation, led them to emphasise systemic, legal barriers to change. One inadvertent consequence of this was that it subjugated the concerns of the service users and minimised practitioners' direct responsibility to respond to them. Similar concerns have been documented in the literature that critiques feminist approaches for politicising the needs of service users at the expense of responding in a meaningful way to their personal circumstances (see for example Payne 2005: 246–9) or for uncritically reproducing dominant power relations (Todd 2005: 137).

Furthermore, this emphasis on structural factors resulted in an overwhelming sense of powerlessness for some practitioners who felt alienated from the means of change. Accordingly, a number of the research participants consistently constructed their roles in limited ways that suggested they had no capacity to respond. This resonates with commentary from other fields of practice where dominant discourses have been identified as heavily represented in social workers' world views (Morley 2004, 2007, Naudi 2006: 118). Alberti (2000) for example, used critical reflection to deconstruct her sense of powerlessness and reconstruct her thinking and practice in ways that allowed her to challenge the misuse of power in a prison setting. By recognising the fragmentation in the prison in which she worked, she was able to transcend her sense of powerlessness in relation to the prison authorities and devise a program that was both more empowering for the prisoners *and* more desirable to the authorities.

With regard to the research presented in this book, one of the ways in which dominant discourses undermined participants' accounts was through the belief that changes must occur through broader structural means such as legislative reform in order to be meaningful. This has the effect of devaluing counselling as a medium of change. This discourse supports the dominant interests as it resulted in counsellors/advocates not exploiting opportunities to advocate for change to their full potential. This dichotomy between macro change and micro practice mirrors the experiences of other practitioners who are working in other contexts, such as international development (Rubensohn 2008). One author, for example, discusses her assumptions that she could not contribute towards global justice by working in a local context. Critical reflection assisted her to question the emphasis she had placed on international social work in relation to local practice in terms of the capacity of these modes to contribute to a global social justice agenda. This ultimately challenged the artificial dichotomy she had constructed between macro and micro approaches through conceptualising 'opportunities for social activism and humanitarian work in the Australian setting' (Rubensohn 2008: 79).

This kind of transformation in thinking similarly enabled the practitioners who participated in this study to transcend dominantly constructed dichotomies between macro modes of working such as policy development, legislative reform, public advocacy, and community development and education, and micro modes of practice such as individual counselling and advocacy. For these participants, reconstruction involved finding opportunities for social activism and social change within the context of working at a micro level with individuals as counsellors/advocates. Reconstruction also enabled them to be more attentive to the processes that informed their work (rather than purely focusing on outcomes) (Fook 2002: 1–18), and develop more complex and multi-dimensional perspectives of their roles (Tsang 2003). Such reconstructions exposed the limitations and disempowering implications of legal discourses that only recognise and value legislative change. Recognition of the ways that dominant legal discourses had colonised participants' accounts was therefore instrumental in creating sites for resistance and change (Fook 2002: 94–6).

Research indicates that practitioners often do not recognise their own capacity to exercise power (Napier and Fook 2000). This resonated with the research participants' initial presentations of their critical incidents, which, when deconstructed, unearthed the unintended consequences for practitioners of seeing themselves as powerless in the face of abstract legal and structural processes. Examples such as these can also be found in the literature. Cosier, (2008: 53) for example, has analysed the notion of 'the disempowered advocate' and suggests that 'a person's ability to empower others can be limited by their own disempowered state'. If practitioners see themselves as disempowered, 'this may inhibit their ability to adequately advocate for their clients. Social workers may think that seeking to empower themselves is self-serving, but on the contrary this may be important, as it may increase their ability to empower their clients' (Cosier 2008: 57).

In this research, participants' accounts indicate that reconstruction enabled them to gain a greater sense of personal empowerment through creating alternative narratives that emphasise their agency for resistance and change (Fook and Askeland 2006: 48–50). They deconstructed their own identities as powerless, passive, ineffectual workers, and constructed other narratives that privileged the active support functions of their roles. The initial desire to eschew power expressed by some participants transformed into a discovery made by another practitioner that their power 'neither can, nor should be, repressed' (Tseris 2008: 37). This involved the development of a more nuanced and sophisticated understanding of power that recognises that power can be used in productive ways; an observation documented by others (see for example Fook and Askeland 2006, Gardner et al. 2006, Tseris 2008). Practitioners also became aware of how, through their participation in discourse, they used and resisted power thus enabling them to change their actions. These reconstructed accounts confirm Fook's (2004) contention that practitioners from inter-professional groups who engage in critical reflection experience a transformative process, including developing a more holistic sense of personal and professional identity. As Fook and Askeland (2006: 51) state:

> individual workers can use critical reflection to reconstitute themselves as potentially powerful, able to exercise agency in influencing situations. This involves a revaluing of self through: shifting the sources of self-value from social environment to themselves; valuing characteristics which were formerly thought to be non-professional; and reintegrating these characteristics into their professional identities.

Furthermore, practitioners' changed views of the victims/survivors they were working with, from powerless receptacles of unjust structural processes to responsible agents capable of exercising power, agency, and resistance, contributed to more helpful and holistic understandings of power and identity. As others have acknowledged, while clients may have been subjected to great social disadvantage and oppression, 'this should not be interpreted to mean that [they are] *powerless*' (Cosier 2008: 56, italics in original). Reconstruction of the narrative to consider service users as possessing 'great *potential* for power' overcomes the unintended disempowering inference of 'labelling the client as powerless' (Cosier 2008: 56, italics in original). A 'client's disempowered position is not seen to be a characteristic implicit in himself/herself (and therefore unchangeable), but rather is a socially constructed position, (created and therefore able to be altered) through the ways in which others interact with the client' (Cosier 2008: 56).

The participants, who developed an understanding of the ways in which they personally contributed to shaping the identities of service users through their practice and use of language, made quite radical shifts. In one case, the mother who was initially seen by the practitioner as powerless and victimised, became seen as someone who took action to protect her daughter from further abuse (Morley 2012). Similarly, a number of other authors have identified practitioners' capacity to reconstruct the identities of themselves and their clients in more empowered terms (see for example Evans 2008: 7, Wieczorek 2008). This process of identity reconstruction, along with the other examples of critically reflective learning that enabled practitioners to identify and resist participation in unhelpful discourses, and to subsequently create opportunities to reconstruct narratives that emphasise practitioners' capacity for resistance and change, is assisted by the theoretical underpinnings that inform the critical reflection process (Fook 2012, Fook and Gardner 2007: 22–39). Some of the principles of critical postmodern thinking about identity (Fook 2012: 70–71, Healy 2000: 54, Sands 1996, Seidman 2004: 212) therefore provide a crucial aspect to the practice of critical reflection that enables practitioners to transform their capacities to envision agency and power to bring about change.

Conclusion

Ultimately, this chapter has explored how critical reflection on practice might develop possibilities for change. The discussion has focused on the two most significant themes including: 1) that even in the most disempowered contexts, it is possible for practitioners to envision agency and power to bring about change; 2) and that critical reflection is a powerful tool in assisting practitioners to connect with this sense of agency. An exploration of these themes has illustrated that critical reflection did in fact indicate various possibilities to enhance change practices with the legal system. The broader implications of these significant themes were discussed and it was evident that insights drawn from critical postmodern analysis were an important ingredient to assist the participants to work towards emancipatory practice in challenging contexts. The following chapter summarises the most fundamental ways that feminist practices were enhanced by utilising critical postmodern theory.

Chapter 10
Critical Postmodern Theory: Enhancing Feminist Practices and Prospects for Change

Introduction

This chapter explicates how critical postmodern theory was integral to enabling the practitioners to reconstruct their practice, and explores some of the contextual considerations when thinking through the implications of the research. Critical postmodern thinking assisted participants to enhance feminist practice and improve prospects for emancipatory change. This observation may be particularly useful for practitioners who want to incorporate feminist ideals into their work, despite operating in contemporary contexts that may be hostile to goals and values of feminism.

Critical Postmodernism: An Important Ingredient for Contemporary Feminist Practice

As noted in Chapter 3, historically, feminist theorists and practitioners have used modernist, emancipatory ideals to guide their work. While these ideals remain constant, questions have been raised about the continuing capacity of modernist feminist approaches to produce progressive social change. Some writers have noted that the 'burgeoning body of literature on feminist social movements within history, political science, and sociology' since the 1970s has been largely ignored by some sectors of society (Kenney 2003: 179). Others contend that violence against women appears to have been largely unchanged by decades of feminist activism, and that the 'gains' of the feminist movement have largely 'failed' to deliver the change they promised (Carmody 2003: 199). Over the past two decades, feminism has been subjected to a harsh backlash (Bell and Klein 1996: xxiv–xxvi, Dominelli 2002: 54–5, Seidman 2004: 209, Weeks 2003) and we have also seen the rise of a global neo-liberalism that is hostile to feminist values, practices and services (Dominelli 2002: 41–62, Morley and Macfarlane 2008, Phillips 2008) that has resulted in many of the gains made by feminist movements being actively dismantled or threatened (Corrigan 2006, Featherstone 2005, Morley and Macfarlane 2008). The context in which feminist practitioners work is always changing and some have argued that feminist practices have lost their contemporary relevance (Carmody and Carrington 2000, 2003, Featherstone 2005, Lawrence 1992, Parton and O'Byrne, 2000: 20–21, Seidman 2004: 208–17,Wise 1995: 85–101). Others have argued more specifically that feminist theory's 'influence on social work, particularly day to day practice … is limited' (Healy 2000: 37).

In providing a response to some of these concerns, participants' accounts suggest that drawing upon insights from critical postmodern theory may enhance the applicability of feminist emancipatory ideals to practice and increase practitioners' capacities to achieve progressive social change (Eisler 2004, Goldberg Wood and Tully 2006, Todd 2005). While asserting the continued importance of feminist analyses of sexual assault and the legal system, this section explores how the participants broadened and enhanced their notions of feminist practice and theory by engaging with critical postmodern ideas.

The participants' accounts indicate that critical reflection, informed by critical postmodern analysis, enabled them to achieve the emancipatory aims of feminist practice in a number of ways. These included i) questioning dichotomous thinking; ii) reconstructing more holistic notions of professionalism; iii) reconstructing modernist notions of power; iv) reconstructing modernist notions of identity; v) reconstructing oppositional power relations; and vi) embracing diversity. Each of these will now be discussed with an emphasis on elucidating how critical postmodern thinking provided opportunities to transcend the limitations of modernist structural analysis and to develop practices that enhance the capacity of feminist approaches to meet emancipatory goals.

i) Questioning Dichotomous Thinking

Critical postmodern analysis proved to be an important inclusion for assisting practitioners to overcome some of the dichotomous constructions inherent in their initial feminist thinking. For example, an unintended consequence of using a structural/feminist framework was that practitioners were often drawn into dichotomous thinking. This assumes that the world can be divided into mutually exclusive and diametrically opposed categories such as feminist practitioners versus the police, and the victim/survivor versus the legal system.

Thinking about the world in dichotomous ways is a feature of modernist thinking (see for example Featherstone and Fawcett 1995, Fook and Napier 2000: 216). Feminism has historically used the gendered categories of masculinity and femininity to determine that, in the context of a patriarchal society, men are powerful and women are powerless, and that men are privileged while women are oppressed. The construction of dichotomous categories establishes, and is reflective of, hierarchical power relationships. Locating our experiences within the construction of these dichotomies arguably bolsters dominant power relations (Fook and Morley 2005, Morley 2005). Critical reflection, which draws upon critical postmodern analysis, was instrumental in highlighting the unhelpful nature of this binary thinking for practice, and in reconstructing more holistic alternatives.

For example, implicit within the participants' initial stories, was a binary 'us and them' construction that assumed that the counsellor/advocate role was completely separate from other involved professionals. Making this distinction more pronounced, many participants indicated a polarised understanding of the situation in which they were faced with the option of either aligning with the medical, legal, or child protection professionals whom they saw as oppressive and incompetent, or aligning with the victim/survivor whom they were committed to supporting. Consequently, participants frequently referred to the need to situate themselves as a buffer between the victim/survivor and the police as well as other professionals involved. This hid an implicit assumption about two mutually exclusive sides in which they were united with the victim/survivor in opposition to the police and other professionals.

The ways in which the participants conceptualised the advocacy component of their roles was also indicative of how they perpetuated these dichotomies. From a modernist, feminist perspective, advocacy is assumed to involve two protagonists and aims to represent the interests of the least powerful person or group to the more powerful side (Fook 2012). This was assumed in the participants' practices when they unwittingly located the victim/survivor as the weaker party in opposition to the legal and medical systems or personnel. These power dynamics are assumed to be fixed and therefore constitute 'deterministic views [which] fail to account for contradictions' (Fook 2002: 9). They cannot, for example, account for the ways in which 'victims' can and do display strength and courage, and may demonstrate other powerful characteristics in different contexts and at different times despite their experience of victimisation. Using postmodern principles to reflect critically on the construction and implications of these artificial dichotomies created opportunities to construct participants' interpretations differently, and in more complex terms.

ii) Reconstructing the Notion of Professionalism

Artificial dichotomous constructions were particularly evident in participants' initial accounts when they talked about their roles. For instance, service users were often implicitly assumed to be separate from, and powerless in relation to, workers and systems. Furthermore, despite most of the participants having a professional education and status, when invoking the notion of hierarchy they consistently assumed that the medico-legal professionals they worked with were more powerful. This was especially the case for participants whose professional identity was social work; a phenomenon acknowledged by other social workers (Lyons and Taylor 2004). This is arguably linked to a broader devaluing of social work, particularly when contrasted with other professionals who have closer disciplinary alignments with scientific and medical bodies of knowledge that are socially constructed as superior (Davies and Leonard 2004: x, Pardeck and Murphy 1993, Taylor and White 2000: 3–28). The quest for professional recognition is something with which social work seems to struggle, particularly as it has been regarded as a 'women's profession' operating in a largely masculinist context (Lyons and Taylor 2004). Indeed, the professional status of social work has been identified as a priority by the Australian Association of Social Workers, which is currently lobbying the Australian federal government to ensure that all practising social workers are registered following the introduction of initiatives such as Medicare-rebated services for specialised mental health accredited workers. However, the participants in this research generated alternative understandings of these issues that suggest different possibilities for action.

Critical reflection was used to evaluate some of the limitations of feminist analyses that unwittingly devalue the professional standing of social work through comparing it with other professions. Reconstructing this dichotomy suggests that understanding the nature of internalised oppression (Mullaly 2002: 123–5) may be more pertinent for social work practitioners who, unlike some other professionals, often aim to reduce power disparities between themselves and their service users (Healy 2000: 22–4). By respecting service users and positioning them as experts on their own experiences, social workers may feel reluctant to acknowledge their own expertise, due to concerns about creating inequitable power relations between themselves and the people with whom they work (see for example Tseris 2008).

Moreover, many women's services have grown out of community development and social activism (Weeks 2003). Critical reflection on implicit assumptions made by participants indicates that, consistent with feminist aims, most practitioners aimed to create an anti-professional culture that is consistent with this history. This anti-professional culture is designed to diminish hierarchical power relations between feminist workers and services users, and avoid the aspects of professionalism that contribute to dominating and alienating the victim/survivor with whom they work (Astbury 2006: 20, Healy 2000: 22–4). However, deconstruction highlights that a by-product of this commitment may be that some social workers feel less worthy than other professionals, as they define their practice and their professional standing in oppositional terms to the dominant construction (Fook and Morley 2005, Morley 2005).

Critical postmodern analysis was therefore useful in highlighting how participants' overt rejection of the neo-liberalist discourse about professionalism was nullified by their unintended affirmation of this discourse through taking an oppositional (and devalued) stance. Others have made similar observations about social work being displaced by masculinist constructions of professionalism that privilege scientific, evidence-based, technical/rational applications of knowledge over more reflective, intuitive, experiential, practice-based approaches to knowledge building (Davies and Leonard 2004, Fook and Askeland 2007, Kicuroski 2008, Taylor 2006, Todd 2005).

However, rather than constructing the current context which privileges the evidence-based approach in opposition to critical practice (which may ironically marginalise critical practice), a reconstructed response that resists these unhelpful dichotomies, highlights the value of critical reflection as a process for developing new insights into professional practice (Baldwin 2004, Fook 2012, Taylor 2006) and recognises that critical reflection is crucial in developing strong evidence-based practice (Fook and Gardner 2007: 195). It could be argued, for example, that professionalism need not be contrary to our critical goals: in some circumstances, 'professionalism may involve boosting the status of the professional so that the needs of service users are better met. Professionalism can also therefore promote client interests' (Fook and Napier 2000: 219).

A critically reflective epistemology of practice may rejuvenate feminist goals in a number of ways. It validates practical wisdom as a legitimate source of knowledge thereby valuing practical experience and experiential learning. It allows practitioners to be acknowledged as experts in their own right and values the artistic and intuitive aspects of professional practice, not just the technical applications of knowledge (Davies and Leonard 2004, Fook 1996: 4, Fook and Gardner 2007: 9–10, Napier 2006). With a growing recognition that society will require practitioners who are able to respond to complexities, uncertainties and ambiguities, critically reflective practice represents a theoretically sophisticated, yet egalitarian and participatory-based practice that is appropriately engaged with the interests of practitioners and the needs of service users (Fook and Askeland 2007, Mezirow 1997, Taylor and White 2006).

However, despite using critical reflection to reconstruct more useful views of professionalism, some practitioners have acknowledged that there is a 'paradox between wanting to distance [themselves] from the "expert role" (Green et al. 2006: 451) while seeking to draw from the "legitimacy" that comes with being considered a "professional"' (Wieczorek 2008: 19). This indicates how seductive these dominant discourses of professionalism can be.

The embrace of dominant constructions of professionalism and expertise, and the initial adoption of an anti-professional response by the participants in this research, may be linked to modernist beliefs that power is inherently oppressive (see for example Smith 2008: 28–32). Indeed, as highlighted in the literature review, feminist analyses have convincingly highlighted the links between gender, power and violence through examining structural power disparities between men and women, and the impact of patriarchal institutions and relations in Western societies (see for example Malloch 2004). A critical postmodern interpretation of the participants' accounts suggests, however, that such an analysis may reinforce a perception that power is something that feminist practitioners do not have, and would not want to have, because power is seen as the domain of the dominant groups (Fook and Napier 2000: 216). This may produce a complicity with oppression among feminist practitioners, ultimately contributing to a sense of powerlessness for both practitioners and the people they seek to support (Fook 2012: 58–9, Minow 1985). Reconstructing these modernist notions of power, which contributed to practitioners' sense of powerlessness, will be explored in more detail next.

iii) Reconstructing Modernist Notions of Power

Critical postmodern analyses extend feminist thinking by reconstructing the ways in which power is conceptualised. In this research, participants' original accounts reflected the assumption that power is a tangible commodity or possession, finite and hierarchical in nature, and embedded in formal structures or accorded to people through professional status. For all the participants, this understanding of power had unintended, disempowering outcomes since participants constructed themselves, and initially their service users, as being without power in relation to more powerful entities; a tendency that has been noted elsewhere (Fook 2004, Fook and Gardner 2007: 4–5, Morley 2004). Deconstructing notions of power suggests that these ideas may have led practitioners to believe that their power is reduced when they try to equalise their relations with service users because the giving of power, from this perspective, always incurs a deficit for the person or group giving it (Fook 2002: 53–60, Healy 2000: 44–5).

Drawing on Foucauldian notions of power, which construct power as exercised or enacted, (Healy 2000: 43–5, Fook, 2012: 60) enabled practitioners to recognise that power is also inscribed within discourse, rather than exclusively residing in social structure (Allan 2009, Fook 2004, Fook, 2012, Purvis and Hunt 1993). Power in this sense is also the capacity to influence, manipulate or re-author discourse (see for example Parker et al. 1999, Smith 2008: 32–4). For some participants, this reconstruction of power occurred through the rejection of the implicit assumption that egalitarianism means a reduction of power for someone else. As acknowledged elsewhere (Fook 2012: 61–2), practitioners' accounts revealed that power may operate differently and be used in various ways in different contexts, and in relation to different people. Participants' reconstructed accounts additionally rejected initial assumptions about power from being an unequivocally negative force, to recognise that it can also be productive. Critical postmodern thinking also enabled practitioners to reconstruct power in more fluid and contextual terms, which allowed them to understand that they could assist services users to exercise power through influencing the discourse surrounding their situations. In this way, critical postmodern theory contributed to practitioners understanding power as being embedded in social interactions and contexts, not just in social structures, and that what is important about power is how it is used and expressed (Fook 2012: 62, Healy 2000: 43–5).

Such a reconstruction of power enabled feminist practitioners to develop greater agency: that is the ability for practitioners to be more directly involved in the processes of social transformation and change (Allan 2009). This agency enabled practitioners to rethink the ways in which they had unwittingly participated in unproductive, oppositional power relations with other legal and medical professionals who were involved in their case scenarios. This redefinition of power is intimately connected to the reconstruction of practitioners' modernist understandings of identity, which will be discussed next.

iv) Reconstructing Modernist Notions of Identity

Critical postmodern thinking also contributed to extending participants' understanding of identity. Their initial assumptions indicated hierarchical views about power and identity in which they identified themselves as relatively powerless in the face of abstract, patriarchal structures and relations, and assumed their service users to be even more powerless. Participants saw that their powerless identities were fixed, unchanging and universal across different contexts and this was often expressed in terms of feeling excluded. The structural factors that produced practitioners' sense of powerlessness and exclusion were assumed to consistently permeate every aspect of their identity as a permanent state of being.

The view that service users were even more disempowered than themselves was expressed through their belief that practitioners must advocate for them. This hid an implicit assumption about the identity of their service users – that they are vulnerable and in need of protection. While this appropriately unites counsellors/advocates with victims/survivors, and puts them on the victims/survivors' 'side', it does so in opposition to dominant power relations that they assumed to be inaccessible and impervious to change. This confirms the argument that feminism's focus on women's relative disadvantage renders the possibility of making women's relative advantage invisible (Eveline 1994). As Seidman (2004: 212) explains: 'Postmodern feminism often draws on poststructural approaches to language as a system of signs whose coherence rests upon internal relations of difference. From this perspective, "women" acquire meaning only in its contrasting relation to "men" in a particular language system.'

Conversely, participants had repeatedly constructed other professionals, such as the police and forensic medical officers, as universally powerful and as one-dimensional, whose problematic behaviour was static and unchanging from one context to the next. This is consistent with modernist feminist theorising that constructs identity in terms of binary, structural categorisations that do not allow for movement, change or contradiction (Fook 2012: 83–4, Sands 1996, Seidman 2004: 204).

Critical postmodern theorising abandons grand narratives, conceptualising identity as situational, socially constructed, and locally and discursively produced (Fook 2012: 154, Sands 1996, Seidman 2004: 212). Deconstruction of participants' presentation of their own subjectivities and that of their service users highlighted the gaps, distortions, missing discourses and exceptions to the original narratives of themselves and their service users as powerless, passive victims, and elucidated the many ways in which these modernist constructions of identity had contributed to a further sense of disempowerment. When participants reconstructed their accounts using critical postmodern ideas about multiple, relative and fluid identities to reconstruct the identities of the other professionals by considering other factors (Fook 2012: 154, Sands 1996), they were thereby freed to consider other possible interpretations that helped to diffuse their sense of powerlessness and exclusion.

Drawing on critical postmodernism perspectives to reconstruct participants' narratives regarding their service users enabled them to recognise that identity can change from one context to another (Healy 2000: 43–5, Sands 1996, Seidman 2004: 212). This promoted opportunities to emphasise different aspects of service users' identities, reconstructing them as more empowered. Privileging different aspects of their original descriptions enabled practitioners to build more holistic narratives about service users and to relocate them within the discourse.

This enabled more complex and sophisticated practice responses and provided a means of acknowledging the relative disadvantage of victims/survivors in the context of the legal system, without contributing to it from the way they were theorising and responding to it. Critical postmodern perspectives therefore enhanced modernist feminist constructions of identity by creating the conceptual space to retain an acknowledgement of the structural problems with the legal response. This yielded the multitude of ways in which the system appears to produce a secondary victimisation of service users whilst avoiding further contributing to discourses that construct service users and practitioners in disempowered terms.

With more complex and multi-dimensional understandings of identity, it was possible for practitioners to attend appropriately to victims/survivors' experiences of victimisation, but also acknowledge their strength and agency. It became possible to see that victims/survivors' experiences of the legal system can be disempowering, while simultaneously creating opportunities for healing, validation and empowerment. Critical postmodern thinking provides feminist practitioners with a means for validating victims/survivors' experiences of oppression without inadvertently reinforcing their marginalisation or contributing to the construction of an oppressed identity.

Using critical postmodern perspectives to deconstruct dichotomous thinking and reconstruct participants' initial modernist understandings of power and identity similarly contributed to the reconstruction of unproductive, oppositional power relations between participants and other professionals. This will be discussed in the following section.

v) Challenging Oppositional Practices

Critical postmodern thinking highlighted that modernist feminist practice casts other professionals involved in the legal process as oppositional and universally problematic. This belief was often expressed by participants through locating blame with other professionals for the difficulties that transpired in the situations they described. During the telling of their initial stories, all of the participants defined their roles and approaches to practice as completely separate from those of the other professionals involved, thus defining themselves by their differences to the dominant constructions. As Fook and Napier (2001: 216) explain, our initial thinking or constructions of a problem may 'constitute stumbling blocks to creative, meaningful, assertive and effective practice'.

However, critical postmodern theories draw attention to the artificially constructed nature of the binary categories, and how participants' acceptance of these dichotomies ironically bolstered the perceived power of the other professionals in relation to themselves and their service users (Fook 2012). This highlighted how their *intentions* to empower worked against their practice, which may have unintentionally quashed their *capacity* to empower. Recognition of this confirms the argument that emancipatory principles do not automatically translate into emancipatory practices (Fook 2000: 5–11).

Recognising the limitations of their initial constructions assisted participants to think about other professionals in less oppositional terms and to develop an interpretation that more greatly valued their contributions. This stance has been referred to as the skill of divergence: 'opening ourselves up to the ideas of others, especially when these provide a new angle or vision' (Mezirow 1991: 369 cited in Fook 2004: 26). It enabled participants to recognise that they might have missed the ways in which other professionals could have assisted the victims/survivors. Critical reflection meant that the differences between the participants and the other professionals did not have to be seen as a threat to equity (Fook 2002: 82–5). In fact, the variety of contributions offered by different professionals could be reconstructed as beneficial to services users. Participants also realised that accepting the viewpoints of others, which may have even contradicted their own, did not mean relinquishing their own position. This parallels findings from a project that explored how critical reflection could be used to research practice in a mental health setting, particularly in relation to supervision. One of the main differences critical reflection had made to practice was the creation of more collaborative and collegial relationships through valuing diversity (Gardner 2013).

Further challenging oppositional practices, participants took responsibility for their tendency to blame other professionals while casting themselves as blameless and passive. They recognised that an unintended manifestation of feminist practice can be that it encourages practitioners to be at 'loggerheads' (Olivia, Interview 2) with systems and their representatives. Participants initially felt that not to operate in confrontational or adversarial ways would be tantamount to preserving dominant power relations, or to betray their unity as feminist practitioners. This was evident when some discussed the anti-professional, feminist culture of the CASAs, and how this can at times contribute to unnecessary, oppositional and adversarial relations between counsellors/advocates and other professionals involved with the legal response to sexual assault (Healy 2000: 87–90).

The need to be united in sisterhood is a cornerstone of modernist feminism, yet critical postmodern thinking extends the possibilities for challenging dominant power relations without adopting dichotomous hierarchies that inhibit the capacity to challenge. Deconstruction suggests that one of the consequences of practitioners seeing themselves as separate from, while also blaming, other professionals is that they contribute to their own sense of oppression and powerlessness. This also casts the problem as external, which exonerates the participants, yet locates the other professionals as being in control, powerful and active. Neglecting to examine how they themselves contributed to the situation was disempowering for the participants. Taking responsibility for their contribution to the difficulties reconstructs practitioners with the agency to create a different, more empowering response (Alberti 2000, Ellerman 1998, Fook 2004, Morley 2004, 2007, Rossiter 2005).

The notion of valuing difference also enabled a number of participants to relocate their relationships with other professionals into a discourse of teamwork and commonality. For some, this involved seeing that even though they offered different skills and insights than the legal and medical professionals involved, they were all potentially working towards the similar goal of responding to the victim/survivor, albeit from different perspectives. For some participants, critical postmodern ideas deconstructed the dichotomies that feminist thought had created between themselves and other professionals and created new discourses that emphasised collaboration and points of commonality. This was integral to counsellors/advocates feeling more empowered and being able to conceptualise new approaches to practice.

Another part of this process involved participants rethinking the value of their roles and contributions as counsellors/advocates. It involved uncovering more positive narratives concerning their practice while presenting their knowledge as different and valuable. Emphasising the value of the counsellor/advocate role and their shared purposes with other professionals, including the notion that everyone involved is providing a service to the victim/survivor, enabled the unearthing of discourses of mutuality.

This created new practice opportunities, which cultivated more complex alliances and challenged the oppositional power relations that permeated participants' initial presentations of their scenarios. Changing the ways in which participants relate to other professionals may change the ways that they relate back to them as practitioners. Drawing on ideas from critical postmodern perspectives therefore creates possibilities for change, whereas participating in oppositional power relations did not often prove conducive to achieving or enhancing feminist practice aims.

vi) Embracing Diversity

In participants' original accounts, a key recurring issue was that the dichotomous, feminist constructions of power and identity did not seem to be able to acknowledge difference without it becoming a threat to equity. As Seidman (2013: 217) explains:

> Feminism seems to be caught in a dilemma. On one hand there is the apparent necessity to invoke the category of women to resist male dominance. On the other hand, every appeal to "women" and to specify the meaning of female gender identity has the effect of excluding and disempowering some women.

Critical postmodern thinking highlighted the possibilities to continue feminist aims of empowering women by universalising their experiences of victimisation and poor legal processes, without disenfranchising those women who consider other dimensions of their identities more significant than gender (Seidman 2013: 217). Some Indigenous victims/survivors, for example, may experience problems caused by colonialism and racism more profoundly than gender discrimination in the legal system (Bennett et al. 2013, Pettman 1992, Pine 1996,). Critical reflection questions the usefulness of privileging gender as the primary dimension of difference, to suggest instead ways that practitioners might account for and respond adequately to diverse experiences. Whilst a postmodern emphasis on celebrating diversity has been interpreted as a challenge to the universal gendered analysis of oppression (Bell and Klein 1996: xxvi, Bulbeck 1994, Sands and Nuccio 1992) and therefore implicated in fragmenting universal feminist arguments, the emphasis on sameness and commonality has been criticised for excluding women with diverse experiences and backgrounds (Hare-Mustin and Marecek 1994). Questions are additionally raised about the potential for modernist feminist analysis to exclude children or men, in denying their experiences as victims/survivors of violence perpetrated by other men. Postmodernism provides an opportunity to discuss gender differences within the category of victim/survivor. It is noteworthy, for example, that much of the feminist literature reviewed in this study dominantly constructs victims/survivors as women. Accordingly, the introductory chapters of this study specifically locate the study within the context of women's experiences of sexual assault. However, within my small sample only two of the six participants chose to reflect on an incident concerning a female victim/survivor. Three of the case studies concerned child sexual assault, and one narrative concerned a young man with an intellectual disability. Postmodern thinking enables this diversity within the category of victim/survivor to be more appropriately acknowledged (Seidman 2013). Given that '[p]ostmodernism presents itself as a celebration of the multiplicity of individual experiences' (Kermode and Brown 1996: 376), it does not need to conceptualise women (or indeed victims/survivors) as a homogenous group in order to respond appropriately to their experiences, both shared and diverse. Women experience various intersecting oppressions, both through gender and other categories of difference. Recognising this can provide the 'conceptual space' (Rossiter 2005:1) to legitimate a variety of stories, voices and cultural experiences that have been unintentionally disenfranchised by modernist feminist discourses. This 'offers empowerment to women who can otherwise be smothered … by the idea of a sisterhood' (Pine 1996: 6) and the capacity to put into practice the emancipatory aims of feminist frameworks by improving their capacity to respond to all victims/survivors (Mullings and Schulz 2006, Weber 2006: 24).

Contextual Considerations

The preceding discussion has shown how critical postmodern analyses can extend feminist thinking and practice by enabling it to transcend modernist constructs. This parallels other work, by Philadelphoff-Puren (2004), for example, who uses Butler's (1997: 92) 'politically consequential renegotiations of language' and Derrida's (1988) discussion of iterability to uncover problems with traditional feminist responses to non-consent. Derrida's concept of iterability, which is defined as: 'the positive condition of possibility for language use as such: it designates the capacity of every mark to be repeated (reiterated) in new contexts not governed by the intention of the speaker or writer' (Philadelphoff-Puren 2004: 245) is relevant here, as it problematises feminist strategies such as 'no means no' and evaluates them as discursively and politically impossible. Iterability instructs that it is inevitable for a women's 'no' to be reinterpreted in a way that conflicts with her original designation. As Philadelphoff-Puren (2004: 246) explains, 'the possibility of transforming a woman's "no" into a "yes" is thus part of the *general* economy of iterability, rather than a consequence of a particular form of politico-sexual organisation'.

Philadelphoff-Puren (2004) goes on to explain that recontextualisation can create new strategies to respond to this problem of misinterpretation of meaning. Recontextualisation, which requires any resistance or mark of refusal to be understood in the specific context or 'total speech situation' (Austin 1976: 52 cited in Philadelphoff-Puren, 2004: 247) in which it occurs, carries the possibility that the complainant's refusal may be understood as authentic. If iterability always links the expression of 'no' to new contexts, then it can never be understood as a solitary sign. As such, 'if the word is non-unitary, then women are never undermined in a single discourse, discipline or institutional location' (Philadelphoff-Puren, 2004: 254). One of the implications of Philadelphoff-Puren's (2004) work, and of the research participants' development of new theory and practice, is the rethinking of some of the unintended consequences of former thought and practice. Feminist theory in this sense is 'neither finished nor the truth but [is] partial and changing' (Featherstone and Fawcett 1994/5: 75).

For Philadelphoff-Puren (2004), feminist strategies that do not take account of iterability (Derrida 1998) have resulted in women's refusal to engage in sexual contact almost certainly being interpreted as consent during sexual assault trials. Similarly, examining the limitations of some modernist, linear, universal thinking, the research process in this study has shown the potential for feminist thinking inadvertently to devalue smaller acts of resistance and change. Such thinking also contributed to practitioners' sense of powerlessness and alienation from the means of change, set up oppositional power relations that can contribute to a sense of fatalism for practitioners, and ironically, contributed to a lack of change despite emancipatory intentions.

This parallels research conducted by other feminists concerned with the totalising implications of universal feminist analyses (Almeras 2001,

Carmody 2003, Carmody and Carrington 2000, White 2006). Carmody and Carrington (2000), for example, evaluated the success of social policy initiatives that have been influenced by feminist activism in preventing sexual violence against women. While these initiatives focused on making sexual violence a public issue rather than a private matter, the findings indicate that 'many prevention strategies have been shaped by unarticulated discourses about sexuality which have focused primarily on women managing the risk of the unethical behaviour of men' (Carmody 2003: 199). Recommendations have been made for further research into 'how to prevent sexual violence by promoting its opposite: the inculcation of ethical sexual practices' (Carmody 2003: 200, see also Carmody and Carrington 2000: 354–6). Developing this further, Carmody (2003: 199) proposes an 'alternative conception of sexual ethics … based on Foucault's work on ethics, sexuality, governmentality and power as productive and in a constant state of negotiation'. She argues that 'deterministic' feminist approaches have undermined women's sexual desire and pleasure by placing emphasis on women's need to avoid sexual oppression (Carmody 2003: 200–201). She examines the potential for an 'erotics of consent' (Carmody 2003: 201) instead, exploring how 'ethical sexual subjectivity' can contribute to the elimination of violence against women. In doing this, however, Carmody is arguing for an 'invigorated debate about prevention' which resists modernist feminist constructions that have influenced anti-violence policy and practice (Carmody 2003: 213). She concludes that: 'There is a need to understand how the dominant gender order continues to limit the possibility of more egalitarian relations between women and men' and to consider the 'fluidity of power relations and the role of individual and collective resistance to dominant discourses concerning sexuality and violence' (Carmody 2003: 213).

Similarly, Lancaster and Lumb (1999) document related concerns about the capacity of feminist analyses to contribute to progressive social change. They explore the disparity between feminist academic writing about child sexual abuse and the daily focus of practitioners who work with the male perpetrators of this abuse, arguing that '[m]en, according to a patriarchal analysis, are caught in an unchanging and unchangeable impasse. Suggestions that men can modify their behaviour without societal change are viewed with scepticism, yet society is analysed in terms which exclude change' (Lancaster and Lumb 1999: 125). They continue to argue: 'If one accepts the analysis that patriarchy suggests an unchanging set of relationships, it could be argued that it is illogical to undertake work which is based on the premise of change' (Lancaster and Lumb 1999: 128). They ultimately contend that radical feminist critique 'does not offer a framework for change' (Lancaster and Lumb 1999: 125).

It would be anti-intellectual to avoid questioning and naming the limitations of modernist feminist theorising for practice in contemporary contexts. As Ellermann (citing Lemert and Gillian 1998: 39) explains, '[i]t is the paradoxical nature of knowledge that gives rise to alternative discourses: "Knowledge is gained only by the criticism of knowledge."' However, when discussing these unintended consequences of feminist theory and practice, I feel extremely concerned for the potential of intellectual debates, which are necessary for improvement and development, to be used in ways that harm feminist emancipatory goals or contribute to the backlash movements against feminism. This level of anguish is heightened by the current Australian context that has witnessed an increasing retreat from feminist principles in the human services sector (Morley and Macfarlane 2008, Phillips 2006); a trend that is also apparent in other Western, industrialised, capitalist countries (Featherstone 2005). Feminist literature argues that feminist values appear to be at odds with the current political culture. The contemporary privileging of scientific, technocratic and economic discourses in social policy means that ideals such as gender equity and social justice, which are essentially intrinsic in nature, are not considered a valuable commodity in the 'free' market (Davies and Leonard 2004: iv). In Australia, three terms of a neoliberal federal government under former Prime Minister John Howard, resulted in policies that replaced social services underpinned by structural and feminist analytical frameworks with those that privileged uncritical, individualised understandings of social problems (Phillips 2006). Whilst there have been some improvements under the Rudd and Gillard Labour Governments, including: the introduction of paid maternity leave; an explicit use of the term misogyny and a broadening of the understanding of this term after a passionate address from former Prime Minister Julia Gillard about the behaviour of the Opposition; and a royal commission into child abuse that is exposing large-scale, institutional cover-up of childhood sexual assault, the dominance of anti-feminist approaches have dismantled much of the infrastructure that feminists had fought hard to establish (Pini and Brown 2004: 161).

While my intention in this research has always been to enhance feminist practice, it has also involved examining its limitations for creating change practices with and within the legal system. However, I do not wish to contribute to recent trends in the field of sexual assault to move away from gendered understandings of violence against women. This shift has resulted in the privileging of psychological approaches concerned with individualising trauma responses. Counsellors/advocates in some CASAs are now being recast as trauma specialists who rely heavily on therapeutic and traditional expert models of service delivery. Research indicates that despite practitioners having an awareness of feminist analyses that take account of the broader social context, most privilege psychologically-based interventions and techniques in their practice. As Lancaster and Lumb (1999: 125) state, 'radical feminist understandings of the patriarchal nature of society and a specific sociological interpretation of the nature of child sexual abuse … appear to be qualified by, and in some senses actually contradicted by, the reality of day-to-day work'. In some cases, the abandonment of feminism has been more explicit and reference to feminist principles, philosophy and practice, has been entirely deleted from organisations' mandates (see, for example, Barwon CASA Annual Report, 2006/2007). While Lancaster and Lumb (1999: 120) remind us of the perils of polarising structural and individual explanations, this side-lining of feminist practice has the capacity to obscure the social, political, historical and gendered causes and consequences of sexual assault, and recast it as a private, individual problem (Morley and Macfarlane 2008, Phillips 2006, Staples 2007).

More broadly, contemporary practice contexts are often seen to be fraught with increasingly bureaucratic, regressive and over-regulated procedures thought not to be ideal for critical practice (Davies and Leonard 2004 iv–vi, Fook 2000, 2004, 2007b: 373, Fook and Askeland 2007, Leonard 1997, Mezirow 1997: 8). Given that free market ideology has commodified social work services, and new practice technologies that objectify service users have flourished in a context where professional legitimacy is linked to scientific discourses of 'technocratic managerialism', the potential to marginalise critical practice is manifest (Davies and Leonard, 2004: x, Fook 2007b: 373, Taylor and White 2000). The increase in state and corporate power reflects a worldwide trend where global capitalism, patriarchy and neo-colonialism disenfranchise and dominate structurally marginalised groups resulting in economic exploitation, poverty, war, terrorism, racism and social exclusion (Drevdahl 1999, MacDonald 1996). While this environment might mean that many practitioners feel alienated from the means of social change in their work (Morley 2004), at the same time, paradoxically, new forms of political resistance are emerging (Davies and Leonard 2004: ix), and there are greater calls for critical reflection (Fook 2013, Munro 2011). Participants' accounts of their transformative learning journeys demonstrate critical reflection as one form of resistance among many 'counter forces' that are developing (Davies and Leonard 2004: ix).

In summary, participants' accounts suggest that it is necessary to draw on modernist emancipatory theoretical frameworks, such as feminism, for ethical guidelines and critical values to orientate practice towards social change, while also using postmodern principles and critique in order to confront 'the tragic failure of this tradition' (Davies and Leonard 2004: ix). The research indicates that critical reflection can be an important tool for practitioners to improve feminist practice and achieve its emancipatory ideals in contemporary contexts.

Chapter 11
Final Reflections and Concluding Comments

This final chapter summarises and concludes the book by highlighting the significance of the research in terms of the contributions it makes to feminist practice, critical postmodern practice and critical reflection in social work and related fields. It explores some of the potential ethical issues posed by this type of the study and ultimately makes recommendations for further research.

Can Critical Reflection be Harmful for Participants?

The process of conducting this research has been both humbling and emancipatory for me (and, I hope, for the other practitioners who participated). Examining the contributions that my own thinking had made to particular discourses that were unhelpful for my practice and contrary to my goals was, at times, very difficult. However, realising that I had the capacity to change these was thoroughly liberating. This is perhaps why the challenges of critical reflection have been referred to as a 'double-edged sword' (Fook and Askeland 2007: 521). Creating possibilities to reconstruct powerlessness and develop strategies to address problems that were apparently insurmountable, while at the same time confronting deeply held assumptions can be enlightening, but may also cause considerable anxiety for participants (Fook 2007b, Fook and Napier 2000: 212). As Brookfield (1990: 178) explains:

> Questioning the assumptions on which we act and exploring alternative ideas is not only difficult but also psychologically explosive … Beginning to recognise and then critically question key assumptions is like laying down charges of psychological dynamite. When these assumptions explode and we realise that what we thought of as fixed ways of thinking and living are only options among a range of alternatives, the whole structure of our assumptive world crumbles.

Nevertheless, Fook (2004: 23) notes that '[t]he novelty of presenting, sharing, and learning from students' own practice experience, is seen as very validating, and they report increased confidence in their own judgment and creative abilities'. Most practitioners involved in this research were enthusiastic about doing so, however, for at least one, the process of destabilising particular assumptions seemed to be personally difficult. While she was able to reconstruct various aspects of her practice, at times she indicated that she was feeling quite 'stuck' and indicated at one point that she was happy with her modernist (structural/feminist) theory and saw its limitations as a compromise.

The potential to cause harm to participants by challenging deep-seated assumptions is a risk associated with using critical reflection as a research methodology. As one facilitator puts it, critical reflection can potentially cause people to feel 'exposed as incompetent, like an imposter, suddenly finding oneself in conflict with the cultural values of the agency and experiencing a loss of innocence when we realise that solutions to our dilemmas are not always readily forthcoming' (Baker 2013: 117). My awareness that a person's identity is an 'evolving construction that manifests itself during conversations in which narratives or stories are told' (Sands 1996: 177) reminded me of the responsibility I have as a researcher not to be passive, but to work constructively towards progressive change. As the person to whom the stories were being told, I recognised that I was implicated in the construction of the participants' narratives (see for example Frost 2006, Langellier 1989). As Sands (1996: 179–80) explains, '[w]hatever the other's role – researcher, friend, or therapist – and whatever posture the other appears to take – supportive, passive, cooperative, or disengaged – she or he participates in or influences the self-narrative'. Although the need to respect and validate the participants' experiences was clear, I also felt I had a responsibility to gently challenge some of the assumptions that I believed were exacerbating their sense of powerlessness (Fook 2004, Morley 2007). However, in keeping with the emancipatory aims of critical theory, I also resisted imposing the particular constructions that I was privileging based on my critical perspective. Consistent with critical practice, my role at this point, both as a critically reflective researcher and facilitator of transformative learning and practice, was to discuss various constructions, options and theoretical viewpoints, but ultimately to respect participants' positions, and their interpretations of reality (Mezirow 1997: 6–8, Morley 2013a). This approach to co-constructing dialogue involves 'remain[ing] open and responsive' to participants and working 'creatively' with 'a degree of uncertainty' (Powell: 2002: 28). I hope that this went some way towards reducing the potential for harm, while also challenging the participant who felt 'stuck'. The critically reflective process can certainly be unsettling for anyone who undertakes it but in all the accounts rendered here it was a hopeful rather than harmful journey.

Logocentrism

At times, some of the participants demonstrated logocentric thinking (Derrida cited in Gregory 2007). One of the consequences of this is the omission of alternative understandings that do not support the dominant construction of a particular situation (Kicuroski 2008). Logocentric thinking may well have limited this research, restricting the range, type and depth of reconstructed practices that emerged from the critical reflection process. While part of my role as a critically reflective researcher is to challenge this, as Brookfield (1995: 33) cautions:

'No matter how creative I might be in taking mental leaps and looking back on experiences from unfamiliar vantage points, I am always trapped inside my own meaning schemes and perspectives'. Hence, another unavoidable limitation of this research is that the critically reflective process, which relies primarily on the researcher and research participants as the key instruments of data generation, will always be partial, incomplete and continuing, as different people read and engage with this work from their own perspectives.

Has my Presence in the Research been a Limitation?

Another potential limitation, or ambiguity, in using the critical reflection method was that I was trying to understand not only the other research participants' experiences, as traditional approaches to research aim to do, but also how they have constructed these experiences, so that I could then work with them to deconstruct and reconstruct the knowledge that we were collaboratively developing from the process (Morley 2008a, 2013a). While one of the goals of critical reflection is transformative learning and most social research involves some form of intervention with the people we are researching, I was aware of how potential ethical problems, and my own limitations as a researcher, were involved in purposely trying to 'transform' my participants and myself.

Moreover, during the deconstruction stage of the research process, I was conscious of privileging particular narratives and making certain assumptions about how practice *should* be. For example, when participants discussed their hesitation to challenge police over inappropriate and dismissive conduct towards service users, there was an implicit judgement in the questions that I posed to them that the practitioners *should* have challenged them. So, although the process was open to a degree, it was not completely relativist in postmodern terms (Rossiter 2005). While this may address some of the criticisms initially levelled against Schon's original construction of reflective practice as apolitical in nature (Taylor forthcoming), it does raise questions about my level of involvement in the research and my level of influence over my representation of the participants' accounts. Critical reflection on my own practices as a researcher and close supervision of transcriptions of the deconstruction and reconstructive interviews have indicated that I was guided by critical perspectives as I had intended, but a paradox remains between empowering participants to think as 'autonomous agent[s] in a collaborative context' (Mezirow 1997: 8), which is one of the goals of critically reflective learning, and the imposition of the researcher's own ideas and judgments.

One of the ways in which I tried to counteract the power relations associated with my researcher role was to simultaneously participate in the research as one of 'the researched'. The decision to include my own story and share the deconstruction and reconstruction of my thinking and practice with the other participants was important in creating a respectful, non-judgmental, open and trusting culture. These conditions have been identified as a central component of the environment required for critical reflection (Fook 2004, Fook and Gardner 2007: 188–92, Gardner et al. 2006), and my position as an insider in the research (White 2001). My inclusion as a research participant also provided me with the opportunity to make reference to particular themes inherent in my own practice and share what I had learned from the process of critically reflecting on it thus enabling participants to identify similar themes in their own practice. This assisted them to legitimise, normalise and theorise their reconstructions by making the links between their experiences and the broader social environment (Fook 2004) as well as model the critical reflection process and appropriate self-disclosure (Fook and Askeland 2007). Another strategy was to 'promote the wider involvement of the participants in the research process' (Powell 2002: 25) by developing a shared construction with participants of their alternative, reconstructed accounts. As Powell (2002: 28) explains, 'the researcher plays a much more facilitative role with expertise to share in the joint process of knowledge construction as a basis for achieving change'.

However, a further implication of this lies in the fact that during the research process I constantly made decisions that influenced the direction of discussions with the participants. This included which assumptions were to be identified for deconstruction, which practices were to be targeted for reconstruction, and how I decided to assemble and present the data. I have been aware of bringing forward particular narratives that I have deemed more useful for creating possibilities for change. In addition, given the sheer volume of data produced by this inductive methodology, including all this material in the book was not possible. I have therefore had to make decisions about what material to emphasise and which to exclude (Morley 2013a).

Thankfully, postmodernism recognises that any representation of knowledge will necessarily be partial, limited by the perspectives, values and assumptions of the person constructing the discourse, and 'legitimised through an operation of power rather that the 'truth status' that is being claimed' (Tseris 2008: 33). Taylor (2006: 75 citing Taylor and White 2000, 2001) makes similar observations, drawing parallels between social work practice and qualitative research because both:

> are engaged in forms of social inquiry that have to make sense of ambiguous and indeterminate situations ... Practitioners just like researchers are implicated in the work they are engaged in. They do not simply observe in a neutral fashion and gather objective facts about people and their "problems", they construct versions of cases and, in this sense, make knowledge about patients and service users.

My involvement in the construction of participants' accounts, in the development of the research problem, and just about every other facet of the research, may be considered as biasing and contaminating the findings from the perspective of more traditional, objectivist paradigms (Loftus et al. 2011). However, drawing on critical and constructivist research paradigms, I have argued that my reflexive positioning has in fact been a strength that has contributed to the greater depth and richer outcomes of this research (Morley 2013a, White 2001). Taking a reflexive stance has aided me to identify my own active influence on the research, the type of knowledge I have created, and the processes I have used to produce it (Fook 1999b, Fook and Askeland 2006: 45, Taylor 2006). I have therefore engaged in a parallel, critically reflective process, which enabled me to 'examine myself examining' the data (Jones 1990: 195), and in which I used critical postmodern perspectives to guide what the deconstruction and reconstruction process should achieve (Fook 2004).

Recommendations for Future Research

It is possible that some of the issues I raise here may be addressed by future research. Given the points noted above regarding my positioning in the research, future studies could expand on some of the considerations of using critical reflection as a research methodology. This would help to address the gap in empirical studies by providing an evidence base to support the use of critical reflection as a method of inquiry (Fook et al. 2006, Hargreaves 2004, Ixer 2000, Mamede and Schmidt 2004, Stein 2000). Such research could explore some of the subtleties of the transformational process, for example: What accounts for the changes? What styles of facilitation might be particularly conducive for various types of participants? How might using critical reflection in research be different from using it as an educational tool? Arguably, the role of educator is different from that of researcher, given that the participants would be engaging in processes of critical reflection for different purposes. How might the facilitator's role vary when using critical reflection in these differing roles and contexts?

Since logocentric thinking was identified as a potential limitation of this research, future studies into how logocentric thinking could be challenged in respectful ways would be informative. Fook and Gardner (2007: 191) note that some people seem to be more able to engage in critical reflection than others, yet we do not really know why this is the case. Consistent with Fook and Gardner's (2007: 190–92) contention, my research points to the need to explore the relationship between individual participants' personalities and learning styles, and the practice of critical reflection. Are there ways in which the culture and values of critical reflection can be developed to be more inclusive, and what might be some of the barriers to this in contemporary workplaces?

Furthermore, examining the type of conditions or learning cultures that might enhance participants' ease in subjecting their practice to critical reflection could be an area for future research. Related research has already been conducted that identifies how a culture of 'critical acceptance' is needed for critical reflection (Fook et al. 2000: 231), 'referring to a type of respectful climate in which it is safe to challenge old ideas and try new ones' (Fook et al. 2006: 16), and where all involved are acknowledged to be both teachers and learners in the critically reflective process (Fook 2007b, Mezirow 1997). Further research could focus on the culture or conditions that are needed to support critical reflection within particular workplaces. This could be particularly pertinent in the many contemporary workplace cultures that work against critical reflection (Fook 2007b: 373, Mezirow 1997, Napier 2006), especially those with cultures of 'silence, individualism and secrecy' (Brookfield cited in Fook and Askeland 2007: 532).

This research concentrated solely on generating new practice possibilities in the context of sexual assault and the legal system. Future studies could replicate this research in a variety of fields of practice, particularly in other environments in which practitioners feel disempowered, or other contexts that are seen as restrictive for critical practice. Further research could also focus on how practitioners could take what they have learned from participating in this research project and apply it to other challenging practice situations and contexts. What sort of conditions would support this? What would practitioners need? How might they become self-directed learners able to reflect critically on particular incidents, and transfer this knowledge to other fields and contexts? Based on some of the positive outcomes of this research, future studies could also focus on how we can expand the use of critical reflection in practice. Similarly, the participants' accounts suggest a need to explore how critical reflection might be supported in practice in the longer term. For example, is the transformative knowledge gained by participants through critical reflection sustainable in contexts seen as challenging for critical practice? What are the opportunities and threats to sustaining and perpetuating the knowledge gained through critical reflection and critical practice?

Finally, given that one of the main outcomes of this research was its demonstration that critical reflection can enable practitioners to envision agency and power to bring about change, future research could follow up with the same participants to explore their capacity to *exercise* agency and power to bring about change. Based on the new awareness that participants developed, it could be pertinent to examine how the envisaging of agency leads to changes in the actions and practices of participants, and what forms the changed practices take. For example, how does practitioners' awareness of their capacity for agency change the way in which they engage with the judicial system? How might their new awareness create opportunities to influence legal processes and outcomes for victims/survivors more effectively? Given the outcomes of this study, it seems imperative to undertake further research that explores and documents the impact of participants' changed awareness.

Concluding Comments

The research presented in this book has explored counsellors/advocates' perceptions of their capacities to deal with and change the legal system's responses to victims/survivors of sexual assault. Initially, the research focused on exploring structural change both within and without the legal system, because much of the literature in the field of sexual assault tends to emphasise social, structural and legislative reform as the primary sites for change. A view of existing research in this field predominantly included feminist critiques of legal responses to sexual assault because it has been feminist scholars who have most comprehensively articulated the concerns of practitioners and described the impact of the inadequacies of the legal system on victims/survivors of sexual assault.

Given the extent and nature of the structural problems highlighted by the existing research, a key theme to emerge was the contention that the legal system must be changed in order to be more responsive to the women who report crimes of sexual assault. Overwhelmingly, researchers have contended that substantial legislative changes, in addition to broader social changes (which require patriarchy to be dismantled), are the necessary conditions for the legal system to become more just in response to victims/survivors of sexual assault. While this view of the required change reflects the feminist analyses that inform it, the theoretical framework of this study, which also drew on critical postmodern perspectives, highlighted how some aspects of modernist, feminist thinking can inadvertently contribute to practitioners feeling powerless to challenge the oppressive aspects of the legal system (Fook 2002: 6–10, Healy 2000: 37–56). Ironically, some feminist ideas can contribute to practitioners feeling paralysed by structural determinism and consequently alienated from the means of change (Morley 2009, 2011, 2012).

Critical postmodern perspectives were used to explore practitioners' lack of agency to change the legal response to sexual assault because this theoretical combination may enable practitioners to develop alternative conceptualisations of the problem by transcending some of the unintended, yet disempowering consequences of feminist solutions (Fook and Morley 2005, Morley 2005). Consequently, the initial focus of the research was broadened to include the goals of understanding the ways practitioners construct and are constructed by their roles in their work with the legal system, and uncovering discourses about their personal sense of agency. Approaching this research from a critical postmodern perspective, it was my contention that changing the ways in which we construct the problem, and our practice options in relation to it, may free practitioners to work in ways they had not previously considered. The research explored the ways in which critical postmodern perspectives might enable practitioners to envisage addressing the structural problems of the legal system at a micro level, and thereby connect them with a more localised means of social change.

Critical reflection was the vehicle that enabled me to put the emancipatory potential of critical postmodern thinking into practice. In this research, critical reflection, which has predominantly been used as an educational tool (see for example, Argyris and Schon 1976, Fook 2002, Mezirow and Associates 1990), was adapted to be applied as a research methodology (Morley 2008a). One of the contributions of this research project is that it expands the use of critical reflection in different ways and for different purposes, and validates its use as a methodology for researching possibilities for change. The research demonstrates that critical reflection – as both an educational process and a research tool – is effective in assisting people to be able to envisage change, even when they are feeling overwhelmed and disempowered.

Critical reflection, which uncovers the ways in which our thinking may be imbued with unhelpful (dominant) constructions (Fook 2002: 98), was chosen as the method of inquiry for the research because its principles are epistemologically congruent with the feminist and critical postmodern theoretical frameworks that underpin this study (Fook 2004, Morley 2013). It enabled the practitioners to explore how they conceptualised change to the legal system and to formulate new practice strategies that transcended their initial constructions of the problem. The practitioners who participated in this research reflected on a critical incident or case from their practice that expressed some of the typical difficulties they had experienced with the legal system. The first stage of the research deconstructed the hidden values and assumptions in participants' accounts of their practices. The second stage reconstructed their thinking and practice in a range of creative ways as participants unearthed their capacities to envisage possibilities for emancipation in situations where they had previously felt powerless to act.

This research is significant because participants' accounts clearly demonstrate that critical reflection on practice did indicate various possibilities for change to the legal system. These included changes in how practitioners constructed themselves and the identities of their service users; changes to how they thought about the problems with the legal system; changes to how they thought about power; and changes to how they saw themselves in relation to the legal system and to other professionals involved in the legal process. These changes occurred largely through the critically reflective processes of: questioning dichotomous thinking; reconstructing more holistic notions of professionalism; deconstructing modernist notions of power and identity; reconstructing oppositional power relations; and embracing diversity.

More generally, and perhaps most significantly, participants' accounts indicated a clear capacity to think about agency and change. This outcome makes a major contribution to feminist theory and practice because it rejuvenates possibilities of achieving the emancipatory aims of feminist analyses. This is particularly important given that recently we have seen a decline in faith in the transformative power of feminist thinking to produce emancipatory outcomes (Bulbeck 1994), and a questioning of the continued relevance of feminist analyses (Featherstone 2005). Significantly, participants' accounts reinforce the importance of gendered, social and political analyses, yet also indicate how feminism might be enhanced by incorporating critical postmodern ideas and critical reflection in order to be responsive to contemporary contexts (Morley 2009, 2011, 2012). The incorporation of postmodern and critical perspectives enabled practitioners to overcome the sense of fatalism engendered by their use of traditional feminist analyses. Transcending this fatalism was an important precursor to revitalising feminist practice in ways that created emancipatory possibilities.

Consequently, the two major themes that arose from participants' accounts were: 1) that even in the most disempowering contexts, it is possible for practitioners to envision their own agency and power to bring about change; and 2) that critical reflection is a powerful tool in assisting practitioners to connect with this sense of agency. Insights drawn from critical postmodern theory were an important ingredient in assisting feminist practice to achieve emancipatory aims in contemporary contexts. The implications of the new knowledge produced by this research are therefore significant, not only for the subject of sexual assault, but also for a range of fields of practice where social workers feel overwhelmed and disempowered by seemingly insurmountable structural barriers to change. This research is relevant to fields such as domestic violence and work with children and families where practitioners wrestle with similar difficulties with the legal system as those working with the victims/survivors of sexual assault. It might also be relevant for a variety of feminist practitioners who struggle with the sometimes limiting effects of traditional feminist analyses on practice.

More broadly, however, the knowledge generated by this research has implications for the ways in which practitioners respond to the many social problems requiring active, creative and critical responses, by helping them to transform their thinking about change and how it can be achieved. In any field of practice where structural factors appear to dominate and to alienate practitioners from the means of change, the knowledge gained from this critically reflective research could be used to develop alternative thinking and practices about the possibilities for change. The outcomes of this research could also be used to inform new ways of responding to situations where modernist critical theorising has resulted in paralysis because the structural problems seem too difficult to negotiate. Moreover, this research has implications for individual counselling practices by providing ways to reconstruct narratives about oppression and injustice in ways that allow people to respond differently, or to reconstruct 'damaged personal identities' (Fook unpublished). This creates opportunities for empowerment through uncovering the ways dominant power structures and relations operate, while generating the potential to transform the ways in which individuals resist, challenge and change the structures, and themselves in relation to them. This research also provides many concrete examples of enacting the theoretical combination of feminist principles with critical and postmodern ideas in practice. This is an original contribution to knowledge, given the dominance of modernist feminist perspectives in the literature.

Another implication of this research is that critical reflection can protect practitioners from burnout, increase their capacity to stay in their roles for longer, and help them to develop more hopeful perspectives on their work. This is attributed to the understanding that when practitioners see possibilities in their practice for change, they experience a sense of hope, inspiration and empowerment. Conducting this research and critically reflecting on my own practice certainly helped me to address the frustrations I experienced as a practitioner (which initially motivated me to undertake the research). The research has inspired my confidence that there are meaningful and practical ways to resist the inadequacies of the current legal responses to sexual assault in ways that can make a difference to the devastating processes and outcomes experienced by many complainants. While structural changes for a more equitable society and legislative improvements must continue to be pursued, it is heartening to know that we do not have to wait for those broader structural changes to occur before we can envision practices of agency and change. Participants' accounts indicate that structural change is not the only way to form more appropriate legal responses or achieve more effective support for victims/survivors of sexual assault who have the courage to pursue legal justice. This also has significant implications for other fields of practice.

It is my view that the other practitioners who participated in this research also experienced a greater sense of increased agency than they had originally thought. Critical reflection was an important catalyst in freeing participants from hegemonic, restrictive assumptions that limited practice and blocked their capacity to think about change (Brookfield, 2000). As one participant commented when reflecting on the research process: 'I can see it totally clearly now … how much all of that was in my head … how I was constructing that for myself, without them doing that for me. Do you know what I mean? It was all in me' (Barbara, Interview 2). Foucault (1980) affirms this when contending that: 'people … are much freer than they feel, that people accept truth as evidence, some themes which have built up at a certain moment during history and that this so-called evidence can be criticised and destroyed' (cited in Rossiter 1996: 29).

The changes in thinking that emerged from participants' critical reflection on their accounts hold significant implications for action. Importantly, the challenge now will be to expand this research by exploring how the changes to thinking, and the development of possibilities to envision agency and power to bring about change, result in changes in action. For Frière (1970 cited in Fook and Napier 2000), critical reflection is 'central to engagement in a liberation process. What he termed "conscientisation" … in his thinking inseparable from "transformative action" … refers to a process where people gain knowledge and find a springboard to active reflection on the oppressive conditions of their lives' (Fook and Napier 2000: 9).

Given the implications of this study, further research is now needed to explore how the new awareness gained from this critical reflection might result in enhanced capacity to *exercise* agency and power to bring about changes in practice. Such research would build on the outcomes achieved by this research, which include:

- finding concrete ways to locate the means of social change with individual practitioners;
- empowering practitioners to resist dominant, constructions of 'reality' that previously limited their capacity to think about change;
- assisting practitioners to overcome the fatalistic beliefs that restricted their aspirations for critical practice;
- liberating practitioners to develop more active and empowered subjectivities; and,
- creating the possibilities for practitioners to imagine their power and agency to work more effectively for emancipation and social justice.

Ultimately, the research demonstrates the power of critical reflection to equip practitioners to think outside the confines of their perceptions, to rethink their experiences and reimagine the possibilities for emancipatory change. This is of vital importance in contemporary practice contexts where injustices are deeply engrained, and the obstacles to change formidable. In this research, the practitioners' use of critical reflection goes some way towards addressing what feminist social activist bell hooks is seeking, when she states: 'There must exist a paradigm, a practical model for social change that includes an understanding of ways to transform consciousness that are linked to efforts to transform structures' (hooks 1989: 118). The critical reflection process provided a mechanism for the research participants to do precisely this. Professor of Law, Bill Quigley (2007: 28) states 'Give your creative thoughts free reign, for it is only in the hearts and dreams of people seeking a better world that true social justice has a chance' (Quigley, 2007: 28). It is my hope that this book will be used to inspire the imagination and action of anyone who is engaged in the struggle for a more socially just world, in ways that are not restricted to dismantling structures, but through considering the infinite possibilities that can emerge from reconstructed consciousness.

Appendix 1
Deconstruction Questions

1/ What were the main themes and patterns to emerge from your experience? What terminology or patterns of communication reoccur? What labels have you used to describe your experience? What are the binary opposite or dichotomous categories in your account?
2/ Who are all the potential players (individuals, groups, the legal system, lawyers, police, etc.) involved in the situation or potentially affected by it?
3/ Whose perspectives are dominantly represented and whose are absent? What interpretations or explanations were made and whose were they?
4/ What interpretations or explanations were made and whose were they?
5/ How were you represented in your account? How did you influence the situation? How did you influence your construction of your account?
6/ How might the situation have been interpreted differently and how might it have been interpreted by different players?
7/ What knowledge and assumptions are implied and used in your account? How do they relate to (e.g.) practice theory, value and belief systems; paradigms; human behaviour; moral and ethical codes; social and political systems and change; power; gender and cultural considerations? Are they relevant and appropriate to the situation at hand? Where do these assumptions originate? What roles or positions do they support? What players stand to gain or lose from holding them, and what power and social functions does holding these assumptions perform? What practices, systems or structures are upheld by these assumptions?
8/ What gaps or biases or emphases are there in your description? What perspectives are missing, distorted or devalued? What actions or assumptions support these biases?
(Adapted from Fook, J. 2012. © *Social Work: A Critical Approach to Practice*. 2nd Edition. London: Sage, 107, with the kind permission of SAGE and the original author.)

Appendix 2
Reconstruction Questions

1/ How does what happened in your incident compare with what you intended to do, or what you assumed you were doing? Was the theory you thought you were using different to what was implied by your actions and interpretations? Did your actions fit your theory?
2/ How does your experience of this situation compare with past experiences? What are common themes and patterns? What aspects of it can be applied to other situations?
3/ How do the different types of theory and knowledge you used in this situation relate to each other?
4/ What further questions arise out of your theory and practice as a result of your experience and reflection?
5/ What needs to change in your assumptions, theory, actions, interpretations, skills, as a result of these reflections?
6/ What strategies can you use to make these changes? How do these strategies fit with your changed theories and interpretations?
7/ How do the main assumptions underlying your practice compare with the more formal theoretical perspectives? What do you need to change about the way you see or use these theories, as a result of your reflections?
8/ How would you label or categorise (or relabel or recategorise) your own theory as a result of this comparison? What is your version or your terminology for the theory upon which you practice?
9/ What is your reformulated theory of (or assumptions about) power resulting from your reflection?
10/ How can you frame your own theory so that what you have learned is transferable to other situations and contexts?
(Adapted from Fook, J. 2012. © *Social Work: A Critical Approach to Practice*. 2nd Edition. London: Sage: 123, with the kind permission of SAGE and the original author.)

References

Adams-Curtis, L. and Forbes, G. 2004. College women's experiences of sexual coercion: A review of cultural, perpetrator, victim, and situational variables. *Trauma, Violence and Abuse*, 5 (2), 91–122.

Agger, B. 1998. *Critical Social Theories*. Boulder/Oxford: Westview Press.

Alberti, S. 2000. Changing the system through casework: A critical incident analysis, in *Breakthroughs in Practice: Theorising Critical Moments in Social Work*, edited by L. Napier and J. Fook. London: Whiting and Birch, 38–48.

Aldunate, R. 1995. Fair go? Only if you speak the lingo and look the part, in *The Project for Legal Action against Sexual Assault: Legalising Justice for All Women*, compiled by M. Heenan. Paper presented at the National Conference on Sexual Assault and the Law, Melbourne, Australia, 28–30 November, 176–83.

Alfrero, L.A. 1972. *Conscientization, New Themes in Social Work Education*. New York: International Association of Schools of Social Work.

Allan, J. 2003. Theorising Critical Social Work, in *Critical Social Work: An Introduction to Theories and Practices*, edited by J. Allan, B. Pease, and L. Briskman. Crow's Nest, NSW: Allen and Unwin, 32–51

Allan, J., Briskman, L. and Pease, B. (eds) 2009. *Critical Social Work*. 2nd Edition. Crows Nest, NSW: Allen and Unwin.

Allan, J., Pease, B. and Briskman, L. (eds) 2003. *Critical Social Work: An Introduction to Theories and Practices*. Crows Nest, NSW: Allen and Unwin.

Allen, J. 2013. Using critical reflection to research spirituality in clinical practice, in *Critical Reflection in Context: Applications in Health and Social Care*, edited by J. Fook and F. Gardner, London and New York, 154–65.

Allen, S. 1996. Sexual assault law reform. Paper presented at the Balancing the scales: National conference on sexual assault, Perth, Australia, 21–22 June.

Almeras, D. 2001. Violence against women: Men and the social imaginary. *Development*, 44 (3), 54–8.

Argyris, C. and Schon, D. 1976. *Theory in Practice: Increasing Professional Effectiveness*. San Francisco: Jossey-Bass.

Arnd-Caddigan, M. and Pozutto, R. 2006. Truth in our time. *Qualitative Social Work*, 5 (4), 423–40.

Askeland. G.A. 2013. The challenges of using critical reflection to develop contextually appropriate social work, in *Critical Reflection in Context: Applications in Health and Social Care*, edited by J. Fook and F. Gardner. London and New York: Routledge, 143–54.

Astbury, J. 2006. *Services for Victim/Survivors of Sexual Assault: Identifying Needs, Interventions and Provision of Services in Australia.* Melbourne: Australian Institute of Family Studies.

Australian Law Reform Commission 1994. *Equality before the Law: Justice for Women/Australia.* Sydney: Law Reform Commission.

Australian Law Reform Commission 2010. *Family Violence – A National Legal Response* (Report No. 114). Sydney: Australian Law Reform Commission.

Avakame, E. 1999. Females' labour force participation and rape: An empirical text of the backlash hypothesis. *Violence Against Women*, 5 (6), 926–49.

Baistow, K. 1994/5. Liberation and regulation? Some paradoxes of empowerment. *Critical Social Policy*, 42, 34–46.

Baker, J.G. 2013. *Cringe*-ical reflection? Notes on critical reflection and team supervision in a statutory setting, in *Critical Reflection in Context: Applications in Health and Social Care*, edited by J. Fook and F. Gardner. London and New York: Routledge, 177–26.

Baldwin, M. 2004. Critical reflection: Opportunities and threats to professional learning and service development in social work organizations, in *Social Work, Critical Reflection and the Learning Organization*, edited by N. Gould and M. Baldwin. Aldershot: Ashgate, 41–56.

Bargen, J. and Fishwick, E. 1995. *Sexual Assault Law Reform: A National Perspective.* Canberra: Office for the Status of Women.

Barwon Centre Against Sexual Assault 2006/07. Unpublished Annual Report.

Beazer, M. 2008. Media watch: DPP raps judges over sex-crime insensitivity. *Legal Date* [Online]. Available at: doi:http://search.informit.com.au/fullText;res=AGISPT;dn=20092003 [accessed 5 June 2009] 20 (3), 8.

Beech, A., Fisher, D. and Ward, T. 2005. Sexual murderers' implicit theories. *Journal of Interpersonal Violence*, 20 (11), 1366–89.

Beichner, D. and Spohn, C. 2005. Prosecutorial charging decisions in sexual assault cases: Examining the impact of a specialized prosecution unit. *Criminal Justice Policy Review*, 16 (4), 461–98.

Bell, D. and Klein, R. 1996. *Radically Speaking: Feminism Reclaimed.* North Melbourne: Spinifex Press.

Benner, P. 1984. *From Novice to Expert: Excellence and Power in Clinical Nursing.* Menlo Park: Addison Wesley.

Berlin, S. 1990. Dichotomous and complex thinking. *Social Service Review*, 64 (1), 46–59.

Bohner, G., Eyssel, F., Pina, A., Siebler, F. and Tendayi, V. 2009. Rape myth acceptance: cognitive, affective and behavioural effects of beliefs that blame the victim and exonerate the perpetrator, in *Rape: Challenging Contemporary Thinking*, edited by M. Hovarth and J. Borwn, Devon, UK: Willan Publishing, 17–45.

Boud, D., Keogh, R. and Walker, D. 1985. *Reflection: Turning Experience into Learning.* London: Kogan Page.

Brookfield, S. 1990. Using critical incidents to explore learners' assumptions, in *Fostering Critical Reflection in Adulthood*, edited by J. Mezirow. San Francisco: Jossey-Bass, 177–93.

Brookfield, S. 1995. *Becoming a Critically Reflective Teacher*. San Francisco: Jossey-Bass.

Brookfield, S. 2000. Transformative learning as ideology critique, in *Learning as Transformation*, edited by J. Mezirow and Associates. San Francisco: Jossey-Bass, 125–48.

Brookfield, S. 2001. Repositioning ideology critique in a critical theory of adult education. *Adult Education Quarterly*, 52 (1), 7–22.

Brookfield, S. 2005 *The Power of Critical Theory.* San Fransisco: Jossey-Bass.

Brown, C.G. 2012. Anti-Oppression Through a Postmodern Lens: Dismantling the Master's Conceptual Tools in Discursive Social Work Practice. *Critical Social Work*, 13 (1).

Brown, J.J. 2007. Sex crimes in suburbia: The recent legal and scientific advances in the assistance given to victims of sexual assault. *On Crime and Law* [Online]. Available at: http://business.highbeam.com/2382/article-1G1-170279534/sex-crimes-suburbia-reflecting-rape-forty-years-ago [accessed: 17 March 2013].

Brownmiller, S. 1975. *Against Our Will: Men, Women and Rape*. New York: Simon and Schuster.

Bryson, V. 2002. *Feminist Debates: Issues of Theory and Political Practice*. 2nd Edition. Basingstoke: Palgrave.

Bulbeck, D. 1994. Where to now? The contemporary loss of faith in feminism's transformative power. *Social Alternatives*, 12 (4), 10–12.

Butler, J. 1989. *Gender Trouble: Feminism and the Subversion of Identity*. New York: Routledge.

Butler, J. 1992. Contingent foundations: Feminism and the question of postmodernism, in *Feminists Theorize the Political*, edited by J. Butler and J. Scott. New York: Routledge, 3–21.

Butler, W. 1997. *Excitable School*. London and New York: Routledge.

Campbell, R. 2006. Rape survivor's experiences with the legal and medical systems: Do rape victim/advocates make a difference? *Women Against Violence*, 12 (1), 30–45.

Campbell, R. and Wasco, S. 2005. Understanding rape and sexual assault: 20 years of progress and future directions. *Journal of Interpersonal Violence*, 20 (1), 127.

Campbell, R., Wasco, S., Ahrens, C., Sefl, T. and Barnes, H. 2001. Preventing the 'second rape': Rape survivors' experiences with community service providers. *Journal of Interpersonal Violence*, 16 (12), 1239–59.

Carbone-Lopez, K. 2005. The 'usual suspects': How race affects decision to report rape victimization. *Journal of Ethnicity in Criminal Justice*, 3 (4), 29–47.

Carmody, M. 2003. Sexual ethics and violence prevention. *Social and Legal Studies*, 12 (2), 199–216.

Carmody, M. and Carrington, K. 2000. Preventing sexual violence? *The Australian and New Zealand Journal of Criminology*, 33 (3), 341–61.

Carpenter, C.R. 2006. Recognising gender-based violence against civilian men and boys in conflict situations. *Security Dialogue*, 37 (1), 83–103.

Centre Against Sexual Assault House. 2007. Sexual assault – statistics. Royal Women's Hospital [Online]. Available at: http://wch.org.au/casa/info.cfm?doc_id=4004 16 [accessed: August 2008].

Child Safety Services. 2009. *What Ifs – Responding to Specific Investigation and Assessment Matters*. Queensland Government [Online]. Available at: http://www.childsafety.qld.gov.au/practice-manual/inverstigation-assessment/faqs.html#anc-56 [accessed: 4 June 2009].

Clay-Warner, J. and Burt, C. 2005. Rape reporting after reforms: Have times really changed? *Violence Against Women*, 11 (2), 150–76.

Cook, K. 2002–3. Rape Law.Consent@FreeAgreement.co.uk: An assessment of the legal definition of consent, in the light of the current review of sexual offences law. *Contemporary Issues in Law*, 6 (1), 7–22.

Corbett, L. and Larcombe, W. 1994. Lunar landscapes: The dark side of sexual assault and the law. Paper presented at *Women and the Law Conference.* Canberra, Australia, September 22–24, 131–42.

Corrigan, R. 2006. Making meaning of Meagan's law. *Law and Social Inquiry*, 31 (2), 267.

Cosier, W. 2008. What part of 'No' don't you understand?: Social work, children and consent, in *Critical Reflection: Generating Theory from Practice*, edited by R. Pockett and R. Giles. Sydney: Darlington Press, 145–61.

Cossins, A. 1995. On stone throwing from the feminist sidelines: A critique of Helen Garner's book, The first stone. *Melbourne University Law Review*, 20 (2), 528–61.

Cossins, A. 2003. Saints, sluts and sexual assault: Rethinking the relationship between sex, race and gender. *Social and Legal Studies*, 12 (1), 77–103.

Cripps, K. 1995. Criminal injuries compensation: Recommendations for change, compiled by M. Heenan. *The Project for Legal Action against Sexual Assault: Legalising Justice for All Women*. Paper presented at the National conference on sexual assault and the law, Melbourne, Australia, 28–30 November, 48–4.

D'Alessio, S. and Stolzenberg, L. 2002. Race and the probability of arrest. *Social Forces*, 81 (4), 1381–97.

D'Arcy, M. 1995. Experiences of victims/survivors of sexual assault with the police and court, compiled by M. Heenan. *The Project for Legal Action against Sexual Assault: Legalising Justice for All Women*, paper presented at the National Conference on Sexual Assault and the Law, Melbourne, Australia, 28–30 November, 135–42.

D'Arcy, M. 1996. Just desserts? The sentencing of sexual offenders. Paper presented at Balancing the Scales: National Conference on Sexual Assault, WA Sexual Assault Referral Centre, Perth, Australia, 20–21 June.

Davies, L. 1999. Protecting Paedophiles: Gender Bias in Child Abuse Prosecutions. *The Australian Feminist Law Journal* 12, 95–101.

Davies, L. and Leonard, P. (eds) 2004. *Social Work in a Corporate Era: Practices of Power and Resistance.* Aldershot: Ashgate.

D'Cruz, H. and Jones, M. 2004. *Social Work Research: Ethical and Political Contexts*. London: Sage.

Dekeseredy, W. and Joseph, C. 2006. Separation and/or divorce sexual assault in rural Ohio: Preliminary results of an exploratory study. *Women Against Violence*, 12 (3), 301–11.

Denzin, N. and Lincoln, Y. 2000. *Handbook of Qualitative Research.* 2nd Edition, Thousand Oaks: Sage.

Derrida, J. 1976. *Of Grammatology* (trans. G Spivak). Baltimore: Johns Hopkins University Press.

Derrida, J. 1980. *Structure, Sign and Play* (trans. A Bass). Chicago: Chicago University Press.

Derrida, J. 1988. *Limited Inc.* (trans. S. Weber). Evanston, IL: Northwestern University Press.

Dewey, J. 1916. *Democracy and Education: An Introduction to the Philosophy of Education*. New York: The Free Press.

Dewey, J. 1933. *How We Think: A Restatement of the Relation of Reflective Thinking to the Educative Process*. Boston: Heath.

DiAngelo, R. 1997. Heterosexism: Addressing internalized dominance. *Journal of Progressive Human Services*, 8 (1), 5–21.

Doherty, K. and Anderson, I. 2004. Making sense of male rape: Constructions of gender, sexuality and experience of rape victims. *Journal of Community and Applied Social Psychology*, 141 (2), 85–103.

Dominelli, L. 2002. *Feminist Social Work Theory and Practice*. New York: Palgrave.

Donat, P. and D'Emilio, J. 1998. A feminist redefinition of rape and sexual assault: Historical foundations and change, in *Confronting Rape and Sexual Assault*, edited by M. Odem and J. Clay-Warner. Wilmington DE, USA: S. Books, 35–48.

Douglas, H. 2005. She knew what was expected of her: The white legal system's encounter with traditional marriage. *Feminist Legal Studies*, 13 (2), 181.

Drevdahl, D. 1999. Sailing beyond: Nursing theory and the person. *Advanced Nursing Science*, 2 (4), 1–13.

Du Mont, J. Miller, K. and Myhr, T. 2003. The role of 'real rape' and 'real victim' stereotypes in the police reporting practices of sexually assaulted women. *Violence Against Women*, 9 (4), 466–86.

Du Mont, J. and Myhr, T. 2000. So few convictions: The role of client-related characteristics in the legal processing of sexual assault. *Violence Against Women*, 6 (10), 1109–36.

Easteal, P. 1996a. The cultural context of rape and reform, in *Without Consent: Confronting Adult Sexual Violence*, edited by P. Easteal. Proceedings of a conference held in Melbourne 27–29 October 1992, Canberra: Australian Institute of Criminology, 1–34.

Easteal, P. 1996b. Masculocentric reality: The limits of law reform and choices for the future. Paper presented at Balancing the Scales: National Conference on Sexual Assault, WA Sexual Assault Referral Centre, Perth, Australia, 20–21 June.

Eisler, R. 2004. Pragmatopia: Revisioning human possibilities. *Tikkun*, 19 (6), 44–6.

Ellermann, A. 1998. Can discourse analysis enable reflective social work practice? *Social Work Education*, 17 (1), 35–44.

Ellis, C. and Bochner, A. 2000. Autoethnography, personal narrative, reflexivity: Researcher as subject, in *Handbook of Qualitative Research*. 2nd Edition, edited by N. Denzin, and Y. Lincoln. Thousand Oaks: Sage, 733–68.

Erlich, S. 2001. *Representing Rape: Language and Sexual Consent.* London and New York: Routledge.

Evans, M. 2008. When worlds collide: Understanding the intersection of the personal and the professional in social work practice, in *Critical Reflection: Generating Theory from Practice*, edited by R. Pockett, and R. Giles. Sydney: Darlington Press, 1–14.

Eveline, J. 1994. The politics of advantage. *Australian Feminist Studies*, 19, 129–54.

Fawcett, B. 2008. Women and violence, in *Addressing Violence, Abuse and Oppression: Debates and Challenges*, edited by B. Fawcett and F. Waugh. New York: Routledge, 7–16.

Featherstone, B. 2005. Feminist social work: Past, present and future, in *Social Work: A Critical Turn*, edited by S. Hick, J. Fook and R. Pozzuto. Toronto: Thompson Education Publishing, 203–17.

Featherstone, B. and Fawcett, B. 1994. Feminism and child abuse: Opening up some possibilities? *Critical Social Policy*, 42, 61–80.

Featherstone, B. and Fawcett, B. 1995. Oh no! Not more 'isms': Feminism, postmodernism, poststructuralism and social work education. *Social Work Education*, 14 (3), 25–43.

Fileborn, B. 2011. *Sexual Assault Laws in Australia*. Australian Centre for the Study of Sexual Assault, Australian Institute of Family Studies, Melbourne.

Filipas, H. and Ullman, S. 2001. Social reactions to sexual assault victims from various support sources. *Violence and Victims*, 16 (6), 673–92.

Flanagan, J. 1954. The critical incident technique. *Psychosocial Bulletin*, 51 (4), 327–58.

Fook, J. 1993. *Radical Casework: A Theory of Practice*. Sydney: Allen and Unwin.

Fook, J. 1996. The reflective researcher: Developing a reflective approach to practice, in *The Reflective Researcher: Social Workers' Theories of Practice Research* edited by J. Fook. Sydney: Allen and Unwin, 1–8.

Fook, J. 1999a. Critical reflexivity in education and practice, in *Transforming Social Work Practice: Postmodern Critical Perspectives*, edited by B. Pease and J. Fook. Sydney: Allen and Unwin, 195–208.

Fook, J. 1999b. *Reflexivity as Method.* Bundoora: La Trobe University.

Fook, J. 2000. Critical perspectives on social work, in *Contemporary Perspectives on Social Work and the Human Services: Challenges and Change*, edited by I. O'Connor, P. Smyth and J. Warburton. Sydney: Longman, 128–38.

Fook, J. 2002. *Critical Social Work.* London: Sage.

Fook, J. 2004. Critical reflection and transformative possibilities in *Social Work, in a Corporate Era: Practices of Power and Resistance*, edited by L. Davies and P. Leonard. Ashgate: Aldershot. 16–30.

Fook, J. 2007a. Reflective practice and critical reflection, in *Handbook for Practice Learning in Social Work and Social Care*, edited by Lishman, J. London: Jessica Kingsley, 363–75.

Fook, J. 2007b. Uncertainty: The defining characteristic of social work? in *Social Work: A Companion for Learning*, edited by M. Lymbery and K. Postle. London: Sage, 30–50.

Fook, J. 2008. Foreword: Critical reflection and the professional task, in *Critical Reflection: Generating Theory from Practice*, edited by R. Pockett and R. Giles. Sydney: Darlington Press, vi–viii.

Fook, J. 2011. Developing Critical Reflection as a Research Method, in *Creative Spaces for Qualitative Researching: Living Research*, edited by J. Higgs, A. Titchen, D. Horsfall and D. Bridges. Rotterdam: Sense Publishers, 55–64.

Fook, J. 2012. *Social Work: A Critical Approach to Practice.* 2nd Edition. London: Sage.

Fook, J. 2013 Critical Reflection in Context: Contemporary Perspective and Issues, in *Critical Reflection in Context: Applications in Health and Social Care*, edited by J. Fook and F. Gardner. London and New York: Routledge. 1–11.

Fook, J. (unpublished). A New Direction for Critical Social Work Research, Unpublished paper.

Fook, J. and Askeland, G. 2006. The 'critical' in critical reflection, in *Critical Reflection in Health and Social Care*, edited by S. White, J. Fook, and F. Gardner. Maidenhead: Open University Press, 40–53.

Fook, J. and Askeland, G. 2007. Challenges of critical reflection: Nothing ventured, nothing gained. *Social Work Education*, 26 (5), 520–33.

Fook, J. and Gardner, F. 2007. *Practicing Critical Reflection: A Resource Handbook.* Maidenhead: Open University Press.

Fook, J. and Gardner, F. (eds) 2013. *Critical Reflection in Context: Applications in Health and Social Care.* London and New York: Routledge

Fook, J. and Morley, C. 2005. Empowerment: A contextual perspective, in *Social Work: A Critical Turn*, edited by S. Hick, J. Fook and R. Pozzuto. Toronto: Thompson, 67–85.

Fook, J. and Napier, L. 2000. From dilemma to breakthrough: Retheorising social work, in *Breakthroughs in Practice: Theorising Critical Moments in Social Work*, edited by L. Napier and J. Fook. London: Whiting and Birch, 212–27.

Fook, J., Ryan, M. and Hawkins, L. 2000. *Professional Expertise: Practice, Theory and Education for Working in Uncertainty.* London: Whiting and Birch.

Fook, J., White, S. and Gardner, F. 2006. Critical reflection: A review of contemporary literature and understandings, in *Critical Reflection in Health and Social Care*, edited by S. White, J. Fook, and F. Gardner. Maidenhead, 3–20.

Forcey, L.R. and Nash, M. 1998. Rethinking feminist theory and social work therapy. *Women and Therapy*, 21 (4), 85–99.

Francis, B. 2000. Poststructuralism and nursing: Uncomfortable bedfellows? *Nursing Inquiry*, 7, 20–28.

Fraser, H. and Briskman, L. 2005. Through the eye of a needle: The challenge of getting justice in Australia if you're indigenous or seeking asylum in *Globalisation, Global Justice And Social Work*, edited by I. Ferguson, M. Lavalette and E. Whitmore. London: Taylor & Francis, 109–24.

Frazier, P. and Haney, B. 1996. Sexual assault cases in the legal system: Police, prosecutor and victim perspectives. *Law and Human Behaviour*, 20 (6), 607–28.

Frost, S. 2006. Recasting individual practice through reflection on narratives in *Critical Reflection in Health and Social Care*, edited by S. White, J. Fook, and F. Gardner. Maidenhead: Open University Press, 107–17.

Gans, J. 1995. Fact-finding and rape law reform, in *The Project for Legal Action against Sexual Assault: Legalising Justice for All Women*, compiled by M. Heenan. Paper presented at the National Conference on Sexual Assault and the Law, Melbourne, Australia, 28–30 November, 221–27.

Garcia, V. and McManimon, P. 2011. *Gendered Justice: Intimate Partner Violence and the Criminal Justice System*. Maryland: Rowman & Littlefield Publisher, Inc.

Gardiner, L. and Roberson, M. 1995. Fishing expeditions: Questioning the legal dragnet: The one that got away OR client files and confidentiality: Legal and ethical issues for sexual assault counsellors, *The Project for Legal Action against Sexual Assault: Legalising Justice for All Women*, compiled by M. Heenan. Paper presented at the National Conference on Sexual Assault and the Law, Melbourne, Australia, 28–30 November, 228–38.

Gardner, F. 2013. Using critical reflection to research practice in a mental health setting, in *Critical Reflection in Context: Applications in Health and Social Care*, edited by J. Fook and F. Gardner. London and New York: Routledge, 28–43.

Gardner, F., Fook, J. and White, S. 2006. Critical reflection: Possibilities for developing effectiveness in conditions of uncertainty, in *Critical Reflection in Health and Social Care*, edited by S. White, J. Fook and F. Gardner. Maidenhead: Open University Press, 228–40.

Geiger, B., Fischer, M. and Eshet, Y. 2004. Date-rape-supporting and victim-blaming attitudes among high school students in a multiethnic society: Israel. *Journal of Interpersonal Violence*, 19 (4), 406–26.

Gil, V. and Anderson, A. 1999. Case study of rape in contemporary China: A cultural-historical analysis of gender and power differentials. *Journal of Interpersonal Violence*, 14 (11), 1151–71.

Gilmore, K. 1995. Violence against women: Crimes, not misdemeanours, in *In the Shadow of the Law: The Legal Context of Social Work Practice*, edited by P. Swain. Sydney: Federation Press, 46–58.

Goldberg Wood, G. and Tully, C.T. 2006. *The Structural Approach to Direct Practice in Social Work: A Social Constructionist Perspective*. 3rd Edition. New York: Columbia University Press.

Golding, J., Fryman, H., Marsil, D. and Yozwiak, J. 2003. Big girls don't cry: The effect of child witness demeanor on juror decision in a child sexual abuse trial. *Child Abuse and Neglect*, 27 (11), 1311–21.

Gouldner, A. 1970. *The Coming Crisis of Western Sociology*. New York: Basic Books.

Goodman, J. 1998. Ideology and critical ethnography, in *Being Reflexive and Critical in Educational and Social Research*, edited by J. Smyth and G. Shacklock. London: Falmer Press, 50–66.

Grace, A.P. 1997. Where critical postmodern theory meets practice: Working in the intersection of instrumental, social, and cultural education. *Studies in Continuing Education*, 19 (1), 51–70.

Graham, R. 2006. Male rape and the careful construction of the male victim. *Social and Legal Studies*, 15 (3), 187–208.

Grant, P. 2001. The power of uncertainty: Reflections of pre-service literacy teachers. *Reflection*, 2 (1), 237–48.

Graycar, R. 1994. Gendered assumptions in family law. Paper presented at the Gender Awareness Seminar. Family Court of Australia, Kooralbyn.

Green, R., Gregory, R. and Mason, R. 2006. Professional distance and social work: Stretching the elastic? *Australian Social Work*, 59 (4), 449–61.

Gregory, R.J. 2007. Borderline attributions. *American Journal of Psychotherapy*, 61 (2), 131–47.

Grey, A. 2007. Not-so-uniform evidence law: Reforming Longman Warnings. *Current Issues in Criminal Justice*, 19 (2), 172–82.

Griffin, M. 2003. Using critical incidents to promote and assess reflective thinking in pre-service teachers. *Reflective Practice*, 4 (2), 207–20.

Grix, J. 1999. Laws, truth and other lies: Women, sexual assault and the criminal justice system. *Australian Feminist Law Journal*, 12, 83–93.

Haag, E. 2000. *Beyond Sexual History: Rethinking the Role of Victim Characteristics in the Successful Prosecution of Sexual Assault Cases*: Southern Sociological Society.

Habermas, J. 1979. *Communication and the Evolution of Society*. (trans T. McCarthy). Boston: Beacon Press.

Hare-Mustin, R. and Marecek, J. 1994. Feminism and postmodernism: Dilemmas and points of resistance. *Dulwich Centre Newsletter*, 4, 13–19.

Hargreaves, J. 2004. So how do you feel about that? Assessing reflective practice. *Nurse Education Today*, 24, 196–201.

Harvey. A., Garcia-Moreno, C. and Butchart, A. 2007. Primary prevention of intimate-partner violence and sexual violence: Background paper for WHO expert meeting, 2–3 May, 2007, World Health Organization.

Hastings, J. 2002. Silencing state-sponsored rape in and beyond a transnational Guatemalan community. *Women against Violence*, 8 (10), 1153–81.

Healy, K. 1998. Participation and child protection: The importance of context. *British Journal of Social Work*, 28, 897–914.

Healy, K. 2000. *Social Work Practices: Contemporary Perspectives on Change*. London: Sage.

Heaney, T.W. and Horton, A.I. 1990. Reflective engagement for social change, in *Fostering Critical Reflection in Adulthood*, edited by J. Mezirow. San Francisco: Jossey-Bass, 74–98.

Heath, M. 2005. *The Law and Sexual Offences against Adults in Australia* (Issue No. 4). Melbourne: Australian Centre for Study of Sexual Assault.

Heath, M. 2007. Lack of conviction: A proposal to make rape illegal in South Australia. *Australian Feminist Law Journal*, 27, 175–92.

Heath, M. and Naffine, N. 1994. Men's needs and women's desires: Feminist dilemmas about rape law reform. *Australian Feminist Law Journal*, 3, 30–52.

Heenan, M. 1995. Victims' experiences of the police code of practice, in *The Project for Legal Action against Sexual Assault: Legalising Justice for All Women*, compiled by M. Heenan. Paper presented at the National Conference on Sexual Assault and the Law, Melbourne, Australia, 28–30 November, 282–91.

Heenan, M. 1997. Sex crimes and the criminal justice system. *Australian Feminist Law Journal*, 9, 90–95.

Heenan, M. 2002–2003. Reconstituting the 'relevance' of women's sexual histories in rape trials. *Women Against Violence*, 13, 4–17.

Heron, B. 2005. Self-reflection in critical social work practice: Subjectivity and the possibilities of resistance. *Reflective Practice*, 6 (3), 341–51.

Heron, J. 1996. *Co-Operative Inquiry: Research into the Human Condition*. London: Sage.

Heslop, L. 1997. The (im)possibilities of poststructuralist and critical social nursing inquiry. *Nursing Inquiry*, 4, 48–56.

Hess, P. 1995. Reflecting in and on practice, in *Practitioner-Researcher Partnerships: Building Knowledge from, in and for Practice*, edited by P. Hess and E.J. Mullen. Washington: NASW Press, 113–29.

Hick, S., Fook, J. and Pozzuto, R. (eds) 2005. *Social Work: A Critical Turn*. Toronto: Thompson Education Publishing.

Holmes, C.A. and Warelow, P.J. 2000. Some implications of postmodernism for nursing theory, research and practice. *Canadian Journal of Nursing Research*, 32 (2), 89–101.

hooks, b. 1989. *Talking Back: Thinking Feminist, Thinking Black*. Toronto: Between the Lines.

Hovdestad, E. 2001. Seeking justice: The strategy of the national social action program. *Journal of Social Distress and the Homeless*, 10 (1), 105–21.

Hunter, C. 1995. The women's justice outreach service models a quality legal service, in *The Project for Legal Action against Sexual Assault: Legalising Justice for All Women*, compiled by M. Heenan. Paper presented at the National Conference on Sexual Assault and the Law, Melbourne, Australia, 28–30 November, 245–50.

Hurst, M. 1995. Counselling women from a feminist perspective, in *Issues Facing Australian Families*. 2nd Edition, edited by W. Weeks and J. Wilson. Melbourne: Longman, 245–57.

Ife, J. 1997. *Human Rights and Social Work: Towards Rights Based Practice*. Cambridge: Cambridge University Press.

Ixer, G. 2000. Assessing reflective practice: New research findings. *Journal of Practice Teaching in Health and Social Work*, 23 (3), 19–27.

Jarvis, S. and McIlwaine, F. 1997. A Crisis of witnessing: Sexually assaulted women in the psychiatric and legal systems. *Domestic Violence and Incest Resource Centre Newsletter*, 3, 3–8.

Jenkins, S. 1996. Integrated approaches to sexual abuse. Paper presented at Balancing the Scales: National Conference on Sexual Assault, WA Sexual Assault Referral Centre, Perth, Australia, 20–21 June.

Jones, H. and Cook, K. 2008. *Rape Crisis: Responding to Sexual Violence*. Dorset, UK: Russell House Publishing.

Jones, M. 1990. Understanding social work: A matter of interpretation. *British Journal of Social Work*, 20, 181–96.

Jordan, J. 2004. Beyond belief?: Police, rape and women's credibility. *Criminal Justice* 4 (1), 29–59.

Jordan, J. 2008. *Serial Survivors: Women's Narratives of Surviving Rape*. Sydney: The Federation Press.

Jordan, J. 2012. Silencing rape, silencing women, in *Handbook on Sexual Violence* edited by J.J. Brown and S.L Walklate. London & New York: Routledge, 253–86.

Kappler. K.E. 2012. *Living with Paradoxes: Victims of Sexual Violence and their Conduct of Everyday Life*. Germany: VS Verlag.

Kaspiew, R. 1995. Rape lore: Legal narrative and sexual violence. *Melbourne University Law Review*, 20 (2), 350–82.

'Kate' 1998. Desperately seeking justice: Systemic abuse and gendered crimes. *DVIRC Newsletter*, Winter Edition.

Keilty, J. and Connelly, G. 2001. Making a statement: An exploratory study of barriers facing women with an intellectual disability. *Disability and Society*, 16 (2), 273–91.

Kellehear, A. 1993. *The Unobtrusive Researcher*. Sydney: Allen and Unwin.

Kenney, S.J. 2003. Where is gender in agenda setting? *Women and Politics*, 25 (1–2), 179–207.

Kermode, S. and Brown, C. 1996. The postmodernist hoax and its effects on nursing. *International Journal of Nursing Studies*, 33 (4), 375–84.

Kicuroski, T. 2008. Borderline personality disorder and binary thinking: Challenging power dynamics and practice, in *Critical Reflection: Generating Theory from Practice*, edited by R. Pockett and R. Giles. Sydney: Darlington Press, 62–76.
Kirkwood, M. and Cecil, D. 2001. Marital rape: A student assessment of rape laws and the marital exemption. *Violence Against Women*, 7 (11), 1234–53.
Koch, T. and Harrington, A. 1998. Reconceptualizing rigour: The case for reflexivity. *Journal of Advanced Nursing*, 28 (4), 882–90.
Kolb, D.A. 1984. *Experiential Learning.* Englewood Cliffs, NJ: Prentice Hall.
Konradi, A. 2001. Pulling strings doesn't work in court: Moving beyond puppetry in the relationship between prosecutors and rape survivors. *Journal of Distress and the Homeless*, 10 (1), 5–28.
Kumar, M. 1995. Justice Sally Brown: Educating the bench. *Polemic*, 6 (2), 93–8.
Laing, L. 2008. Violence, criminal justice, the law, policy and practice, in *Addressing Violence, Abuse and Oppression: Debates and Challenges*, edited by B. Fawcett and F. Waugh. New York: Routledge, 67–79.
Lancaster, E. and Lumb, J. 1999. Bridging the gap: Feminist theory and practice reality in work with perpetrators of child sexual abuse. *Child and Family Social Work*, 4, 119–29.
Langellier, K. 1989. Personal narratives: Perspectives on theory and research. *Text and Performance Quarterly*, 9 (4), 243–76.
Larcombe, W. 2002. The 'ideal' victim v. successful rape complaints: Not what you might expect. *Feminist Legal Studies*, 10 (2), 131–42.
Larcombe, W. 2005. *Feminism, Rape Law and Romance Fiction.* Leichhardt, NSW: Federation Press.
Lawrence, M. 1992. Women's psychology and feminist social work practice, in *Women, Oppression and Social Work: Issues in Anti-Discriminatory Practice*, edited by M. Langan and L. Day. London: Routledge, 32–48.
Lea, S. and Auburn, T. 2001. The social construction of rape in the talk of a convicted rapist. *Feminism and Psychology*, 11 (1), 11–33.
Lehmann, J. 2006. Telling stories … and the pursuit of critical reflection, in *Critical Reflection in Health and Social Care*, edited by S. White, J. Fook and F. Gardner. Maidenhead: Open University Press, 201–12
Leonard, P. 1994. Knowledge/power and postmodernism: Implications for the practice of a critical social work education. *Canadian Social Work Review*, 11 (1), 3–19.
Leonard, P. 1997. *Postmodern Welfare.* London: Sage.
Leonard, P. 2004. The uses of theory and the problems of pessimism, in *Social Work in a Corporate Era: Practices of Power and Resistance*, edited by L. Davies and P. Leonard. Aldershot: Ashgate, 3–15.
Lesnick, A. 2005. The mirror in motion: Redefining reflective practice in an undergraduate fieldwork seminar. *Reflective Practice*, 6 (1), 33–48.
L'Heureux-Dube, C. 2001. Beyond the myths: Equality, impartiality and justice. *Journal of Social Distress and the Homeless*, 10 (1), 87–104.

Lievore, D. 2005. *No Longer Silent: A Study of Women's Help-Seeking Decision and Service Responses to Sexual Assault*. Canberra: A Report prepared by the Australian Institute of Criminology for the Australian Government's Office for Women, Commonwealth of Australia.

Lifschitz, R. 1995. The Macarthur Sexual Assault Service: Advocacy in practice, in *The Project for Legal Action against Sexual Assault: Legalising Justice for All Women*, complied by M. Heenan. Paper presented at the National Conference on Sexual Assault and the Law, Melbourne, Australia, 28–30 November, 239–44.

Lipp, A. 2007. Developing the reflexive dimension of reflection: A framework for debate. *International Journal of Multiple Research Approaches*. 1 (1), n.p.

Loftus, S., Higgs, J. and Trede, F. 2011 Researching living spaces: Trends in creative qualitative research, in *Critical Spaces for Qualitative Researching: Living Research*, edited by J. Higgs., A. Titches., D. Horsfall and D. Bridges. Rotterdam: Sense Publishers, 3–12.

Logan, T., Evans, L., Stevenson, E. and Jordan, C. 2005. Barriers to services for rural and urban survivors of rape. *Journal of Interpersonal Violence*, 20 (5), 591–616.

Lonne, B. 2008. National president's report to the AASW Annual General Meeting, 9 November 2008 [Online]. Available at: http:www.aasw.asn.au/publications/Annual_Reports/AASW2008_NtlPresReportAGM.pdf [accessed: 19 November 2009].

Lovelock, R. and Powell, J. 2004. Habermas/Foucault for social work: Practices of critical reflection, in *Reflecting on Social Work – Discipline and Profession*, edited by R. Lovelock, K. Lyons and J. Powell. Aldershot: Ashgate, 181–216.

Lyons, K. and Taylor, I. 2004. Gender and knowledge in social work, in *Reflecting on Social Work – Discipline and Profession*, edited by R. Lovelock, K. Lyons and J. Powell. Aldershot: Ashgate, 72–94.

MacDonald, L. 1996. Dismantling the movement: Feminism, postmodernism and political action. *Refractory Girl*, 51 (96), 48–51.

Macey, D. 2000. *The Penguin Dictionary of Critical Theory*. London: Penguin Books.

Mack, K. 1998. Judicial attitudes and women's credibility: Barriers to equality in the law, in *Women and the Law*, edited by A. Thacker. Geelong: Deakin University Press, 145–52.

Maich, N., Brown, B. and Royle, J. 2000. 'Becoming' through reflection and professional portfolios: The voice of growth in nurses. *Reflective Practice*, 1 (3), 309–24.

Maier, S. 2005. Navigating the transformation of rape crisis centres and programs: Experiences, views, and struggles of rape advocates. *Dissertation Abstracts International, A: The Humanities and Social Sciences*, 6 (8), 3161

Maier, S. 2008. 'I have heard horrible stories ...': Rape victim advocates' perceptions of the revictimization of rape victims by the police and medical system. *Violence Against Women*, 14 (7), 786–808.

Malloch, M. 2004. 'Risky' women, sexual consent, and criminal justice, in *Making Sense of Sexual Consent*, edited by M. Cowling and P. Reynolds. Aldershot: Ashgate, 111–25.

Mamede, S. and Schmidt, H.G. 2004. The structure of reflective practice in medicine. *Medical Education*, 38 (12), 1302–8.

Marchant, H. and Wearing, B. 1986. *Gender Reclaimed: Women In Social Work*. Sydney: Hale and Iremonger.

Martin, F. and Angel, K. 1995. Barriers to justice – invisible survivors, in *The Project for Legal Action against Sexual Assault: Legalising Justice for All Women*, compiled by M. Heenan. Paper presented at the National Conference on Sexual Assault and the Law, Melbourne, Australia, 28–30 November, 94–102.

Martin, K., Vieraitis, L. and Britto, M. 2006. Gender equality and women's absolute status: A test of the feminist models of rape. *Violence Against Women*, 12 (4), 321–39.

McCarthy, T. 1995. Battered woman syndrome: Some reflection of the invisibility of the battering man in legal discourse drawing on R *v*. Raby. *Australian Feminist Law Journal*, 4, 141–51.

McCulloch, J. 1998. Sexual assault: The legal process. *Domestic Violence and Incest Resource Centre Newsletter*, 4, 16–18.

McDonald, J. 2005. Neo-liberalism and the pathologising of public issues: The displacement of feminist service models in domestic violence support services. *Australian Social Work*, 58 (3), 275–84.

McKelvie, H. and Heenan, M. 1993. No means no. *Polemic*, 4 (1), 7–11.

Menon, T. 2003. Crime against women in India: Violence within and without. *Philosophy and Social Action*, 21 (9), 17–22.

Mertus, J. 2004. Shouting from the bottom of the well: The impact of international trials on wartime rape for women's agency. *International Feminist Journal of Politics*, 6 (1), 110–28.

Mezirow, J. 1990. How critical reflection triggers transformative learning, in *Fostering Critical Reflection In Adulthood*. San Francisco: Jossey-Bass, 1–20.

Mezirow, J. 1997. Transformative learning: Theory to practice. *New Directions for Adult and Continuing Education*, 74, 5–11.

Mezirow, J. and Associates. 1990. *Fostering Critical Reflection in Adulthood*. San Francisco: Jossey-Bass.

Mezirow, J. and Associates. 2000. *Learning as Transformation: Critical Perspectives on a Theory in Progress*. San Francisco: Jossey-Bass.

Mills, L. 1996. Empowering battered women transnationally: The case for postmodern interventions. *Social Work*, 41 (3), 261–68.

Minow, M. 1985. Learning to live with the dilemma of difference: Bilingual and special education. *Law and Contemporary Problems*, 18 (2), 157–211.

Mitchell, L., Francavilla, D. and Wilson, L. 1995. Telling tales, in *The Project for Legal Action against Sexual Assault: Legalising Justice for All Women*, compiled by M. Heenan. Paper presented at the National Conference on Sexual Assault and the Law, Melbourne, Australia, 28–30 November, 123–34.

Modisett, J. and Dreyer, D. 2005. Prosecuting Mike Tyson: Boxing with the media. *Sociology of Crime, Law and Deviance*, 6, 145–63.

Moffat, L. 1999. Surveillance and government of the welfare recipient, in *Reading Foucault For Social Work*, edited by A.S. Chambon, A. Irving and L. Epstein. New York: Columbia University Press, 219–45.

Monroe, L., Kinney, L., Weist, M., et al. 2005. The experiences of sexual assault: Findings from a statewide victim needs assessment. *Journal of Interpersonal Violence*, 20 (7), 767–76.

Monson, C., Langhinrichen-Rohling, J. and Binderup, T. 2000. Does 'no' really mean 'no' after you say 'yes'? *Journal of Interpersonal Violence*, 15 (11), 1156–74.

Morley, C. 2004. Critical reflection as a response to globalisation? *International Journal of Social Welfare*, 13 (2), 297–303.

Morley, C. 2005. Collaborative social work practice in opposing paradigms: Issues to emerge from a sexual assault and mental health project. *Women Against Violence: An Australian Feminist Journal*, (16), 4–14.

Morley, C. 2007. Engaging practitioners in critical reflection: Issues and dilemmas. *Journal of Reflective Practice*, 8 (1), 16–74.

Morley, C. 2008a. Developing critical reflection as a research methodology, in *Knowing Differently: An Introduction to Experiential and Arts-Based Research Methods* edited by P. Liamputtong and J. Rumbold. New York: Nova Science Publishers, 265–80.

Morley, C. 2008b. Teaching critical practice: Resisting structural domination. *Social Work Education*, 27 (4), 407–21.

Morley, C. 2009. Developing feminist practices, in *Critical Social Work: An Introduction to Theories and Practices*, edited by J. Allan, B. Pease, and L. Briskman. Crows Nest, NSW: Allen and Unwin, 145–59.

Morley, C. 2011. Critical reflection as an educational process: A practice example. *Advances in Social Work and Welfare Education: Special Issue – Critical Reflection Method and Practice*, 13 (1), 7–28.

Morley, C. 2012. How does critical reflection develop emancipatory possibilities for emancipatory change? An example from an empirical research project. *British Journal of Social Work*, 42 (8), 1513–32.

Morley, C 2013a. Some methodological and ethical tensions in using critical reflection as a research methodology. *Critical Reflection in Context: Applications in Health and Social Care*. London and New York: Routledge. 166–78.

Morley, C. 2013b. Using critical reflection to research possibilities for change. *British Journal of Social Work*. Publication pending [Online]. Available at http://dx.doi.org/10.1093/bjsw/bct004 [accessed 18 March 2013].

Morley, C. and Macfarlane, S. 2008. The continued importance of a feminist analysis: Making gendered inequalities visible through a critique of Howard government policy on domestic violence. *Just Policy: A Journal of Australian Social Policy*, 47, 31–8.

Morley, C. and Macfarlane, S 2012. The nexus between postmodernism and feminism: Still a central concern for critical social work. *British Journal of Social Work*, 42 (4), 687–705.

Mullaly, B. 2001. Confronting the politics of despair: Toward the reconstruction of progressive social work in a global economy and postmodern age. *Social Work Education*, 20 (3), 303–20.

Mullaly, B. 2002. *Challenging Oppression: A Critical Social Work Approach.* Ontario: Oxford University Press.

Mullaly, B. 2007. *The New Structural Social Work.* 3rd Edition. Ontario: Oxford.

Mullings, L. and Schulz, A. 2006. Intersectionality and health: An introduction, in *Gender, Race, Class and Health: Intersectional Approaches*, edited by L. Mullings and A. Schulz. San Francisco: Jossey-Bass, 3–17.

Munaaba, F. 2004. Human rights and legal pluralism: Linking women's realities to laws and practices in Uganda. *The East African Journal of Human Rights and Democracy*, 2.2 (1), 1–22.

Murphy, T. and Whitty, N. 2000. What is a fair trial? Rape prosecutions, disclosure and the Human Rights Act. *Feminist Legal Studies*, 8 (2), 143–67.

Mustaine, E. and Tewksbury, R. 2002. Sexual assault of college women: A feminist interpretation of a routine activities analysis. *Criminal Justice Review*, 27 (1), 89–123.

Napier, L. 2006. Practicing critical reflection, in *Skills for Human Service Practice: Working with Individuals, Groups and Communities*, edited by A. O'Hara and Z. Weber. South Melbourne: Oxford University Press, 7–16.

Napier, L. and Fook, J. 2000. Reflective practice in social work, in *Breakthroughs in Practice: Theorising Critical Moments in Social Work*, edited by L. Napier and J. Fook. London: Whiting and Birch, 1–11.

Naudi, M. 2006. Disrupting dominant discourses: Critical reflection and code-switching in Maltese social work, in *Critical Reflection in Health and Social Care*, edited by S. White, J. Fook, and F. Gardner. Maidenhead: Open University Press, 118–31.

Naylor, B. 1985. Sexual assault: The law and the child victim. *Legal Service Bulletin*, 10, 12–17.

Neave, M. 1995. The gender of judging. *Psychiatry, Psychology and Law*, 2 (1), 183–204.

Nelson, T. 1995. Collaboration, co-operation – can it work? Organisational responses to a rape crisis, in *The Project for Legal Action against Sexual Assault: Legalising Justice for All Women*, compiled by M. Heenan. Paper presented at the National Conference on Sexual Assault and the Law, Melbourne, Australia, 28–30 November, 292–97.

Nicholson, L. and Seidman, S. (eds) 1995. *Social Postmodernism: Beyond Identity Politics*. New York: Cambridge University Press.

Nolan, M. and Behi, R. 1995. Alternative approaches to establishing reliability and validity. *British Journal of Social Work*, 4 (10), 587–90.

O'byrne, R., Rapley, M. and Hansen, S. 2006. You couldn't say 'no' could you? Young men's understanding of sexual refusal. *Feminism and Psychology*, 16 (2), 133–54.

Oosterhoff, P., Zwanikken, P. and Ketting, E. 2004. Sexual torture of men in Croatia and other conflict situations: An open secret. *Reproductive Health Matters*, 12 (23), 68–77.

Orth, U. and Maercker, A. 2004. Do trials of perpetrators retraumatise crime victims? *Journal of Interpersonal Violence*, 19 (2), 212–27.

Page, A. 2004. Behind the blue line: Investigating police officers' attitudes toward women and rape. *Dissertation Abstracts International, A: The Humanities and Social Sciences*, 54 (4), 1546–A.

Pardeck, J.T. and Murphy, J.W. 1993. Postmodernism and clinical practice: A critical analysis of the disease model. *Psychological Reports*, 72 (3, part 2), 1187–94.

Pardeck, J.T. and Murphy, J.W. 1998. Renewing social work practice through a postmodern perspective. *Social Thought*, 1. 81 (3), 5–18.

Parker, S. 1997. *Reflective Teaching in the Postmodern World*. Buckingham: Open University Press.

Parker, S., Fook, J. and Pease, B. 1999. Empowerment: The modern social work concept par excellence, in *Transforming Social Work Practice: Postmodern Critical Perspectives*, edited by B. Pease and J. Fook. London: Routledge, 150–59.

Parliament of Victoria Social Development Committee 1998. *First Report upon the Inquiry into Strategies to Deal with the Issue of Community Violence*. Melbourne: Jean Gordon Government Printer, 343–59.

Parton, N. and O'Byrne, P. 2000. *Constructive Social Work: Towards A New Practice*. Houndmills: Macmillan.

Payne, M. 2005. *Modern Social Work Theory*. London: Macmillan.

Pearce, H. 2003. An examination of the international understanding of political rape and the significance of labeling it torture. *International Journal of Refugee Law*, 14 (4), 534–60.

Pease, B. 2002. Rethinking empowerment: A postmodern reappraisal for emancipatory practice. *British Journal of Social Work*, 32, 135–47.

Pease, B. and Fook, J. (eds) 1999. *Transforming Social Work Practice: Postmodern Critical Perspectives*. St. Leonards, NSW: Allen and Unwin.

Pettman, J. 1992. *Living in the Margins*. Sydney: Allen and Unwin.

Philadelphoff-Puren, N. 2004. The mark of refusal: Sexual violence and the politics of recontextualization. *Feminist Theory*, 5 (3), 243–56.

Philladelphoff-Puren, N. 2005. Contextualizing consent: The problem of rape and romance. *Australian Feminist Studies*, 20 (46), 31–42.

Phillips, J. 1996. Sexual, multiple disabilities and the law. *Australian Feminist Law Journal*, 7, 157–62.

Phillips, R. 2006. Undoing an activist response: Feminism and the Australian government's domestic violence policy. *Critical Social Policy*, 26 (1), 192–219.

Phillips, R. 2008. Feminism(s) and domestic violence within national policy contexts, in *Addressing Violence, Abuse and Oppression: Debates and Challenges*, edited by B. Fawcett and F. Waugh. New York: Routledge, 57–66.

Pile, S. 1997. Introduction, in *Geographies of Resistance*, edited by S. Pile and M. Keith. London: Routledge. 1–32.

Pine, D.W. 1996. Post-modernist analysis a valuable tool for feminists. *Refractory Girl*, 51 (96), 4–7.

Pini, B. and Brown, K. 2004. Farm women and femocracy. *Australian Journal of Political Science*, 39 (1), 161–73.

Pockett, R. and Giles, R. 2008. *Critical Reflection: Generating Theory from Practice: The Graduating Social Work Student Experience*. Sydney: Darlington Press.

Porter, S. 1993. Nursing research convention: Objectivity or obfuscation? *Journal of Advanced Nursing*, 18, 137–43.

Powell, J. 2002. The changing conditions of social work research. *British Journal of Social Work*, 32, 17–33.

Purvis, T. and Hunt, A. 1993. Discourse, ideology, discourse, ideology, discourse, ideology, discourse, ideology …! *British Journal of Sociology*, 44 (3), 473–99.

Quigley, B. 2007. Letter to a law student interested in social justice, 1, *DePaul Journal for Social Justice* 1, 7–28.

Reason, P. and Bradbury, H. (eds) 2001. *Handbook of Action Research*. London: Sage.

Reason, P. and Rowan, P. (eds) 1981. *Human Inquiry: A Sourcebook of New Paradigm Research*. Chichester: John Wiley and Sons.

Redmond, B. 2004. *Reflection in Action: Developing Reflective Practice in Health And Social Services*. Aldershot: Ashgate.

Rees, S. 1991. *Achieving Power*. Sydney: Allen and Unwin.

Rosaldo, R. 1994. Subjectivity in social analysis, in *The Postmodern Turn: New Perspectives on Social Theory*, edited by S. Seidman. New York: Cambridge University Press, 171–84.

Rosenau, P.M. 1992. *Postmodernism and the Social Sciences: Insights, Inroads and Intrusions*. Princeton, NJ: Princeton University Press.

Rossiter, A. 1996. A perspective on critical social work. *Journal of Progressive Human Services*, 7 (2), 23–41.

Rossiter, A. 2005. Discourse analysis in critical social work: From apology to question. *Critical Social Work*, 6 (1) [Online]. Available at: http://criticalsocialwork.com/units/social work/cri [accessed: 18 September, 2006].

Rubensohn, R. 2008. International social work versus local practice: The moral dilemma of knowing where to give aid, in *Critical Reflection: Generating Theory from Practice*, edited by R. Pockett and R. Giles. Sydney: Darlington Press, 77–92.

Ruch, G. 2007. Reflective practice is contemporary child care social work: The role of containment. *Child and Family Social Work*, 10, 111–23.

Rumney, P. and Morgan-Taylor, M. 2004. The construction of sexual consent in male rape and sexual assault, in *Making Sense Of Sexual Consent*, edited by M. Cowling and M. Reynolds. Aldershot: Ashgate, 141–69.

Safai, P. 2002. Boys behaving badly: Popular literature on the mis/behaviour of male team sport athletes in North America. *International Journal Review for the Sociology of Sport*, 37 (1), 97–102.

Sands, R. and Nuccio, K. 1992. Postmodern feminist theory and social work. *Social Work*, 37 (6), 489–494.

Sands, R.G. 1996. The elusiveness of identity in social work practice with women: A postmodern feminist perspective. *Clinical Social Work Journal*, 24 (2), 167–86.

Sawyer 1993. Reclaiming social liberalism: The women's movement and the state, in *Women and the State: Australian Perspectives*, edited by R. Howe. Victoria: La Trobe University Press, 1–21.

Schon, D. 1983. *The Reflective Practitioner: How Professionals Think in Action*. New York: Basic Books.

Schon, D. 1987. *Educating the Critically Reflective Practitioner: Toward a New Design for Teaching and Learning in the Professions*. San Francisco: Jossey-Bass.

Scott, D., McCarthy, T. and Gilmore, K. 1991. A tribute to Dora: Supporting adult survivors of child sexual assault: A feminist perspective, in *Incest and the Community, Australian Perspectives*, edited by P. Hetherington. Perth: Centre for Western Australian History, University of Western Australia, 198–213.

Scutt, J. 1990. Confronting precedent and prejudice: Child sexual abuse in the Courts, in *Understanding and Managing Child Sexual Abuse*, edited by K. Oates. Sydney: Harcourt Brace, 312–41.

Scutt, J. 1991. Law reform and child sexual abuse in Australia, in *Incest and the Community, Australian Perspectives*, edited by P. Hetherington. Perth: Centre for Western Australian History, University of Western Australia, 117–38.

Scutt, J. 1995. The voice of the rapist, in *Australian Violence Contemporary Perspectives II*, edited by D. Chappel and S. Egger. Sydney: Australian Institute of Criminology, 299–323.

Scutt, J. 1996. Taking action on invisible crimes: Focusing on the positive, avoiding the negative. Paper presented at Balancing the Scales: National Conference on Sexual Assault, WA Sexual Assault Referral Centre, Perth, 20–21 June.

Scutt, J. 1998. Character, credit, context: Women's lives, judicial reality, in *Balancing the Scales: Rape Law Reform and Australian Culture*, edited by P. Easteal. Annandale, NSW: Federation Press, 159–73.

Segal, L. 1995. Feminism and the family, in *Gender, Power and Relationships*, edited by C. Burke and B. Speed. London: Routledge, 248–66.

Seidman, S. (ed.) 2004. *The Postmodern Turn: New Perspectives on Social Theory*. New York: Cambridge University Press.

Seidman, S. 2013 *Contested Knowledge: Social Theory Today*. 5th Edition. Wiley Blackwell: Sussex.

Shaw, J. and Campbell, R. 2011. Rape crisis centers: Serving survivors and their communities, in *Surviving Sexual Violence: A Guide to Recovery and* Empowerment, edited by T. Bryant-Davis. Maryland: Rowman & Littlefield Publishers Inc., 112–28.

Sjoberg, R.L. and Lindblad, F. 2002. Limited disclosure of sexual abuse in children whose experiences were documented by videotape. *American Journal of Psychiatry*, 159, 312–14.

Smith, D.E. 1990. *The Conceptual Practices of Power: A Feminist Sociology of Knowledge.* Boston, MA: Northeastern University Press.

Smith, R. 2008. *Social Work and Power*. Houndmills: Palgrave Macmillan.

Smyth, J. 1988. Deliberating upon reflection in action as a critical form of professional education. *Studies in Continuing Education*, 10 (2), 164–71.

Smyth, J. and Shacklock, G. 1998. Behind the cleansing of socially critical research accounts, in *Being Reflexive in Critical Educational and Social Research*, edited by G. Shacklock and J. Smyth. London: Falmer Press, 1–13.

Spohn, C., Beichner, D., and Davis-Frenzel, E. 2001. Prosecutorial justifications for sexual assault case rejection: Guarding the gateway to justice. *Social Problems*, 48 (2), 206–35.

Staples, J. 2007. NGOs out in the cold: Howard government policy towards NGOs. *Democratic Audit of Australian Discussion Paper 19* (6), University of New South Wales Faculty of Law Research Series, 27 February [Online]. Available at: http://www.austlii.edu.au/au/journals/UNSWLRS/2007/8html [accessed: 5 September 2006].

Stein, D. 2000.Teaching critical reflection. *Myths and Realities*, 7 [Online]. Available at: http://www.cete.org/acve/docgen.asp?tbl=mrandID=98 [accessed: 8 February 2006].

Stephen, K. 1994. The legal language of rape: A feminist reconstruction of rape. *Alternative Law Journal*, 19 (5), 224–8.

Stephenson, M. 1994. Post-modernism and feminism: A fruitful alliance but, perhaps, a problematic marriage. *South Australian Educational Leader*, 5 (2), 1–5.

Stermac, L., Del Bove, G. and Addison, M. 2004. Stranger and acquaintance sexual assault of adult males. *Journal of Interpersonal Violence*, 19 (8), 901–15.

Stevenson, K. 2000. Unequivocal victims: The historical roots of the mystification of the female complainant in rape cases. *Feminist Legal Studies*, 8 (3), 343–66.

Stromquist, N. 2000. The challenges to emancipation in higher education. *World Studies in Education*, 1 (1), 61–77.

Stuart, D. 1993. No real harm done: Sexual assault: Sexual assault and the criminal justice system, in *Without Consent: Confronting Adult Sexual Violence*, edited by P. Easteal. Proceedings of a conference held in Melbourne 27–29 October 1992, Canberra: Australian Institute of Criminology, 95–106.

Tannin, G. 1996. The competing demands, interests and rights or victims and the accused in sexual offence proceedings: An analysis of the law of corroboration and discovery. Paper presented at Balancing the Scales: National

Conference on Sexual Assault, WA Sexual Assault Referral Centre, Perth, Australia, 20–21 June.

Taylor, C. 2004. *Surviving the Legal System: A Handbook for Adult and Child Sexual Assault Survivors and their Supporters*, Melbourne: Coulomb Communications.

Taylor, C. 2006. Practicing reflexivity: Narrative, Reflection and the Moral Order, in *Critical Reflection in Health and Social Care*, edited by S. White, J. Fook, and F. Gardner. Maidenhead: Open University Press, 73–88.

Taylor, C. (forthcoming). Critically reflective practice, *The New Politics Of Social Work*, edited by M. Gray, and S. Webb (eds). Houndmills: Palgrave Macmillan

Taylor, C. and White, C. 2006. Knowledge and reasoning in social work: Educating for humane judgment. *British Journal of Social Work*, 36, 937–54.

Taylor, C. and White, S. 2000. *Practising Reflexivity in Health and Welfare: Making Knowledge*. Maidenhead: Open University Press.

Taylor, S. 1996. Court licensed abuse and the construction of the 'incest' victim. Paper presented at Balancing the Scales: National Conference on Sexual Assault, WA Sexual Assault Referral Centre, Perth, Australia, 20–21 June.

Temkin, J. 2005 *Rape and the Legal Process*. 2nd Edition. New York: Oxford University Press.

Tesh, S. 1998. *Hidden Arguments: Political Ideology and the Disease Prevention Policy*. New Brunswick: Rutgers University Press.

Thomas, R.A. and Davies, A. 2005. What have the feminists done for us? *Feminist Theory of Organizational Resistance*, 12 (5), 711–40.

Todd, S. 2005. Unfinished fictions: Becoming and unbecoming feminist community organizers, in *Social Work: A Critical Turn*, edited by S. Hick, J. Fook and R. Pozzuto. Toronto: Thompson Education Publishing, 137–52.

Townsend, K. 1996. Sexual assault law: A fair trial or advantage to the accused. Paper presented at the Balancing the scales: National conference on sexual assault, Perth, Australia, 21–22 June.

Tripp, D. 1998. Critical incidents in action inquiry, in *Being Reflexive in Critical Educational and Social Research*, edited by J. Smyth and G. Shacklock. London: Falmer Press, 36–49.

Trounstine, J. 2001. The forgotten minority, in *Women, Gender and Human Rights: A Global Perspective*, edited by M. Agosin. New Brunswick, NJ: Rutgers University Press, 205–18.

Tsang, A. 2003. Journaling from internship to practice teaching. *Reflective Practice*, 4 (2), 221–40.

Tseris, E. 2008. Examining these words we use: 'Participation', 'empowerment', and the child protection role, in *Critical Reflection: Generating Theory from Practice*, edited by R. Pockett and R. Giles. Sydney: Darlington Press, 30–44.

Victorian Law Reform Commission 2008. *Sexual Offences: Final Report: Summary and Recommendations in Plain English.* Melbourne: Victorian Law Reform Commission.

Wadsworth, Y. 1991. *Everyday Evaluation on the Run*. Melbourne: Action Research Issues Association.
Warner, K. 2004. Gang rape in Sydney: Crime, the media, politics and sentencing. *The Australian and New Zealand Journal of Criminology*, 37 (3), 344–61.
Wasco, S., Campbell, R., Howard, A., et al. 2004. A statewide evaluation of services provided to rape survivors. *Journal of Interpersonal Violence*, 19 (2), 252–63.
Washington, P. 1999. Second assault of male survivors of sexual violence. *Journal of Interpersonal Violence*, 4 (7), 713–30.
Webb, C. 1992. The use of the first person in academic writing: Objectivity, language and gatekeeping. *Journal of Advanced Nursing*, 17, 747–52.
Weber, L. 2006. Reconstructing the landscape of health disparities research: Promoting dialogue and collaboration between feminist intersectional and biomedical paradigms, in *Gender, Race, Class and Health: Intersectional Approaches*, edited by L. Mullings and A. Schulz. San Francisco: Jossey-Bass, 21–59.
Weedon, C. 1987. *Feminist Practice and Poststructuralist Theory*. 2nd Edition. Oxford: Blackwell Publishers.
Weeks, W. 2003. Women: Developing feminist practice in women's services, in *Critical Social Work: An Introduction to Theories and Practices*, edited by J. Allan, B. Pease and L. Briskman. Crows Nest, NSW: Allen and Unwin, 107–23.
Wells, L. (2008. Recent statutory reform of consent in sexual offences. *Judicial Officers Bulletin*, 20 (1), 1–3.
Whatley, M. 2005. The effect of participant sex, victim dress and traditional attitudes on causal judgments for marital rape victims. *Journal of Family Violence*, 20 (3), 191–200.
White, S. 2001. Auto-ethnography as reflexive inquiry: The research act as self-surveillance, in *Qualitative Research In Social Work*, edited by I. Shaw and N. Gould. London: Sage, 100–115.
White, S. and Stancombe, J. 2003. *Clinical Judgment in the Health and Welfare Professions; Extending the Evidence Base*. Maidenhead: Open University Press.
White, V. 2006. *The State of Feminist Social Work*. London and New York: Routledge.
Wieczorek, J. 2008. Crossing invisible lines: Professional boundaries, gender and power in social work, in *Critical Reflection: Generating Theory from Practice*, edited by R. Pockett and R. Giles. Sydney: Darlington Press, 15–29.
Wightman, M. 1995. In limbo: Young women, sexual assault and the rest, in *The Project for Legal Action against Sexual Assault: Legalising Justice for All Women*, compiled by Paper presented at the National Conference on Sexual Assault and the Law, Melbourne, Australia, 28–30 November, 251–66.
Wise, S. 1995. Feminist ethics in practice, in *Ethical Issues in Social Work*, edited by R. Hugman and D. Smith. London: Routledge, 85–101.

Wuest, J. 1995. Feminist grounded theory: An exploration of the congruence and tensions between two traditions in knowledge discovery. *Qualitative Health Research*, 5 (1), 125–37.

Yancey Martin, P. 2005 *Rape Work: Victims, Gender, and Emotions in Organisation and Community Context.* New York: Routledge.

Yeatman, A. 1990. *Bureaucrats, Technocrats, Femocrats: Essays on the Contemporary Australian State*. Sydney: Allen and Unwin.

Yeatman, A. 1994. *Postmodern Revisionings of the Political.* New York: Routledge.

Young, M. 1995. Guilty verdicts of juries in childhood sexual assault cases – unsafe or unsatisfactory? In *The Project for Legal Action against Sexual Assault: Legalising Justice for All Women*, compiled by M. Heenan. Paper presented at the National Conference on Sexual Assault and the Law, Melbourne, Australia, 28–30 November, 103–13.

Yurchesyn, K. Keith, A. and Renner, E. 1992. Contrasting perspectives on the nature of sexual assault provided by a service for sexual assault victims and the law courts. *Canadian Journal of Behavioural Science*, 24 (1), 71–85.

Index